CW01496608

The Trade Union Badge – Material Culture in Action

This book is dedicated to the following labour historians who have passed from us in recent years and whose presence and contributions are sorely missed:

Eddie Frow, John Gorman, John Hammond, Arthur Marsh, Harry Murt, Raph Samuel, Greg Smith

The Trade Union Badge –
Material Culture In Action

PAUL MARTIN

Ashgate

Published by
Ashgate Publishing Limited
Gower House
Croft Road
Aldershot
Hants GU11 3HR
England

Ashgate Publishing Company
131 Main Street
Burlington
Vermont, 05401–5600
USA

Ashgate website: http://www.ashgate.com

British Library Cataloguing in Publication Data
Martin, Paul, 1959–
    The Trade Union Badge: Material Culture in Action. — (Perspectives on Collecting)
    1. Labor union emblems—Great Britain—History. 2. Labor union emblems—Collectors and collecting—Great Britain. 3. Badges—Great Britain—History. 4. Labor unions—Great Britain—History.
    I. Title
    331.8'80941

US Library of Congress Cataloging in Publication Data
Martin, Paul, 1959–
    The Trade Union Badge: Material Culture in Action / Paul Martin
        p. cm. (Perspectives on Collecting)
    Includes bibliographical references.
    1. Labor union members—Medals. 2. Badges—Social aspects. 3. Badges—Psychological aspects. 4. Badges—Collectors and collecting. 5. Labor unions—History. 6. Material culture—Social aspects. 7. Material culture—Psychological aspects. I. Title. II. Series.
    CJ5793.L3M37 2002
    331.88'02'7–dc21   2001053579

ISBN 0 7546 0324 5

This book is printed on acid free paper.

Typeset by Manton Typesetters, Louth, Lincolnshire, UK.
Printed and bound in Great Britain by MPG Books Ltd, Bodmin, Cornwall.

Contents

Foreword

The present volume began life as a dissertation for the completion of my two-year study for the Ruskin College History Diploma in 1988. Having served its purpose at that time it remained dormant until a couple of years ago, when I began adding information to it gleaned by collectors and professionals alike in the intervening years. In doing so, and in adding my own additional research, conducted over the years, I found that there was indeed enough material to rewrite it as a book. That noone else had written anything on the subject in the intervening years outside the collecting fraternity (which is a little surprising, given the attention that visual culture in and outside of the labour movement has received during the 1980s and 1990s) compelled me to draw together all of the sources that had been discovered since its inception and bring it to a wider audience.

In my last book, *Popular Collecting and the Everyday Self*, I focused to a considerable degree on the meaning of the minutiae, the flotsam and jetsam of our throwaway consumer society and the contemporary significance of collecting that which was only ever designed to be disposed of, or which had been functionally and technologically superseded. In the present volume, I have concentrated on the historical and contemporary presence and indeed persistence, of the trade union badge. By studying the apparently ephemeral and innocuous material culture of the everyday, we reveal it as symbolic of far greater sociocultural importance than its literal physicality suggests. I have used the trade union badge here as an example of this, both for what it reveals in itself, and also in the hope that it might encourage similar approaches to other material of the everyday. Thus will the 'meaning' of the material culture of our own time be conveyed to future generations, perhaps for some of whom our preoccupation with materialism will not otherwise be properly understood.

Paul Martin, Leicester, June 2001

General Preface to the Series

The study of collecting is a crucial facet in the contemporary turn towards the understanding of social practice, seen as the medium through which individuals and communities create self-identity. Social construction of the meanings of material culture is at the heart of this project, and the collecting process, through which objects are put into meaningful relationships seen as producing knowledge, value, aesthetic and prestige, is central to it. *Perspectives on Collecting* is intended to bring together detailed studies and broader over-views, drawn from the analysis of a wide range of collecting practices, which together will develop a sustained exploration of the field.

Susan Pearce, General Editor
November 2001

Preface

Throughout the book, reference is made to the 'button'. In this book the word has two principal meanings. First, historically, in Britain it was used to denote a lapel badge, irrespective of what it was made from. Hence reference is often found to, for example, 'the docker's button'. This derived from the raised stud-fixing on the reverse of the badge designed to be worn in the once ubiquitous lapel buttonhole of men's jackets. For instance, the National Union of Public Employees (NUPE) headlined a report on the competition for a new badge design amongst its membership in a 1949 issue of its journal *The Public Employee* as: 'NUPE Starts Buttonhole Search'. However, such badges were also often issued with pin fittings and the term 'button' in this sense often became used for the lapel badge generally. Where this is the intended use of the word, it is proceeded by an asterisk *. The second meaning of the word was originally an American one, but is now practically universal. This indicates specifically, a lapel badge made of tin, either with a paper design covered by celluloid, or of a design printed directly onto the tin. Such badges in America were and still are far more widely used than enamel or other kinds of badge. Where no asterisk occurs after the word 'button' it is being used in this sense. For the sake of uniformity, these indicative differences are employed throughout the book. Any other intended meanings of the word, other than the two noted here, are explained where relevant in the text. The necessity of making such distinctions will become apparent on reading.

The number of organisations mentioned in the text are too great for a conventional glossary of initials to be useful. Therefore, they are listed both in full and initials or acronym where they are first mentioned in the text and where they occur in the index.

Acknowledgements

There are inevitably many people who contribute towards the completion of a book such as this and without whom it would be greatly impoverished. My grateful thanks are therefore due to numerous people. For many of the photographs used in this book, I am indebted to the following who responded most enthusiastically to my requests for them: James Bridges of Bonham's, London; Paul Cosgrove; Philip Dunn, registrar at the National Museum of Labour History; Joe Fleming for the use of his badges and Dean Bennett for photographing them; Frank Little of North Lanarkshire Leisure Services Department; Mark Organ; David Pretty; Andrew Redpath; Harry Rubenstein at the National Museum of American History, the Smithsonian Institute and David Yorke.

The following have been indispensable in supplying information and detail at various stages in the research for the book: Lou Adams, general secretary ASLEF; Peter Carter, correspondence secretary of the Trade Union Badge Collectors Society, who ever since I began the original thesis has very helpfully supplied relevant materials for inclusion, quite apart from his numerous articles in the Society's newsletter; S. Cherry, Curator, Cork Public Museum for her cooperation in providing photographs of the Cork Harbour Labourers Guild of St Patrick medallion, which although eventually unused in the book, is of great use in visual presentations; Nick Clark at *Labour Research* for allowing me access to the full range of survey responses to his article on trade union badges; Philip Dunn at the National Museum of Labour History for making available the discussion document *Labour History In Museums*; Andy Durr for allowing me to quote from his most useful unpublished manuscript; Joe Fleming, another collector who generously lent of his time, knowledge and resources for which I am most grateful; Lorna Goldsmith of the Department of Coins and Medals at the British Museum; Ted Hake, dealer in Americana; Peter Ludvigson of the Workers Museum in Copenhagen for documents and articles used in Chapter 6; Mark Organ; R.W. Pollard, secretary, Ancient Order of Foresters, Southampton; David Pretty for information on the Anglesey Workers Union; Andrew Reeves of the Western Australian Museum; Andy Redpath for numerous useful snippets of information and for drawing to my attention both material on the use of badges within public sector unions and Russell's book on the American longshoremen's union which proved to be an important reference source for the likely origins of the quarter badge system; Harry Rubenstein, National Museum of American History; Raphael Samuel, former tutor in history at Ruskin

College, Oxford who acted as my supervisor on the original dissertation, proved a valuable soundboard for my thoughts and queries at that time, and took the project's relevance at face value when many others thought its proposal as a legitimate study was a fetishistic indulgence; Greg Smith for his pioneering work on Australian union badges; Graham Stevenson, national secretary, docks, waterways and fishing group TGWU for drawing my attention to the Kokuro case in Japan; Paul Viney for the supply of material, which though not used in the book was most welcome contextually; David Yorke for his friendly and cooperative responses to my queries; to everyone who has contributed their thoughts and research to the *Trade Union Badge Collectors' Newsletter* over the last fifteen years and all those collectors and activists who were kind enough to take the time to put their thoughts and opinions down on paper in response to my enquiries and questions and who are variously quoted and cited throughout the book. Last here, but always first in my heart and thoughts, is my wife Marie, whose support in every way has been a major contribution to getting the book finished; first for her translation from the French, of some of the text appearing in Chapter 6, and second for her ready acceptance of my excuse for the neglect of domestic matters being due to working on the book! Any omissions or oversights from these acknowledgements are entirely unintentional and I apologise for them here.

List of Illustrations

Introduction

Here We Go, Here We Go, Here We Go (And How We Got Here)

A lot of you may think badges are a rather frivolous subject to have a rule amendment on when we have such important things as privatisation, cuts and wage battles to fight. The fact is we cannot begin to fight those battles until we have recruited those members into the union. We need all the recruitment aids we can get.[1]

The study of the visual is now recognised as being as important as the literature of the labour movement.[2] Before the Second World War, reference to this visual heritage was often cited as a matter of pride, especially amongst craft unions in their commemorative histories.[3] These early histories were often compiled directly from old minute books, largely for the benefit of the members, and the union badge often makes a cursory appearance. For example, an early history of the National Society of Operative Printers Assistants (NATSOPA) in relation to their first badge, issued in 1910, notes that: '... a button hole badge giving a view of Caxton House [the head office] in red and gold with the title of the society in white on a green border, was prepared and sold at 1d each.'[4] Such passing references are sometimes the only clue to the visual culture of an individual trade union's history or even its very existence. The technology that enabled the mass manufacture of vitreous enamel badges arrived in time to capture the flavour of crafts and trades that by the Second World War were already anachronistic or fast fading. Hence small British craft unions with memberships barely countable in their hundreds such as the Organ Builders Trade Society,[5] were moved to display their craft pride through the adoption of their now very rare enamel badge featuring a monogram of the Society's initials. Others such as the equally rare Victorian badge of the obscure Military Cork Head Dress Trade Union, picturing the clasped hands of unity above a tropical pith helmet which in turn sits above a globe symbolising the empire,[6] serve to remind us of the very different conceptions of national identity and world view that prevailed at the turn of the twentieth century amongst all classes. Indeed, as will be seen at various points in the book, the lapel badge can be used as an atlas of British trade union organisation throughout the world. Branches of the British woodworkers, engineers and railway servants unions amongst others, initiated by emigrant tradesmen in search of work or just a new life, issued badges in the white dominions of Australia, Canada and South Africa, whilst the Plumbing Trades Union for one, formed branches in non-imperial, anglophile countries like Argentina. Eventually these 'worker outposts of empire' would be absorbed by, or meta-morphose into, indigenous organisations with their own national characteristics and traditions, but their iconic legacy acts as a compass for the spread of trade unionism throughout the nineteenth-century world.

Yet for three decades after the Second World War, there was little mention, let alone analysis, of the importance of the lapel badge, either as a functional object or as a totem of meaning or heritage. It is probably not coincidental that these years of symbolistic absence were, unlike the twentieth century's first three decades, also years of job security and economic buoyancy in which it was not felt necessary to display the sociocultural cleavage to images and symbols of workplace defence. Other than a few pioneer collectors and labour historians, it was not until the boom in collecting trade union badges in the aftermath of the 1984–85 miners' strike that information on the subject began to grow. The annual miners' galas of course kept banners in the public eye in the Midlands and the North, whilst Klingender's 1947 exhibition and book[7] on the engineer in art, and Hobsbawm's interest in secular ritual[8] cast an academic eye on the form. It was the early 1970s however, which proved significant. Two pioneering studies were published at this time: R.A. Leeson's 1971 study of trade union emblems, *United We Stand*,[9] and John Gorman's survey of extant trade union banners in Britain, *Banner Bright* first published in 1972 . Other similar studies were soon forthcoming and have continued,[10] whilst most recently, Rodney Mace's *British Trade Union Posters* has usefully raised the profile of that particular medium.[11] Leeson's and Gorman's studies were additionally important as academic interest in popular material culture began to be taken more seriously, at least in America.[12] More recently an important study of the American 'Knights Of Labor' (KOL) has been made by Bob Weir.[13] Weir asserts that the KOL 'tried to rebuild community by constructing an entire KOL universe that embraced not only work and ideology, but also badges, parades, picnics, music, poetry, literature, and religion'.[14] In Britain, craft and the new unskilled labourers unions alike in the late nineteenth century sought to similarly assert their presence. The material culture attendant in all of this was, beyond its role as advertisement, an attempt to manifest physically a collective mind-set and attitude, a set of beliefs. The union badge for many became a secular icon which not only publicly attested to the wearer's collective belonging, but was also worn as a personal talisman, to offer reassurance of their self-worth and moral fortitude. Although books have recently been published on the variety and beauty of lapel badges in general,[15] outside of the important articles penned by collector-researchers, largely in their own journals,[16] the present book is the first serious British study of the trade union badge.

The disruption to the post-war consensus on labour relations, particularly the mass demonstrations against the 1971 Industrial Relations Bill (subsequently, Act) which saw the old banners on the streets again (see Chapter 4), also promoted a wider public interest in them. By the 1980s, in the midst of the Thatcherite attack on its rights, the organisational visual heritage of the labour movement became publicly revived.[17] A surge of vintage graphics and maxims, from Victorian union banners reproduced on postcards, to the utopian 'merry England' socialist vignettes of the Victorian illustrator, Walter Crane, reproduced on posters advertising May Day and other communal events became commonplace, replacing the activist, social realist graphics of such materials of the 1960s and 1970s.

Organised labour's visual culture has always centred on its banners and emblems, which are now recognised as important interpretative tools of systems of values and beliefs. It now remains for the role of the badge to be examined. Gorman's work has inspired similar studies as far away as Australia.[18] The opening of the National Museum of Labour History (NMLH) in 1975, based on the collections of Walter Southgate and Henry Fry,[19] fired interest even further. The artefacts of the unions, until this time, were largely discarded once they had served their purpose, and more than a few Victorian union membership emblems and other material were 'rescued' from skips and rubbish sacks by collectors, whilst perhaps not entirely apocryphal horror stories of union branches burning their old banners in spring cleaning exercises circulated amongst collectors and cultural historians alike.[20] A few dedicated collectors and archivists such as Eddie and Ruth Frow, who turned their terraced house into the Working Class Movement Library (and Museum), salvaged what they could.[21] The NMLH in particular alerted unions to the wealth of history to be preserved and has since proved to make unions more mindful of their older regalia and documents. Also importantly, since its foundation in 1973, the Modern Records Centre of the University of Warwick Library in Coventry has built up the largest collection of trade union records in the United Kingdom, although it does not collect artefacts.

This book is submitted to the reader first as an exercise in public history. One important aspect of public history which is especially reflected here in Chapters 4 and 6, can be usefully summarised as history in the making and of the present which surrounds us all in our everyday environments, of which we are all constituent parts. By the very act of living our lives, we contribute to the making of the historical record. Further, it is history made, researched and written about ordinary people, public events, structures, places and heritage outside of the academy, and of which all of the above is exemplary. Public history also uses the resources of the everyday to tell stories, trace paths and make meaning. Hence the very public presence of the lapel badge is a fitting subject for this kind of historical approach.[22] Secondly, this book is presented as an exercise in interpreting everyday material culture as a means of understanding the importance of the context and culture from which it comes.[23] In the spirit of Geertz[24] and Weir,[25] the book is grounded in the idea of 'thick description':

> The key to formulating thick description is to resist temptations to analyze a subject before a requisite number of details are revealed and clear patterns can be discerned. Sometimes such a construction requires the realization that some behaviours have no discernible logic, some meanings are ambiguous, and a few cultural productions can be

appreciated but not fully understood. Often thick description tends to reveal cultural secrets in a deeper, if less determinate way.[26]

I am quite aware of the perceived narrowness of a 'banner and badge' approach[27] towards labour history. As one museum commentator once put it: 'Over the last ten years I have seen many labour history exhibitions that consisted of an art gallery presentation of banners, a print collection of emblems, and a stamp collection of badges, laid out in serried rows.'[28] Therefore, in making a detailed study and asserting the importance of the trade union badge, I would not wish it to be construed as an exclusive view of all of labour history. Nor is it an attempt to narrowly claim or portray 'labour history' as simply the history of the organised labour movement, the academic and museological debate about which is discussed in Chapter 6, even though it is about trade unions. Indeed, there has in the recent past even been some discourse on differentiation between 'trade societies' and 'trade unions'.[29] The 'white, middle-aged maleness' of trade union officialdom which was a particular issue in the 1980s especially, is addressed in Chapter 4. I have simply used an neglected aspect of trade union heritage, the badge, as a vehicle or example with which to highlight how the study of such material can help make the familiar new to us again, through revealing a different dimension to (in this case, trade union) history.

Dick Hebdidge showed how an unassuming mode of personal transport, the motor scooter, was turned by Britain's 'mods' of the early 1960s into a significant cultural symbol.[30] Badges, certainly within trade unions, have been used to symbolise belonging to a particular ethos and set of principles and values in the same way. Badges on a general level can often illustrate micro-contexts of the bigger events of which they were a part. For instance, during the Korean War, Chinese 'volunteer' soldiers would, at Christmas, pin peace dove brooches and other propaganda material onto the wire defences of the Commonwealth contingent of the UN forces. Commonwealth soldiers: 'pinned [them] to the[ir] balaclavas to show that the wearer had been at the sharp end of the war'.[31] It is interesting that military badges are taken seriously in relation to the study of regimental and military history.[32] Even nursing badges have now been accorded their place in history and are recognised as important signifiers of identity. As Baroness McFarlane of Llandaff has noted in her foreword to Jennifer Meglaughlin's *British Nursing Badges*:

> If you want to analyse the value system of nursing as it has evolved, it is portrayed in this volume. [The nurses' badge] ... was seen as something which signified skill and competence to the public, it 'places' a person in the context of their background, standards and values. This is why many nurses still wear a badge denoting their qualification, hospital or association and through it say, 'This is what I am'. It has meaning for both the wearer and the observer.[33]

Trade union badges also serve this purpose and like many military badges and medals, are awarded and worn as 'honours'. As one nursing member delegate to the

1988 conference of the National Union of Public Employees (NUPE) noted: 'Recruitment is vital and so is the NUPE badge. It is a statement that "I'm in NUPE and wear a badge to prove it".'[34] Many nurses, as a cursory glance at their uniform will attest, wear their qualification or hospital badge next to their union badge, thus visually encapsulating the duality of their professional and employment values and publicly presenting them as a unitary identity. Badges can also be read as a means of access. Today, chemically sensitive badges are worn by lab technicians to keep them safe; pass and name badges are often essential in order to access buildings, conferences and offices. The trade union badge was often essential in order to access employment, and by extension, a better standard of living. It is also a springboard for the contemporary historian or sociologist, to examine attitudes, mind-sets and cultural codes within the context of industrial relations. This is a field which, as a particular strand of labour history, has traditionally relied heavily on statistical data and the sometimes arid language of economics. The focus of this book is on trade union badges, both as an organisational device and as a visual semaphore. The book's purpose is to examine the origins, history and use of the lapel badge in trade unions, as a model for a wider and deeper appreciation of the significance of everyday material culture. At the same time, the badge is revealed as a symbol of belonging to a wider system of social values than the purely economic. It is discussed in the context of its use and effect within the culture that produced it. The study is based on Britain, as the birthplace of trade unionism. However, as my research progressed, I found that examples of the use of badges in other countries were equally significant. Therefore, the study has been widened to incorporate these findings, and place the use of the badge in trade unions in an international context. It is hoped that in so doing, its significance will be made even more apparent.

How we got here

Whilst this is the first in-depth study of the trade union badge in Britain, I feel it is necessary to acknowledge the sources from which existing information is derived and to credit those who have made the current work less arduous through their own research. Their results are often made public through collectors' publications and sometimes as a constituent part of wider studies. This acknowledgement is also intended as a sketch of the international landscape in which the book is based.

Britain

Dwarfed by its more opulent cousins, the banners and emblems, the union badge has been largely overlooked for serious research. To date, the most important British work on union badges has been Smethurst and Devine's essay on badges as a means of membership control,[35] which seems to have been the first significant study of its kind, although a compilation of short, illustrated photocopied articles from collectors' magazines was made available in 1987.[36] John Hammond's reference work, *Trade Union Badges*, first published in 1991 is the other key piece of research. This was updated several times, before the author's untimely death in 1997, and continues to be updated by the collector-researchers who have always contributed to it. It lists descriptions of all known British trade union badges, along with some black-and-white illustrations, and can only be a matter of time before it is professionally published with colour illustrations as the audience for such materials widens. A small illustrated booklet on the badges of the 1984/5 miners' strike appeared in 1987,[37] as did a brief survey of past and present uses of trade union badges, in the magazine, *Labour Research*. This also sketched out the process of ordering badges from manufacturers.[38] Trade unions produce features on the badges of their organisations from time to time,[39] whilst union badges have also been used as supportive illustrations in academic labour history.[40] In 1999, a book of colour photographs of mainly pre-Second World War enamel badges; including trade union badges[41] was published, looking at them from the perspective of graphic art. More importantly, a British collectors' group, based around *The Trade Union Badge Collectors' Newsletter* (*TUBCNL*),[42] has been the main source through which new discoveries have been made and in which information on trade union badges has been circulated in recent years (see Chapter 6). Run for and by collectors, and produced in an *ad hoc* photocopied format, as a corpus of information over two decades, the newsletter constitutes a significant body of research, visual and written reference material in the spirit of public history.

Ireland

Historically of course, Ireland has been dominated by British trade union organisations. After 1922 this changed considerably, and whilst British trade unions maintained a dominant position in the North of Ireland, Southern Ireland developed its own distinctive character, its history coming down to us in badge form through such organisations as 'The Officers And Men Of the National Army Trade Union' of the early 1920s, but of which little else seems to be known. The establishment of the Irish Transport Workers Union in 1909 and the legacy of Jim Larkin and the 1913 Dublin general strike tend to be the locus of Irish trade union heritage. The 'red hand' (shaped) badge of the 1913 Dublin strike holds still a powerfully evocative sense of moment. Being intrinsically tied to British organisations for so long, published work on Irish trade union history obviously overlaps with the British. One of the earliest publications about Irish labour iconography dealt with the processions and emblems of the Irish trades guilds of the nineteenth century,[43] and is probably, along with Klingender[44] one of the earliest significant publications of its type. There have in recent years, been a number of important exhibitions in Ireland involving *Soathar*, the Irish Labour History Society. The leading light in promoting the material culture of Ireland's labour movement is Francis Devine, an education officer with the former Irish Transport and General Workers Union (now the Services, Industrial and Professional Trade Union, SIPTU). He has contributed both through writing and engaging in the organisation of museum exhibitions to the wider dissemination of the significance of Irish trade union badges.[45] His work with Smethurst as mentioned above, addresses both British and Irish union badges. There have also been publications approximating to Gorman's work, sometimes tied to museum exhibitions.[46]

Australia

An important book, *Emblems Of Unity: Australian trade union badges* was published in 1992 by Greg Smith,[47] which illustrated nearly nine hundred badges, accompanied by brief descriptions and potted union biographies. This was written to 'visually record officially issued badges and medals from the earliest period to the present accompanied by relevant information and historical background on each union', and to 'encourage the preservation and further study of the use of badges in the development of our trade unions and foster their continual issuing in the future'.[48] The book which followed an Australian museum exhibition on banners, which also featured some badges,[49] was inspired directly by John Gorman's work,[50] whilst union bodies such as the Trades and Labour Council of Western Australia (TLCWA) have published celebratory visual records of union culture, including badges. There have also been synoptic articles in various union journals and collectors' publications which have highlighted the usefulness of badges as interpretative tools in labour history.[51]

North America

In the United States, one major dealer in Americana believes that no major work has yet been published on the badges of the American labour movement, although interest in them is beginning to increase.[52] There has in the past however, been academic research into union labels,[53] and a recent significant book on the culture of the Knights of Labor, devotes a scholarly chapter to their material culture in its widest sense, including badges and regalia.[54] There has also been at least one celebratory union publication, similar to the Australian TLCWA booklet, which is illustrated with trade union ephemera,[55] whilst books dealing with labour graphics, the worker in art and radical movements touch on labour ephemera in passing.[56] One major exhibition, *Symbols And Images Of American Labor*, was staged at the Smithsonian's National Museum of American History, from January to September 1988 subsequently making a three-year travelling exhibition around the US:[57]

> The first half of the exhibit examined how workers expressed their sense of identity through images and symbols ... The second half of the exhibit ... traced how workers as

a distinct group have been characterized in cartoons, magazines, campaign memorabilia, advertising, television, movies and on product labels from the 1800s to the present.[58]

Nothing as specific has apparently been staged since.[59] Canada, intrinsically linked with the US, has seemingly also yet to make any serious study of the transition from British to American-style labour relations and the representation of them through its material culture.

Japan

Other than the above countries, which might be expected to have the most in common with British forms of organisation, there has been at least one important survey. The Japanese National Railway Workers Union (KOKURO), enlisted the assistance of the International Transport Workers Federation (ITF), to which it is affiliated, after its legal right to wear union badges at work was challenged by the privatised railway companies. A survey of international affiliates by the ITF was initiated on KOKURO's behalf and the results published bilingually in both Japanese and English (see Chapter 3 and Appendix 3).[60]

Other Contexts

Other researchers, particularly paranumismatists and those interested in medals and tokens generally have, in the course of their otherwise unrelated work, revealed significant contextual information and groups of material on a regional basis, such as miners' tallies and tokens of other working-class organisations such as friendly societies and the Co-operative Movement, which were common until 1945.[61] Finally, trade union badges have been used as illustrations in other contexts.[62] This indicates the diaspora of interest in trade union badges and allied ephemera, and therefore the breadth and diversity of the interest which has grown in them. The context and continuity of the use and development of the badge in the labour movement however is still largely one of a far from completed jigsaw. As such, it is hoped the present work will encourage further research. The number of instances of the use and relevance of the union badge, tend to surface on a regular basis. As a result, the present work does not claim to be definitive.

Notes

1   K. Allan (Northumberland East Health [Branch]), National Union of Public Employees (NUPE), annual conference report 1984, p. 367. He is proposing the issue of a free 'deluxe' membership badge for all members on joining NUPE.
2   It is acknowledged that there is an ongoing debate about the nature, validity, interpretations of, and approaches towards terms such as 'labour movement', 'organised labour'

and 'labour history'. For the sake of convenience, these terms are used throughout this book to mean the trade union movement, with which it is primarily concerned. However, other approaches are more fully discussed in Chapter 6. See also K. Moore, 'Labour History In Museums: development and direction' in S.M. Pearce (ed.), *Museums And The Appropriation of Culture*, London, Athlone Press, 1994: pp. 142–173 for a specific and detailed overview. For a wider discussion of 'history from below', of which labour history is a key constituent, see e.g. E. Hobsbawm, *On History*, London, Weidenfeld & Nicholson 1997, pp. 266–286.

3   e.g. D.C. Cummings, *The History of The United Society of Boilermakers and Iron and Steel Shipbuilders*, Newcastle upon Tyne, USBI&SS, 1905; S. Higginbottom, *Our Society's History*, Manchester, Amalgamated Society of Woodworkers,1939; J. Nicholson, *A Hundred Years of Vehicle Building 1834–1934: centenary of the National Union of Vehicle Workers*, London, NUVB, 1934; J.R. Raynes, *Engines And Men* (Associated Society of Locomotive Engineers and Firemen), London, Goodall & Suddick, 1921; B. Turner, *A Short History Of The General Union Of Textile Workers*, Heckmondwike, Labour Pioneer & Factory Times Printing Department,1920. Although there are exceptions. See e.g. A. Pugh, *Men of Steel by One Of Them*, London, Iron and Steel Trades Confederation, 1951.

4   R.B. Suthers, *The Story Of NATSOPA 1889–1929*, London, NATSOPA, 1929, p. 35.

5   See K. Sequin, *The Graphic Art of the Enamel Badge*, London, Thames and Hudson, 1999, p. 68 for badge illustration.

6   See A. Marsh and V. Ryan, *Historical Dictionary of Trade Unions Volume 4*, Aldershot, Scolar Press, 1994, pp. 485–486 for the few details known of the union. Such small craft organisations as the Military and Orchestral Musical Instrument Makers Trade Society and the Card Setting Machine Tenters Society, formed in the nineteenth century, were still extant in 1999 with 62 and 88 members respectively (both had issued badges as recently as 1982 and 1972 respectively), whilst the Sheffield Wool Shear Workers Union was still able to see in the new millennium with just 11 members (source: *Whittaker's Almanack*, London, HMSO, 1999). Others such as the London Jewel Case and Display Cabinet Makers Union, formed in 1894, did not quite make it, winding up with just two members in 1986 (although its highest recorded membership had never risen above seventy five, see *Daily Telegraph*, 24 December 1986). The longevity, survival and culture of such small unions would make an interesting study in its own right.

7   F.D. Klingender, *Art And The Industrial Revolution*, (A. Elton, ed.) London, Evelyn Adams & Mackay, 1947/1968.

8   E.J. Hobsbawm, *Primitive Rebels*, Manchester University Press, 1959.

9   Although studies of certificates and emblems in a wider context did already exist, e.g. T.O. Haunch, 'English Craft Certificates', *Ars Quatuor Coronatorum*, Vol. 82, 1969, pp. 169–263.

10 e.g. National Union of Vehicle Builders, *The Badge Emblems and Banner of the National Union of Vehicle Builders 1834–1972*, London, N.U. Vehicle Builders 1972; W. Moyes, *The Banner Book*, Newcastle upon Tyne, Frank Graham, 1974; E. and R. Frow, 'Trade Union Emblems', *North-West Group for the Study of Labour History*, No. 3, 1976, pp. 29–31; J. Smethurst, 'The Manchester Banner Makers', *Northwest Group for the Study of Labour History*, No. 3, 1976, pp. 17–28; T.P. O'Neill, 'Irish Trade Union Banners', in C. O'Danachair (ed.), *Folk and Farm: essays in honour of A.T.*

Lucas, Ireland, Royal Society of Antiquaries of Ireland, 1976, pp. 177–199; C. Muller, *James Sharples Und Das Zertifikat DerAmalgamated Society of Engineers: studien zur Bildkultur Britischer Gewerkshaften,* Hamburg, 1978; E.J. Hobsbawm, 'Man and Woman in Socialist Iconography', *History Workshop Journal,* No. 6, Autumn, 1978, pp. 121–138; E.J. Hobsbawm, *Worlds of Labour,* London, Weidenfeld & Nicholson, 1984, pp. 66–83, N. Emery, *Banners Of The Durham Coalfield,* Gloucestershire, Sutton Press, 1998.

11 R. Mace, *British Trade Union Posters,* Gloucestershire, Sutton Publishing, 1999.

12 e.g. F.E.H. Schroeder (ed.), *Popular Culture in Museums and Libraries,* Ohio, Bowling Green University Press, 1981; E. Mayo (ed.), *American Material Culture: the shape of things around us,* Ohio, Bowling Green State University Popular Press, 1984.

13 R. Weir, *Beyond Labor's Veil: the culture of the Knights Of Labor,* Pennsylvania State University Press, 1996.

14 Ibid., p. xix.

15 e.g. F. Setchfield, *The Official Badge Collectors' Guide,* London, Longman, 1986; Sequin, *The Graphic Art of The Enamel Badge*

16 e.g. F. Devine, 'Who dares wear the red hand badge?', *Liberty,* Journal of the Irish Transport and General Workers Union, 1984, June; J. Smethurst and F. Devine, 'Trade union badges – mere emblems or means of membership control?', *Soathar,* Journal of the Irish Labour History Society, 1981, No. 7. See also *Trade Union Badge Collectors' Newsletter* 1985–2000 *passim* for various articles and information.

17 e.g. T. Brake, *Men of Good Character,* London, Lawrence & Wishart, 1985; I. McDougall, *Labour In Scotland,* Edinburgh, Mainstream Publishing, 1985; J. Gorman, *Banner Bright,* London, Scorpion (revised 3rd edn),1986.

18 A. Reeves, *Badges of Labour Banners of Pride,* Sydney, George Allen & Unwin, 1984.

19 J. Gorman, *Images of Labour,* London, Scorpion, 1985, pp. 11–14.

20 Peter Carter, for instance, relates how the General Secretary of the Amalgamated Union of Woodcutting Machinists allegedly ordered the destruction of some five hundred mint copies of the union's membership emblem when it became part of the Furniture, Timber and Allied Trades Union in the early 1970s. P. Carter, *Trade Union Badge Collectors' Newsletter,* No. 73, Autumn 2000.

21 E. Frow and R. Frow, 'Travels with a caravan', *History Workshop,* No. 2, 1976a, pp. 177–182; *Morning Star,* 3 January 1987, pp. 6–7; E. Frow and R. Frow, 'The Working Class Movement Library', *Social History Curators' Group Journal,* No. 18, 1990/91, pp. 13–14.

22 For further exploration of public history in Britain, see the following: J. Winter, 'Public History and Historical Scholarship', *History Workshop Journal,* 1996, No. 42, Autumn, pp. 169–172; H. Kean, P. Martin and S. Morgan (eds), *Seeing History: Public History in Britain Now,* London, Francis Boutle, 2000; L. Jordanova, 'Public History', *History Today,* Vol. 50 (5) May 2000, pp. 20–21; L. Jordanova, *History In Practice,* Edward Arnold, 2000, pp. 141–171. However, in the US and Australia for instance, public history is more narrowly understood. It relates variously to those working through or with museums or who are focused on family history research, to those who hire themselves out on commission to write corporate or other histories.

23 For a similar recent example both of a subject and of a study to the present one, see A. Clarke, *Tupperware: The Promise Of Plastic In 1950s America,* Washington, DC, Smithsonian Institute, 1999.

24 C. Geertz, *The Interpretation of Cultures*, New York, Basic Books, 1973.

25 Weir, *Beyond Labor's Veil* .

26 Ibid., p. xiii.

27 L. Knowles, 'The portrayal of Labour History in museum displays', *Bias In Museums: Museum Professionals Group Transaction* 22, 1987, pp. 9–10, p. 10.

28 E. King, 'Labour History at The People's Palace', in V. Bott (ed.), *Labour History In Museums*, London, Society For The Study of Labour History / Social History Curators Group, 1988, pp. 11–16, p. 11.

29 R.A. Leeson, 'Business as usual – craft union developments 1834', *Bulletin of The Society For The Study of Labour History*, No. 49, 1984, pp. 15–17.

30 D. Hebdidge, *Subculture: The Meaning Of Style,* London, Methuen, 1985.

31 B. Catchpole, 'The Commonwealth In Korea', *History Today*, Vol. 48, 11, 1998, November, pp. 33–39, p. 35.

32 e.g. R. Williamson-Latham, *British Military Badges and Buttons*, Buckinghamshire, Shire Publications, 1994; Mark Lloyd, *Military Badges and Insignia*, London, Grange Books, 1995; F. Wilkinson, *Badges of The British Army: an illustrated reference guide for collectors*, London, Arms & Armour Press, 1997; P. Taylor, *Collecting Anodised Cap Badges*, London, Pen & Sword Books 1998.

33 J. Meglaughlin, *British Nursing Badges, Volume One: an illustrated handbook,* London: Vade Mecum, 1990, p. 18. Of course there were more coded uses of badges, such as the example of sixth-form public school girls, who allegedly wore golly brooches to indicate that they had '"known" a man in the biblical sense', cited in A. Clayson, *Hamburg: The Cradle of British Rock*, London, Sanctuary Press, 1997.

34 Sister K. Barker (United Sheffield Hospital), NUPE conference report 1988, p. 133.

35 J. Smethurst and F. Devine, 'Trade Union Badges'.

36 V. Graves (ed.), *Trade Union Badges*, Milton Keynes, 1987. A compilation of photocopied articles on badges from various collectors' magazines of the 1980s.

37 B. Seaton, *Justice For Mineworkers Badge Collectors' Guide*, Nottingham, Private publication, 1987.

38 N. Clark, 'Worn With Pride – Union Badges', *Labour Research*, 1987, February, pp. 19–20.

39 e.g. I. Monkton, 'Worn With Pride – The "Badge of Nobility"', *Landworker*, February, 1991, pp. 4–5.

40 e.g. F. Little, 'Summerlee Heritage Trust and the Scottish Railway Strike 1890–91', *Scottish Labour History Review*, No. 5, Winter 1991–Spring 1992, pp. 12–13.

41 Sequin, *The Graphic Art of the Enamel Badge*, pp. 66–73.

42 A full set of which is available for consultation in the library of Ruskin College, Oxford.

43 J. Swift, *History Of The Dublin Bakers And Others*, Dublin, 1947.

44 F.D. Klingender, *Art And The Industrial Revolution*.

45 Especially his article 'Who Dares Wear The Red Hand Badge?', *Liberty*, Journal of the ITGWU,1984, June.

46 B. Loftus, *Marching Workers*, Dublin, Arts Council of Ireland, 1978.

47 G. Smith, *Emblems Of Unity: Badges of Australia's Trade Unions*, New South Wales, Little Hill Press Pty Ltd, 1992a.

48 Ibid., pp. 16–17.

49 A. Reeves, *Badges Of Labour Banners Of Pride*.

50   Ibid., introduction; A. Reeves, *Another Day Another Dollar: working lives in Austral-ian history*, Victoria, McCulloch Publishing, 1988; A. Reeves, *A Tapestry Of Australia: The Sydney Wharfies Mural*, Sydney, Waterside Workers Federation, 1992.

51   e.g. G. Smith, 'Badges Trace The History Of NSW Railways', *Australian Coin Review*, 1985, June, pp. 25–26; G. Smith, 'Badges Of The NSW General Strike 1917', *Journal of The Numismatic Association of Australia*, Vol. 5, 1991, pp. 53–56; G. Smith, 'Union Badges Of The 1913 Ferry Strike', *Australian Coin Review*, 1992, October, pp. 34–35; P. Murphy, 'Sacked For Wearing Their Union Badge', *The Public Transport Worker*, 1993, Winter, pp. 30–31.

52   T. Hake, personal communication, 15 January 1998.

53   E.R. Spedden, *The Trade Union Label*, Baltimore, John Hopkins University Press, 1910.

54   Weir, *Beyond Labor's Veil* op. cit. pp. 231–276.

55   M.B. Schnapper, *American Labor: A Bicentenial History*, Washington, DC, Public Affairs Press, 1975.

56   e.g. W. Cahn, *A Pictorial History of American Labor*, New York, Crown Publishers, 1972; M.B. Schnapper, *American Labor: A Pictorial Social History*, Washington, DC, Public Affairs Press, 1972; R. Oestreicher, 'From Artisan To Consumer: Images of Workers 1840–1920', *Journal of American Culture*, 1981, 4, pp. 47–64; U. Achten, M. Reichelt and R. Schultz, *Mein Vaterland ist International: internationale illustrierte Geschichte des 1. Mai 1886 bis Heute*, Berlin, Asso Verlag, 1986; P.S. Foner and R. Schultz, *Das Andere Amerika*, Berlin, Elefanten Press, 1986; P. Buhle and E.B. Sullivan, *Images Of American Radicalism*, Massachusetts, Christopher Publishing House, 1998.

57   H.R. Rubenstein, 'Symbols And Images Of American Labor: Badges Of Pride', *Labor's Heritage*, 1989a, April, pp. 36–51; H.R. Rubenstein, 'Symbols And Images of Ameri-can Labor: Dinner Pails And Hard Hats', *Labor's Heritage*, 1989b, July, pp. 34–49; S. Molloy, 'Labor History Exhibit', *Solidarity Forever*, newsletter of the American Politi-cal Items Collectors' Labor History Chapter, Summer, 1988, p. 1.

58   Rubenstein, 'Symbols And Images of American Labor: Dinner Pails And Hard Hats', p. 36.

59   H.R. Rubenstein, Division of Social History, Smithsonian Institution, Washington, DC, personal communication, 24 March 1998.

60   National Railway Workers Union of Japan (KOKURU), *Report On An International Survey Of Wearing Trade Union Badges*, London, International Transport Workers Federation (English and Japanese text), 1994. See also Chapter 3 and Appendix 2.

61   e.g. B. Senior, 'Association Badges', *Numismatic Circular*, London, Spink and Sons, Vol. 72, 1964, May, pp. 105–106; R.N.P. Hawkins, *A Dictionary of Makers of British Metallic Tickets, Checks, Medalets, Tallies and Countrs 1778–1910*, London, Baldwins, 1989; S. Minnitt and D. Young, *Tickets, Checks And Passes From The County Of Somerset*, Taunton, Somerset County Library And Museum Services, 1990; N. Cox and A. Cox, *The Tokens, Checks, Metallic Tickets, Passes And Tallies Of Wales 1800–1993: Two Hundred Years of Welsh Paranumismatic History*, Cardiff, Cox, 1994; J. Gardiner, *Checks, Tokens, Tickets and Passes of County Durham and Northumberland* Darlington, self-published, 1996.

62   F. Setchfield, *The Official Badge Collectors' Guide*, London, Longman, 1986, pp. 35, 40–41; D. Froggatt, *Railway Buttons, Badges & Uniforms*, London, Ian Allan, 1986, pp. 58, 117, 126–131; Achten et. al., *Mein Vaterland ist International*.

Chapter 1

Of Emblems, Badges and Banners:
The Triple Alliance

Small things forgotten ... the simple details of past experience which escape historical mention ... simple artifacts ... not deemed important in art historical terms[1]

In this opening chapter, will attempt to put the badge into context with banners and emblems, and to show that as an alliance, they were all equally useful in furthering the union cause. Banners and emblems have been chosen because they are the two mediums through which (other than badges) consciousness, cause and principle have been most commonly materially expressed in social organisations. For instance, as long ago as 1757, freemasons had certificates produced by commercial printers, often heavily embellished with symbols.[2] Various ceramic items such as mugs and plates also have a strong commemorative tradition in the labour movement and have been revived in recent years. Additionally, a modern mixture of graphic satire and social commentary published by companies like Leeds Postcards, pays homage to the Georgian tradition of the political cartoon. Other symbolic and ritualistic regalia can also be found in labour history other than that with which this book deals,[3] but it does not seem to have the breadth of permeation, or the unbroken continuity of banners, emblems or badges from the past to the present.

Many of the emblematic devices found in trade union iconography were inherited from previous generations and other organisations; clasped hands, the beehive, crossed keys, the bundle of sticks, the all-seeing eye for instance, many of which have their origins in the Bible, Aesop's fables and other tomes of antiquity. The world of late Tudor and Stuart England was one in which visual allegory and metaphor often had greater impact than the written word. This was the era of the emblem books in which the symbols most commonly associated with trade union iconography were first generally used.[4] It was an emblem book, for instance, that James Sharples used as a source when designing the membership emblem of the Amalgamated Society of Engineers in 1851.[5] As historian Andy Durr notes:

By the late seventeenth century and early eighteenth century, the emblem in some cases, lost its classic form of words and image, and the genre that had started life as a literary form of language to be supplemented by illustration, had in popular culture become a graphic art, a language of sign and symbol, read and understood by the common people of Europe and the New World.[6]

It was these same symbols and icons that were adopted by the Livery Guilds,[7] Freemasons[8] and Friendly Societies[9] to assert their visual presence, although as Durr has noted: 'Most historians, wherever they are coming from, rarely see voluntary organisations such as the Freemasons and the Trade Unions on the same agenda.'[10] Although numerous British examples of synthesis with and the lineage of craft unionism and ritualism exist, the American Knights of Labor (KOL) exemplify the connection most fervently, not least because they also, unusually, enrolled African Americans, women and unskilled labourers. We are told about Uriah Stephens, the first leader of the KOL, and an ardent advocate of ritual: ' ... his de facto leadership conferred by the title of Grand Master Workman – fashioned an elaborate ritual based on freemasonry.'[11] This ritual was laid down in the Knights' ritual book, the *Adelphon Kruptos*, which was widely available to members after 1878.[12] Like freemasonry, 'Ritual defined "knighthood" as an exalted model of personal behaviour that dictated how members related to each other and how they encountered the outside world.'[13] One KOL activist, Theadore Cuno, wrote in the *New York Times* in April 1882, that:

> The 'working' of an assembly combines the mysticism of the Masonic lodge with the beneficiary element of a mutual aid society and the protective and defensive phases of a trade union after the old English pattern ... All the symbols are important object lessons and have their teachings applied to the labor movement.[14]

Indeed, Terrence Powderly, the KOL's most famous leader, notes in his memoirs how he argued with a Catholic priest, who mistook his Machinists and Blacksmiths Union badge for a Masonic symbol.[15] Ironically, Powderly did in fact die a thirty-third degree freemason.[16] The lapel badge universally, especially where used as an organisational tool, can be seen as the last vestige and paradoxically, both the most innocuous and most effective element of ritual regalia, after more ostentatious iconography and ceremony had fallen from favour. To the early KOL, for an element of whom ritual was always so important,[17] the union badge was a symbol of fraternalism, of conviction and ethos, an aspiration to build a society based on principals of mutuality, cooperatism and brotherhood.[18] The KOL, overall, sought to build a labour way of life, even to the point of substituting for organised religion.[19] The KOL's universalist ideal of trade unionism, self-help and morality, unwieldy though it was, represented a far broader vision than 'straight ahead' trade unionism of the time.[20] Thus ritual and regalia was not in this early organisation broadly associated with exclusivity in any social or occupational sense or in ethos, unlike its contemporary (from 1886), the craftsmen-only American Federation of Labor (AFL), although it was in the nature of the competing ideologies within the KOL that some Local Assemblies (LAs) operated along craft or racially separatist lines. The KOL in fact organised upwards of 10,000 members in Britain (as well as elsewhere in Europe), organising Liverpool dockers in the 1880s and initiating a still-extant British union in the National Union of Stove Grate Workers, based in

Rotherham, South Yorkshire. The British chapters of the KOL had in their enrolment such early labour movement luminaries as the Merseyside dockers' leader James Sexton (see Chapter 3) and Ben Turner of the Trades Union Congress (TUC) and General Union of Textile Workers.[21] As an aspect of British labour history, and as a linchpin in the development of British trade unionism, the KOL is still, half a century after Pelling's article on the subject, under-appreciated.

When trade unions began to emerge publicly, these icons and motifs became sometimes central panels, other times vignettes, sprinkled around symbols of the relevant trade, in their banners. Not only this, but the meanings changed, or were lost:

> Freemasons were following on the tradition of the Emblem writers of word and image. The word came through the catechism and lectures, the image through theatre and artefact. What is of interest here, is that when the great amalgamation of local and regional trade societies took place, the ritual became simplified, the meaning of the pictorial emblem was not taught. However, many of the trade union emblems were sold with their epigrams, the basic principle of the early Emblem writers.[22]

Therefore, as the central icons or symbols to the trade or convictions of the early craft unions were adopted for their emblems, so they were refined further in their uses as symbols on badges. One can trace through this line of exploration, a constant refinement of symbolic devices, which find their ultimate reduction in the form of the lapel badge or ceremonial medallion. An early twentieth-century brass tally (designed for sewing directly onto the clothes) of the Australian Federated Waterside Workers Union, features the initials of the union and 'Brisbane Branch' around the outside, but the centre is taken up by the tied bundle of sticks, without any other motto or maxim. The allegory adopted from Aesop's Fables, for strength in unity, (that a single stick can easily be snapped by a boy, but tied together, they are unbreakable), is visually stated without the need for explanation – it would have been understood by those wearing it, simply in iconic terms. Linguistically also, early maxims and mottoes serve as warnings, such as the 'S.O.M.A' – 'Secrecy, Obedience, Mutual Assistance'[23] –, which is found on many badges of the American Knights Of Labor and has clear overtones of freemasonry therein. In Australia, the eight hours movement is central to its trade union heritage, far more so than similar campaigns in Britain. It was the success of the first eight hours campaign in Melbourne in 1856, which gave birth to the modern Australian trade union movement. Annual eight hours commemoration days were celebrated thereafter throughout Australia. Personalised and highly ornate 'eight-hours committee' medals and badges were awarded to organisers of these celebrations, all of which feature, in common with membership badges of many other Australian trade unions, the recurring motif of the triple eight symbol – eight hours labour, eight hours recreation and eight hours rest,[24] a motif which, in our own globalised and deregulated age, still seems as poignant almost one hundred and fifty years on. The intertwined triple eight motif, therefore, is akin to the clasped handshake of unity, and captures within it the sacrifice, achievement and aspirations, the history of an entire movement, all of which is immediately conveyed by it to those who recognise it.

Many British trade unions in the eighteenth century operated in the guise of friendly societies, which had become partially legal in 1793, during the years in which the Combination Acts were in force, making trade union organisation illegal.[25] The material culture of friendly societies, trade unions and those organisations somewhere in between, is therefore more scarce and often without provenance. Trade union banners and emblems proper however, were first widely used during the early 1800s, especially after the repeal of the Combination Acts in 1824, whereas trade union badges were not to come into their own until the last decade of the nineteenth century. One consequence, however, of the repeal of the Combination Acts, was that trade unions could operate more openly, though caution was of course still necessary. The implementation of the 1797 Unlawful Oaths Act, to prosecute the Tolpuddle Martyrs in 1834, is the most famous example of such necessity. However, in becoming more visually and publicly present, the early trade unions inevitably generated more material culture. One early example of this process, are the trade union beer tokens, which were used by members at lodge meetings, at this early stage still largely held in public houses and taverns. Examples are known to survive from unions such as the Boilermakers,[26] Liverpool Tinplate Workers[27] and the Brushmakers.[28] These were exchanged with the landlord for beer at lodge meetings and redeemed by the union for cash afterwards. As the craft unions progressed into mid-century, they increasingly wished to be seen as respectable, and gave up meeting in taverns.

The oldest banner to be discovered by Gorman was that of the United Tin Plate Workers Society, which is believed to date from 1820,[29] although a flag of the Hawick Stocking Makers dates from 1797, and is thought to be the oldest in Scotland.[30] Although emblematic representations of tramping cards, etc. date from the eighteenth century,[31] the coloured emblems once so common on parlour walls seem to date from around the 1820s as emblems of the Independent Order of Oddfellows Friendly Society are known to date from around this period.[32] The Boilermakers had an emblem by 1836[33] and the Brushmakers by 1839.[34] There is no doubt that banners and emblems were viewed with immense pride, and were not to be handled roughly, or made light of. The Webbs, referring to the emblem, state: 'To him it is some slight connecting link with the other men in his trade or society. To his wife it is the charter of their rights in case of sickness, want of work or death.'[35] To say that the emblem was only 'a slight connecting link' is to underestimate the symbolic power and reverential status of the emblem. Its importance is demonstrated by the monument on the grave of James Amos of the Boilermakers in New Swindon cemetery, where 'upon which at his expressed wish is an engraved metal plate representing the old emblem of the society'.[36] It is said that there were few union activists who did not have an emblem framed on the parlour wall, and Arthur Pugh asserts that: 'That and the union badge or ribbon was the outward and visible sign of the owner's trade union faith.'[37] Bob Weir, writing about the American Knights Of Labor of the late nineteenth century, comments that 'For many Knights, their identity was as much shaped by a dime-sized lapel pin as by the weighty pronouncements of convention delegates.'[38]

The ribbons and sashes used increasingly from the 1870s onwards were generally worn on special occasions by officers of the unions on demonstrations, processions and funerals. Often, they were like the example of the British Steel Smelters, Mill and Tinplate Workers from the 1890s:

> The metal badge [clasp] is 3 inches across and nearly 1½ inches deep, it is embossed with the familiar emblem of unity and friendship, the firm handshake. Attached to the metal clasp is a 6½ inch by 2½ inch reversible silk ribbon. At the foot of the ribbon hangs a 1 inch fringe in gold thread. The blue side of the ribbon was shown at processions and meetings, and the black side at funerals.[39]

The blue side bore the legend 'In union is strength', whilst the black side bore the legend 'In Memoriam' (see Figure 1.1). It was something the individual could wear. It did not have to be mounted on a wall, it could be special to the member himself. By the 1890s, the firm of George Tutill were issuing special sash 'embellishments', as Gorman states:

> Special metal badges could be added to the sashes, emblematic of the union as in the case of the Bristol branch of the National Amalgamated Sailors and Firemen's Union that carried two. One bearing the union motto 'Pull Together' and the other depicting the world and the word 'Unity'.[40]

Such embellishment badges would normally be made of base metal and attached to the sash by sewing them on. These were common amongst friendly societies, although later the embellishments were sometimes of the lithographic button variety. Black ribbons would be pinned on at a lodge meeting by members in respect for a deceased member. The ultimate personalisation of the lapel badge would take this one step further. Pugh has said that sashes, emblems and banners were equal partners in union imagery made manifest; the link with the emblem is further strengthened by the fact that many craft unions adopted them for the designs of their lapel badges. In a description of the Amalgamated Society of Carpenters and Joiners (ASC&J) emblem, the author states that: 'In the centre under the figure of St. Joseph is introduced a shield bearing the arms and surmounted by the crest of the society',[41] and later that: 'the following year [1911] our G.C. [Governing Council] issued the present society badge, which every member is supposed to exhibit on his watch chain or in his jacket lapel.'[42]

The badge that was issued was the same shield as that described in the emblem. From at least 1921, the membership emblem was supplied with elaborate descriptions of its symbolism, a practice that was carried over into the union's journal, in relation to the derivative lapel badge, to at least 1963[43] The Bricklayers and the

Figure 1.1   Ceremonial ribbon and clasp of the British Steel Smelters, Mill and Tinplate Workers Association c.1890s. The reverse in black, was for display at funerals of former members, through which the dangerous nature of the work is all too clearly conveyed. It also exemplifies how the traditional favour or ribbon was being used in conjunction with badges as the ornate metal clasp illustrates.
David Yorke collection.

Boilermakers were other unions which followed this trend, as was the printers assistants' union NATSOPA in 1913.[44] As has been mentioned, it would seem that the craft unions were reaching up to their cathedralised banners and emblems and plucking from them the central shield or vignette which most epitomised and encapsulated the tools and traditions of their trade and placing them on their lapels. In so doing they were able to have with them an attractive symbol of their union membership, which did not have to be left at home on the parlour wall, or carefully rolled up and kept in oilskin-lined containers, only to be brought out on parades. The pride felt when looking at their membership emblem or when marching under the banner could now be kept with them to display as they wished (or indeed, dared).[45]

The mass popularity of the badge in the trade union movement seems to have taken off in the 1890s, although, as we will see in Chapter 2, they existed before this. Medallions are known to have been issued in the last quarter of the nineteenth century, although their detail is not related to any great extent. The train drivers' union, The Associated Society of Locomotive Engineers and Firemen (ASLEF), declared that in 1887: 'we have three hundred medals the size and thickness of a shilling sterling silver.'[46] Also it is recorded that one Matthew Smith when elected district delegate for the Birkenhead No.1 Branch of the Boilermakers Society in 1875, was presented with a gold watch and medallion. What form the gold medallion took, however, is not explained.[47] The idea of introducing the badge into a union often came about as a result of propositions from the branches, rather than from above at national level. Weir notes that as early as 1880:

> Indiana Knights demanded to know where they could get badges and pins like other locals had, a summons that baffled the GEB as no authorized versions existed. In 1881 the leadership relented and appointed a committee to design a badge. The one-inch diameter final product was completed in early 1882. It contained a triangle enclosed by a circle with 'K of L' emblazoned across the middle. Anger erupted when the many orders were delayed due to a manufacturing flaw.[48]

It is noted by the Union of Construction, Allied Trades and Technicians (UCATT), that in 1911, in the November issue of the monthly journal, a resolution was passed from the Newport second branch (probably of the ASC&J whose badge had appeared in 1911): 'That we the members of the above branch consider it advisable to adopt the method of other trade unions in the matter of a badge or button* as a mark of distinction between us and non-unionists.'[49]

The badge was issued in December 1911 at a cost to members of 6d. This implies the badge was becoming popular amongst trade unions, and that in 1911 the ASC&J were by no means the first union to adopt it. It is possible that the idea of the badge was copied from Canada where ASC&J branches had been established some years before.[50] An example of a Canadian ASC&J medal is held by a British collector, which lends credence to this idea. ASC&J branches also existed in the US until 1914, when they merged with the United Brotherhood of Carpenters and Joiners.[51] But as the resolution itself points out, they wanted to adopt 'the methods of other [contemporary British?] unions in the matter of the badge or button*'. It is perhaps also worth noting that the first ASC&J badge bore upon it the symbols of the woodworking trade, but no wording or initials that would signify it as a trade union badge. This could mean any number of things: that to display the union name would lead to dismissal from work, or that the symbol was well known enough in the trade as that of the union not to need lettering. It could even be that it was mimicking the Freemasons in its discretion as it pictured a compass and set square as do many Masonic medals. However, an Australian branch of the ASC&J had been formed in Sydney in 1875, and a round medallion dating from 1912, struck by the Australian branch, pictures the shield as a central design inside a ring bearing the union's full name, and the Latin motto 'Credo Sed Caveo' – 'I Believe, But I Beware'.[52] Another Australian ASC&J fob of a probably similar vintage was made especially for the ship joiners' section.[53] Branches of other unions were also now demanding badges. The following appeared in the quarterly report of the National Amalgamated Society of Operative House and Ship Painters and Decorators in 1914:

> In response to inquiries for badges from many branches, the E.C have approved a design submitted by Messrs. Fattorini and Sons, of Bradford. The badges are specially made to be worn in the buttonhole of the coat, and the pendant to be attached to the watch chain. These bear the name of the Society and the painter's coat of arms, in gilt and enamel, making a highly decorative badge, which every member of the Society should be proud to wear.

The extent of the popularity of these badges is perhaps implied in that, by the Society's 32nd annual report of December,1917, it was reported that stocks were almost exhausted and that henceforth a new design, in the shape of a painter's pallet would be available, bearing the abbreviated title of 'National Painters Society'. Its importance to Society officials can be gauged from their request: 'Will branch officers please draw the attention of members to the above, as we wish our badge to be used by all our members in future.' The extent to which the cathedralisation of the emblem was made more mobile, is demonstrated through the small celluloid and paper button badge issued by the National Union of Gas Workers and General Labourers in the early 1900s. They emulated their elaborate membership emblem design in colour, by transposing a section of it onto a one inch (25 mm) badge (see Figure 1.2).[54] This being a new union, it is perhaps indicative of a desire to imitate the iconography of the craft unions, if not their practices, in order to engender an air of aesthetic legitimacy to their new organisation.

The emblem then, and the banner in many cases, provided the imagery and the visual scope which was adapted for the badge. It was no mere aside to the emblem and banners. Ben Turner of the General Union of Textile Workers, recalled that

Figure 1.2 **Lithograph and tin (button) badge of the National Union of Gas Workers & General Labourers, c.1900s. It is shown here enlarged, picturing a detail from the union's membership emblem. It connotes both a sense of arrival and optimism, especially through its reference to the ideal of the eight-hour day, whilst paying visual homage to the imagery of craft unionism, whose traditional conservatism the 'new unions' of unskilled labourers of the 1890s otherwise ridiculed.**
Joe Fleming collection, photograph Dean Bennett.

workers leaving the mill at night, wearing their union button was 'a real good sight' and 'a sign of independence and progress'. He gives the instance when: 'At one mill, a manager had to meet a deputation of work people and when he saw the buttons on their smocks he surrendered and said "hang it, it's no use talking to yoh, ahd better talk ta t' union folk nah".'[55]

The badge showed that the workers were all union members from a cursory glance at their smocks. It took great courage to wear the union badge at work on many occasions, as will be examined in Chapter 3. Its positive effects though, were to announce their membership and therefore their protection, without having to assert it verbally. Another instance of the membership badge as a symbol of pride and defiance, as well as security and fraternity, is well illustrated in the following passage, which relates to the successful strike in 1912 at Murray's sweet factory over recognition and conditions. The strike had been inaugurated by women in the National Federation of Women Workers, and was supported by male members of the N.U. Gas Workers and General Labourers:

The firm met Mary MacArthur and Mr. Wright of the Gas Workers and General Labourers Union who was representing the men, and a settlement was arrived at, which included full recognition of the union, after which, the workers, men and women, returned
to work, every one of the three hundred wearing their union badge.[56]

The Badge in Context with Emblems

Eric Hobsbawm has described the union badge as 'another non-utilitarian object'[57]
except amongst certain unions, which will be explored in Chapter 3. Turner's
example of the GUTW badge contradicts this, as it was designed to advertise the
union, not as a piece of jewellery. Appendix 1, further proffers the utility of the
ordinary membership badge in the contemporary sense. While banners and emblems had the opportunity to establish a niche in the labour movement throughout
the nineteenth century, the badge, as mentioned earlier, did not make an appearance
until the 1890s in any significant form or numbers. Hobsbawm, drawing on Muller,
states that:

> While in 1889, more than half the membership of the Amalgamated Society of Engineers
> had owned a certificate, in 1916 only 20% did so. And of the 43,000 who joined in 1917,
> only perhaps 750–800 bought one. They were no doubt replaced by the more modern
> membership badge.[58]

Badges probably did in some ways take over the role of the emblem. The peak
popularity of the emblem was between 1870 and 1900, when more than 100,000
were printed and sold.[59] This is due largely to the change in printing techniques
from engraving to lithography and mass production, and colour printing instead of
tinting.[60] Leeson tells us that 'Commercial lithography of the last twenty years of
the [nineteenth] century brought more quickly produced and colourful emblems
with no increase in price ... .'[61] This suggests that the peak popularity of the
emblem culminated shortly after the first introduction of the enamel badge. An
indication of this is made in the accounts of the Federated Wire Drawers Society of
Great Britain for the year 1898, which state that expenditure on emblems was £40
6s 9d, whilst income for sale of them was only £21 6s 8d.[62] Certainly the popularity
of badges was plain to see amongst some conservative craft unions, for which the
membership certificate would normally have been the main focus of iconographical
attention: 'In 1903 The British Steel Smelters, Mill, Iron and Tinplate Workers
Association ordered 2,500 membership badges which they sold at 1s each. By the
end of the year only ten remained and a further 1,000 were ordered.'[63] In 1921 the
Amalgamated Society of Carpenters and Joiners (est.1860), merged with the older
General Union of Carpenters and Joiners (est. 1827), to form the Amalgamated
Society of Woodworkers (ASW), but continued to issue the old ASC&J emblem
with an ASW label stuck over the old name. This suggests that old stock was being
utilised even amongst the craft unions, and that branches had perhaps ordered more

emblems than they could dispose of. It is noted that the General Union of Braziers and Sheet Metal Workers had 'already in 1872 ordered emblems for sale to members and later on bought a supply of badges for the members to purchase',[64] thus illustrating the underlying trend to acquire whatever available means of making trade union sentiment and principle visual and manifest. By the early Edwardian period, badges were becoming as popular as emblems had been in their own time. But this by no means proves that badges had usurped the emblem. True, the ornate emblems and illuminated addresses became gradually less common, but were still produced. Emblems for retirement, merit and long service are still issued, and are still held in the same esteem as they always were. It does not mean though that one ousted the other. Members of unskilled workers unions did not have the same iconographical tradition as the older craft unions, but the utilisation of the badge seems to have been a popular decision with all organisations. There was still, however, a desire for emblems, and that for banners never abated. All three were utilised to their fullest extent, and portrayed trade union sentiment and conviction in all spheres of the member's life. This is borne out when Arthur Pugh states that 'such regalia as banners, emblems and badges had always been an important part of trade union equipment.'[65]

The Badge in Context with Banners

It is not enough to simply say that new manufacturing techniques of the 1890s which facilitated badge production led to their popularity; other plausible explanations can be put forward: 'In the 1890s, something like a banner mania seized working people and not only in their unions. Banners went everywhere to meetings, demonstrations, funerals, even picnics ...'[66] In the year of the great dock strike, 1889, the firm of George Tutill turned out more banners than ever before or since.[67] The new unions sought to announce their arrival with a banner, and in the last decade of the nineteenth century thousands were made. As with emblems these banners represented pride, presence and cause, and as such went everywhere. However, it must have been very cumbersome to carry a hefty silk banner around on so many occasions, as well as there being the risk of damage from high winds and generally adverse weather. This could therefore offer a clue to the popularity of the badge: it was a micro-representation of the banner or emblem, and was far more convenient, adaptable and personalised. It could be worn on day trips and outings without the incumbent duty to look after yards of banner silk and weighty support poles. By contrast, the badge could also belong to every member, whereas the honour of bearing the banner could be awarded to only a few. Another reason could be that of cost: 'Their banners became enterprises of the spirit, large and silken and heavy and expensive; memorials to a certain permanence.'[68] So apart from the burden of carrying these silken cathedralisations around, the cost was escalating. It was claimed that Tutill's, based in City Road, east London, had, since its founda-

Figure 1.3   George Tutill-manufactured medal of the Associated Shipwrights Society c.1900 picturing a ship under construction. The figure of Britannia surmounts the medal clasp, a visual attestation of both the craft pride felt by the Association's members and imperial Britain's dominance of the sea, standing in stark contrast to the British shipbuilding industry of today.
David Yorke collection.

tion in 1837, made 75 per cent of all banners[69] and must have therefore had a virtual monopoly of the banner trade. There is no question of badges superseding the banner, but given the high cost of banners, the inexpensive complement to them would surely have been the badge. This is where Tutill's played another card. As well as the banners that Gorman has studied, Tutill's also issued badges and medals and made all manner of regalia, though banners must have been their biggest earner. The medals that Tutill's made were for the same diverse range of organisations as the banners. They are of a similar design to each other, round or oval in shape, with a sort of star-burst effect (see Figure 1.3), and may well have been standardised as the banners were: 'As late as the 1930s, union men were still ordering the cherished late-Victorian public art enshrined in Tutill's massive catalogue of the 1890s.'[70]

Most of Tutill's medals were ceremonial in nature. That of the Association of Ex-Service Civil Servants, bearing the inscription '20 Years On', would suggest it was issued in 1937, as the Association was formed in 1917.[71] Yet it is not unlike the earlier ones of the Shipwrights and Coal Trimmers which were issued around the turn of the twentieth century. Tutill's medals then, would seem to have been issued with the same cherished public art as their banners from the same periods. Tutill's was selling two-thirds of the triple alliance in the form of banners and medals (badges are also known) and quite probably made emblems as well. They would not have been made if there was no demand, and so reiterates the case for the banner, emblem and badge as being equally sought after by unions to proclaim their presence. Ceremonial medals would not normally have been worn on their own, but would have been pinned to a sash and worn on special occasions.

There would appear to have been some reluctance to wear the ceremonial medal on its own. This was perhaps an unwillingness to give up the custom and opulence of the sash, seeing the new medals and badges as an embellishment to them. This custom is still practised by Orangemen and friendly societies on their parades. Gorman surmises that sashes seem to have died out after the General Strike in 1926[72] and so presumably the medals from that time were independently worn in their own right. A frustrated member of the Amalgamated Society of Engineers wrote to complain that the Workers Union was poaching members, in the June 1913 issue of the *ASE Monthly Journal*: 'Men who have resisted all inducements to join the skilled unions for which they are eligible, are paying their shilling entrance fee and consider themselves trade unionists as soon as they can get a button* in their coats!'[73] Note that it is 'a button* in their coats', rather than an emblem on their wall or a banner at a branch meeting place that is mentioned. This implies that the badge was synonymous with new unionism in the eyes of potential members, and personified the attempt of consolidation of such organisations at this time. The ASE, though responsible for one of the oldest dated badges (see Chapter 2), was still placing more emphasis on the traditional membership emblem, whose sales of which, as previously cited, would soon be on the decline. It does, however, highlight the recognition of iconography, and the badge specifically, as significant to the trade union movement as a whole.

To summarise, it could be argued that the banners were the pride and joy of the branch members and the feelings of pride and identity that were felt when marching with the banner on parades needed to be present to them in a more permanent way. Emblems went some way to solving this, at least they were a permanent symbol that a member could have and mount on the parlour wall, and would be theirs alone, to reassure them of some protection in time of need. However, if the union member wanted something that would convey these sentiments to all, the badge provided the answer. Along with the Albert watch chain fob of the more prosperous artisans, the lapel badge conveyed their pride in miniature. If the banner represented the collective identity and all that it stood for, then the badge represents the personalisation of, and compliance with, that same collective identity. Thus the members had the banners for special occasions, their emblems to admire at home, and their badge in their lapel to consolidate their principles in a discreet visual form, and to assert their pride in union membership for all who cared to see. The badge according to Smethurst and Devine has 'always made the member feel "dressed", instilling a sense of identity and solidarity'.[74] Indeed the silver badges of the Australasian Trained Nurses Association, between 1899 and 1924, bore on their reverse both the member's name and date of joining the Association,[75] thus providing the ultimate personalisation of such an identity symbol. Weir notes that the nineteenth-century Knights of Labor could

> ... fasten their cuffs with KOL cufflinks, adorn their shirts with KOL buttons, check the time on KOL watches, and drink water from KOL glasses ... Knights could don KOL collar stays and watch fobs that proclaimed Knighthood's universalism. Mutuality, unity, brotherhood and identity were there for the viewing[76]

Having discussed the relevance of the badge in relation to banners and emblems, it is now incumbent to investigate its possible origins and to trace some of the more tenable threads that suggest them. In the next chapter we will look at the antiquity of badges and their earliest manifestation in the trade union movement. This will give some grounding for the argument of their importance.

Notes

1 J. Deetz, *In Small Things Forgotten: the archaeology of early American life*, New York, Anchor Books, 1977, p. 16.
2 T.O. Haunch, 'English Craft Certificates', *Ars Quatuor Coronatorum* Vol. 82, 1969, pp. 169–263; A. Durr, 'Rituals Of Association And The Organisation Of The Common People', *Ars Quatuor Coronatorum*, Vol. 100, 1987, pp. 88–108, p. 98.
3 See e.g. Her Majesty's Stationary Office, *Catalogue of a collection of pottery and porcelain illustrating popular British history leant by Henry Willett*, London, HMSO, 1899; H.Willett, 'Museums And Their Uses: a paper read at the Congress of Curators at the Royal Pavilion, Brighton, July 4th 1899', reprinted from the *Brighton Herald*, July 8th 1899 (Sussex Pamphlets, Brighton Reference Library SO40 SU.8); P. H.J.H. Gosden, *The Friendly Societies In England 1815–1875*, Manchester, Manchester University Press, 1961; K. Boney, 'The Liverpool Society of Bucks', *Apollo: the magazine of the arts,* January, 1962, pp. 8–10; J. Stubbs, and T.O. Haunch, *Freemason's Hall: The Hall and Heritage of The Craft*, London, The United Grand Lodge of Freemasons of England, 1983; W.G. Cooper, *The Ancient Order of Foresters Friendly Society: 150 years 1834–1984*, Southampton, Hampshire, AOF, 1984; P. Carter, 'Fund Raising For Disaster Relief', *Trade Union Badge Collectors' Newsletter*, No. 71, Spring 2000; C. Kightly, *The Customs And Ceremonies Of Britain: an encyclopaedia of living traditions*, London, Thames and Hudson, 1986, pp. 80–81; A. Durr *Popular Art: The Emblems and Associa-*

tions of Mutual Aid, unpublished manuscript, 1988. Readers are advised that the published catalogue accompanying the exhibition of the same name in 1988, is merely a descriptive list of the objects exhibited. An unpublished 37-page A4 manuscript with accompanying illustrations of the same title in my possession was prepared, but was not, according to Durr, ultimately published. Information cited from this source will hereafter be referenced as 'Durr MS' and from which a number of antiquarian references have been used in this chapter. I am grateful to Andy Durr for permission to quote from his MS; A. Durr, *Popular Art: The Emblems And Associations Of Mutual Aid*, published exhibition catalogue, University of Brighton, 1988. For examples within early friendly societies, Masonic lodges, village clubs and political commemoration. See J. Gorman, *Images of Labour*, London, Scorpion, 1985, pp. 30, 186; J. Swift, *History of The Dublin Bakers And Others*, Dublin, 1947 for examples of early trade unions.

4 See e.g. R. Freeman, *English Emblem Books*, London, Chatto & Windus 1948, 1967 edition; H. Peacham, *Minerva Brittanica or a Garden of Heraldic Devises* (1612 facsimile), Leeds, Scolar Press, 1966; E.H. Gombrich, *Symbolic Images*, Oxford, Phaidon Press, 1972, 1985 edition; R. Wittkower, *Allegory And The Migration Of Symbols*, London, Thames & Hudson, 1977, 1987 edition; H. Diehl, *An Index of Icons In English Emblem Books 1500–1700*, Oklahoma, University of Oklahoma Press, 1986; M. Tung, 'From Heraldry To Emblem: a study of Peacham's use of heraldic arms in Minerva Brittanica', *Word And Image*, Vol. 3, No. 1, 1987, pp. 86–93; D. Russell,'The Emblem And Authority', *Words And Image*, Vol. 4, No. 1, 1988, pp. 81–87.

5 Durr MS, p. 7.

6 Ibid., p. 8.

7 See for instance Swift, *History of The Dublin Bakers*; J. Bromley and H. Child, *The Armorial Bearings Of The Guilds of London*, London, Frederick Warne & Co., 1960.

8 Prior to their formalisation in 1717, in the Grand Lodge of England, freemasons had acted as a kind of proto-trade union through the Society of Masons in the sixteenth and seventeenth centuries. See A. Durr, 'The Origin of The Craft', *Ars Quatuor Coronatorum*, No. 96, 1983, pp. 170–183; A. Durr, 'Rituals of Association and the Organisation of the Common People', *Ars Coronatorum*, No. 100, 1987, pp. 88–108. Durr believes there is little doubt that friendly societies copied masonic ritual: Durr, 'Rituals of Association', p. 99. Durr's papers are published in the transactions of the English Freemasons, *Quatuor Coronati*, 2076 research lodge. They are accessible via the library of the United Grand Lodge of England, London.

9 W. Sutherland and W.G. Sutherland, 'Emblems of the Friendly Societies of Great Britain', in W. Sutherland and W.G. Sutherland (eds), *The Sign-Writer And The Glass Embosser*, Manchester, The Decorative Art Journal, 1898; Cooper, *The Ancient Order of Foresters Friendly Society*.

10 Durr MS, p. 1.

11 Weir, *Beyond Labor's Veil*, p. 9.

12 Ibid., p. 10.

13 Ibid., p. 21.

14 Cited in ibid., p. 44.

15 Cited in ibid., pp. 69–70.

16 Cited in ibid., p. 66.

17 See ibid., pp. 19–66.

18 See ibid., pp. 64–66.

19 Ibid., pp. 67–101.

20 Ibid., Preface.

21 H. Pelling, 'The Knights of Labor In Britain 1880–1901', *Economic History Review*, second series, Vol. IX, Numbers 1, 2 and 3, 1956–1957, 1956, pp. 313–331; see also E.J. Hobsbawm, 'General Labour Unions In Britain 1884–1914', *Economic History Review,* second series, No. 1, 1949, pp. 123–142.

22 Durr MS, p. 24.

23 D. Yorke, personnal communication 1998.

24 See G. Smith, *Emblems Of Unity*, pp. 17, 92, 101–104, 167 174–176, 230, 259–260; A. Reeves, *Badges Of Labour Banners Of Pride*, Sydney, George Allen & Unwin, 1984, pp. 15, 36; T. Prichard, 'The Eight Hour Day Campaign In Australia', *Trade Union Badge Collectors' Newsletter,* No. 57, December, 1996.

25 But see Durr, 'Rituals of Association', pp. 93, 97, 99–100 for linguistic and conceptual qualifications.

26 J.M. Mortimer, *The History of The Boilermakers Society, Vol. 1: 1834–1906*, London, George Allen & Unwin, 1973, pp. 44–47; the 1848 rules demanded sobriety.

27 T. Brake, *Men of Good Character*, London, Lawrence & Wishart, 1985, pp. 176–177.

28 W. Kiddier, *The Old Trade Unions*, London, George Allen & Unwin, 1930, p. 35; See also P. Carter, 'Trade Union Beer Tallies', *Trade Union Badge Collectors' Newsletter*, No. 44, June, 1994, pp. 3–4. Kiddier records that the pot ticket was 'a metal disc about the size of a penny' (Kiddier, *The Old Trade Unions*, p. 35). The 1806 articles of the London Brushmakers Society state 'That on every meeting night, each member shall receive a pot ticket at eight o' clock, a pint at ten, and no more' (article V1, Kiddier, *The Old Trade Unions*, p. 37). Brake notes that the Liverpool Tinplate Makers Society threepenny beer tokens were stamped from 20-gauge brass, and that their minute book records that as late as 1860 'that 100 drink checks be made and that Wm Tower make them'. It was not until 1868 that the Society abandoned meeting in pubs (Brake, *Men of Good Character*, pp. 176–177). In some working men's clubs, the use of beer tokens was only discontinued around 1970, due to decimalisation (Cox and Cox, *The Tokens, Checks, Metallic Tickets, Passes And Tallies Of Wales 1800–1993*, p. 218).

29 J. Gorman, *Banner Bright*, London, Allan Lane, 1973, p. 68.

30 I. McDougall, *Labour In Scotland*, Edinburgh, Mainstream Publishing, 1985, p. 30.

31 The appearance of iconographical and allegorical representations on tramping cards in the eighteenth and nineteenth centuries had its twentieth-century invocation as well. Gorman relates the competition held annually from 1907 to 1955 in the London Society of Compositors (LSC) to decide on the illustration of the annual membership card. This arose from 'an outcry against one year's card which was described as a monstrosity and offended the craft pride of the display compositors' (Gorman, *Images of Labour*, pp. 111–112). A first prize of five pounds with second and third prizes of one pound and ten shillings respectively, were awarded for the best designs. The winning design was adopted for use on that year's card whilst an order was placed with the firm for which the winning entrant worked. After the amalgamation between the LSC and the Printing Machine Minders Trade Society in 1955, to form the London Typographical Society (LTS), the competition continued, but only until 1963 when the LTS amalgamated with the Typographical Association to form the National Graphical Association. This serves to illustrate the diversity of, and pride in, labour iconography and the equation of the dignity of labour that it implicitly represents.

32   Leeson, *United We Stand*, p. 11.

33   Ibid., p. 20.

34   Ibid., p. 8.

35   S. and B. Webb, *History Of Trade Unions*, London, Longman, 1950, p. 450. The Amalgamated Society of Woodworkers are a good example of the continuation of the emblem and its interchangability with the badge. In 1928 a member's emblem was introduced for long service, seventeen years after the introduction of the first badge in 1911. This was replaced in 1940 by a silver badge. The Union of Construction, Allied Trades and Technicians (UCATT) with which the ASW amalgamated in 1971, issued a certificate denoting twenty-five years' service in an official capacity, being first issued in 1980. It was replaced in November 1987 by a badge. Although it could be argued that this shows a preference for using badges by replacing emblems with them, it also shows that emblems are thought of as significant, as the example above shows their intermittent reintroduction. See J. Hardman, *UCATT Viewpoint*, November 1987.

      The 'V.C of the ASE' (Amalgamated Society of Engineers) merit emblem was presented to Frank King in 1962. The same emblem, which is very similar to the first Amalgamated Engineering Union emblem issued in 1920, was still in use in the 1980s. This itself has strong similarities to the Amalgamated Society of Engineers emblem of the 1890s (see Gorman, *Images of Labour*, p. 75). In the 1960s, the Amalgamated Society of Painters and Decorators (ASP&D) issued a membership emblem, the roots of the design of which are firmly in the early 1900s (see ASP&D Annual Report, December 1963, back cover). The examples used show the continuing popularity of the emblem and its thematic loyalty to the emblems of the nineteenth century.

36   Cummings, *The History Of The United Society Of Boilermakers*, p. 37.

37   Pugh, *Men Of Steel*, p. 340.

38   Weir, *Beyond Labor's Veil*, p. 231.

39   'Gold, Silver And Silk Badges For Steelworkers', *Man and Metal*, Vol. 49, No. 7, July, 1972, p. 172.

40   Gorman, *Images of Labour*, p. 188.

41   Higginbottom, *Our Society's History*, p. 340.

42   Ibid., p. 180.

43   The ASC&J became the Amalgamated Society of Woodworkers in 1921, by amalgamating with the General Union of Carpenters and Joiners. On this occasion an elaborate explanation of the union's emblematic heraldry was written by a 'Bro. Herbert Crompton of Chicago USA'. He describes at length the meanings behind the gules, chevron, roses, scallop shell, compasses and motto. See *The Woodworkers Journal*, September, 1963, pp. 417–418.

44   R.B. Suthers, *The Story of NATSOPA 1889–1929*, London, NATSOPA, 1929, p. 43.

45   For instance see the account of the 1919 Vale of Glamorgan agricultural workers strike related in D.A. Pretty, *The Rural Revolt That Failed: Farm Workers Trade Unions In Wales 1889–1950*, Cardiff, University of Wales Press, 1989, pp. 129–134 and the photograph of participants that appears on the dust jacket, all wearing the badge of the National Agricultural and Rural Workers Union (NARWU)... .

46   J.R. Raynes, *Engines And Men* (Associated Society of Locomotive Engineers and Firemen), London, Goodall & Suddick, 1921, p. 63.

47   Cummings, *History of the United Society of Boilermakers*, pp. 93–95.

48   Weir, *Beyond Labor's Veil*, pp. 243–244.

49   Hardman, *UCATT Viewpoint.*
50   Ibid.
51   Rubenstein, 'Symbols And Images of American Labour: Badges of Pride', p. 44.
52   Smith, *Emblems Of Unity*, p. 31. Perhaps the earliest example of an Australian branch
     of a British union being formed is the Amalgamated Society of Engineers. The Austral-
     ian branch was formed on '8th October 1852 aboard the ship "Francis Walker", en
     route to Sydney. Further branches were established in Melbourne in 1859, Ballarat in
     1861, Williamstown in 1863, Newcastle in 1861, Adelaide in 1864, Sandhurst in 1865,
     and Ipswich in 1865. By 1866 membership of these eight branches was over four
     hundred.' The ASE like its British parent became the Amalgamated Engineering Union
     (AEU) in 1920 and remained a branch of the British union until 1968, when it became
     independent until 1972. It then amalgamated with the Boilermakers and Blacksmiths
     Society of Australia (Smith, *Emblems of Unity*, pp. 33, 22). It issued at least one ASE
     medallion, of a type unissued in Britain, whilst its AEU badges were much the same as
     the British ones. The export of organisation was facilitated during the First World War,
     when the Australian Munition Workers Association was founded in England by 'sev-
     eral thousand [Australian] munitions workers sent to England to work in munitions
     factories'. The ornate badge of the Association was made by 'Bladon, London' (Smith,
     Emblems Of Unity, pp. 65).
53   Smith, *Emblems of Unity*, p. 32. The Australian branch eventually amalgamated with
     other unions in 1942 to form the Building Workers Industrial Union of Australia
     (Smith, *Emblems of Unity*, p. 93).
54   See C. Muller, *James Sharples und das Zertifikat der Amalgamated Society of Engi-
     neers: Studien zur Bildkultur Britischer Gewerkshaften*, Hamburg, 1978, p. 266 for
     illustration.
55   B. Turner, *A Short History Of The General Union Of Textile Workers*, Heckmondwike,
     Labour Pioneer & Factory Times Printing Department, 1920, p. 188.
56   Anon. *Fifty Years of the National Union of General and Municipal Workers Union*
     (1889–1939), London, NUG&MW, 1939, p. 51.
57   E.J. Hobsbawm, *Worlds of Labour*, London, Weidenfeld & Nicholson, 1984, pp. 73–4.
58   Ibid.
59   Leeson, *United We Stand*, p. 6.
60   Ibid., p. 16.
61   Ibid., p. 18.
62   Federated Wire Drawers Society of Great Britain accounts 1898. I am grateful to Peter
     Carter for passing this on to me.
63   'Gold, Silver And Silk Badges For Steelworkers', p. 182.
64   Brake, *Men of Good Character*, p. 215.
65   Pugh, *Men of Steel*, p. 529.
66   G.A. Williams, introduction to J. Gorman, *Banner Bright,* London, Allen Lane: 1973,
     p. 12.
67   Ibid., p. 12.
68   Ibid., p. 6.
69   Ibid.
70   Ibid.
71   A. Marsh and V. Ryan, *Historical Directory of Trade Unions, Volume 1*, Hampshire,

Gower, 1980, p. 20; an example of the medal is held in the collection of a British collector known to the author.

72   Gorman, *Images of Labour*, p. 188.
73   R. Hyman, *The Workers Union*, London, Clarendon Press, 1971, p. 71.
74   Smethurst and Devine, 'Trade Union Badges – Mere Emblems or Means of Membership Control?', p. 93.
75   Smith, *Emblems of Unity*, p. 44.
76   Weir, *Beyond Labor's Veil*, p. 233.

Chapter 2

The Lapel Emblazoned: The Origins and Development of the Trade Union Badge

Have a nice white rosette or a neat star, but by all means don't have a rosette the size of a dinner plate, the same as we have seen at some of the demonstrations of late (have nothing gaudy).[1]

At the Knights of Labor's 1880 convention, Terence Powderly [the KOL leader] was besieged by supplicants clamoring for 'some sort of badge' to signify Knighthood. He tried to avoid them, as the 1880 KOL was still a secret organization containing strict ritualists who felt he had already tinkered too much with time honoured practices. Nonetheless, one year later, the Grand Assembly approved an official badge.[2]

Rosettes and Ribbons

White rosettes were the personal emblem of choice for the South Yorkshire Miners Association at the 1873 Chesterfield demonstration. The custom of wearing ribbons, rosettes and sashes is one which was common amongst trade unionists from the earliest times. Such desire for collective recognition through 'fancies', 'favours', 'cockades', etc. goes back far in time. General Gordon in 1779 suggested to his Protestant Association, for the meeting in St. George's Fields, that 'they should wear blue cockades in their caps that they may know each other.'[3] Before the Manchester Bastille dinner in 1791, celebrants were warned against 'wearing cockades or badges of distinction to avoid disturbance',[4] whilst R.A. Leeson tells us that at the turn of the eighteenth century, after the Combination Acts had been passed 'radical workers wore the green ribbon, memento of the Agitators of Cromwell's army and the rebels at Sedgemoor ... '[5] A 'badge' in such instances as these could mean virtually anything.

The signifying of place or rank in a procession or demonstration by wearing a cockade or a coloured rosette or ribbon would be considered dignified by union officials, and no doubt helped the marshals to form up the march in the correct order. This, though, is not to assume that the muteness of a simple coloured rosette was the predecessor of a more articulate, engraved or printed slogan in the form of a badge. Commemorative tokens in Britain date from the mid-sixteenth century[6] and political tokens are known to date from at least the eighteenth century, the most

21

celebrated examples being issued by Thomas Spence.[7] Metal 'badges' of some description are believed to date from around the early seventeenth century.[8] There are three main strands which can be pointed to that may lead to more insight on this question. First, the rosette, favour or ribbons, etc: these can be traced back in time with reasonable continuity. Early union examples of ribbons are held by the National Museum of American History in Washington, DC, of organisations such as the House Painters Society, which was worn in a New York procession to commemorate the completion of the Erie Canal in 1825, and of the Glass Cutters Trade Union Society of 1840.[9] In Britain ribbons were still being worn by the agricultural labourers at least, in the 1870s:

> The members used to have a piece of blue braid around their hats to show that they were members of the union. That was in the days before the badge was thought of. There were four letters upon the braid only, 'NALU' which stood for the National Agricultural Labourers Union.[10]

In 1880s America meanwhile, the Knights Of Labor developed extremely ornate and grandiose ribbons of office.[11] In the 1930s, button badges were issued attached to ribbons, demanding the six-hour day[12] and so, even when more developed means of iconic expression were developed, the older ones such as ribbons and rosettes were still utilised. It is interesting to note that even nowadays with all the sophistication of the enamel badge and other devices, that the rosette, one of the oldest forms of the badge is still around. Often seen on the lapels of parliamentary candidates at election time, used as awards in agricultural shows, gymkhanas, and exhibitions and shows of all types, its traditional use still persists. As already mentioned however, this is not to negate the fact that metallic items either as keepsakes or for actual appendage to clothing were not used, and therein lie two other strands of ancestry to the contemporary badge. Records show that in the mid-nineteenth century, at the dawn of the trade union movement in Australia, based on the campaign for the eight-hour day 'unionists were identifying themselves, usually in the form of different coloured ribbons or rosettes, with the organising committee members wearing hand-engraved silver badges, from at least the 1880s.'[13] In the early 1830s, Robert Owen's Grand National Consolidated Trades Union issued suitable ribbons for wearing at the funeral of fellow members. They featured the words 'In memory of our Departed BROTHER' 'Resurgam', whilst other designs for use in the centre of rosettes, referred to as 'badges' were also made. They were advertised thus:

> The following are specimens of Union Badges and centres for rosettes, printed on silk by Brother Harding, 10 Grafton Street, Soho. The badges are sold at 11/2d. and the centres at 1d. each. As all these little emblems and tokens of respect have a tendency to inspire the mind with the kindlier feelings, we thought it probable that our country [i.e. those outside of London] brothers would like to see them in print.[14]

Metal Badges

Papal dispensation was given in the twelfth century to the authorities in Rome to make pewter badges featuring St. Peter and St. Paul which were worn by pilgrims as a sign of devotion.[15] Certainly, by the fourteenth century, brooches bearing the effigy of saints – 'pilgrim badges' – had become commonly worn by those travers-ing the established routes to pay their devotions to their favoured saints, such as Thomas Becket. Some are of quite large size, such as those held in the Neish Pewter Collection, formally displayed in Harvard House, Stratford-upon-Avon. By 1522, a writer of emblem books, Alciata, was suggesting that after reading his *Emblematica*: 'painters, goldsmiths and founders can fashion objects which we will call badges and which we fasten on our hats, or else bear as trade marks … .'[16] By the late seventeenth and early eighteenth centuries, large badges made of various metals such as pewter, silver and brass are found to have been used on civil uniforms. In the private fire insurance companies of this period, mention is made of badges, usually for the arm of the tunic. The Hand-In-Hand Insurance Company issued a 'blue cloth tunic with silver buttons with a silver plate on the left sleeve showing the locked hand device of the company embossed on it',[17] and the instruc-tion to the wearers was 'cloathes [sic] and badges must be worn constantly.'[18] Furthermore:

> On a fire proposal form by the Sun Fire office in 1710 it stated: 'For the further encouragement of all the persons there are actually employed in the service of the office, thirty lusty able-bodied firemen, who are clothed in blue liveries, and having silver badges with the sun mark upon their arms, and twenty able porters likewise, who are always ready to assist in quenching fires and removing goods having been given bonds for their fidelity'.[19]

Christian Muller asserts that the wearing of badges in the secular realm seems to point quite clearly to the Guilds and Corporations.[20] He believes that it was a drive for legitimacy which led early unions to copy the Guilds and Masons' custom of badge wearing. He cites the instance of the Fraternity of London Building Workers who in 1605 produced 'tin badges' which pictured crossed shovels on the obverse and the member's name on the reverse for the Feast of the Trinity. Union badges, he continues, were the final step in the challenge to the issuing of badges by employ-ers associations.[21] Certainly, at the exhibition, *British Trade Union Badges*, held at the British Museum in 1986, there was an example of a medallion of the Worship-ful Company of Needle Makers from 1777, and another of the Worshipful Com-pany of Joiners, dating from the mid-nineteenth century. Additionally, Ted Brake illustrates an apprentice's badge of the Tin Plate Workers Company, dated 1747, the obverse bearing the company's arms, the reverse inscribed: 'Tho' Cooke bound May 14th in the year 1747'.[22] Muller cites the survival of such 'over-sized badges' in the annual rowing competition of the Fishermen's Company in London.[23] He may be referring here to the Doggett Coat and Badge race, originally competed between the Thames Watermen as part of their coming out of apprenticeship ceremony. This race was inaugurated in 1716 by the actor Thomas Doggett, to commemorate the accession to the throne of George I (and continues today in an amended form). The coat was a long tunic, originally orange and later changed to scarlet, and had sewn to its sleeve a large oval silver (later pewter) badge, which was the prize of the winner of the race.[24] Henry Pelling in *A History of British Trade Unionism*, cites the eyewitness account of one of those who watched a demonstration parade in support of the London dockers' strike in 1889: 'there were also better off sympathisers such as the Watermen who paraded in long scarlet coats, pink stockings and velvet caps, with huge pewter badges at their breasts like decorated amphibious huntsmen.'[25] It would seem from this description that by the 1880s the badge had cased to be attached to the arm as was traditional, and had been transferred to the breast, as was common with rosettes, etc. The above examples show that 'badges' of one kind or another were commonly used long before the ascent of the union badge, but as a form of iconography it illustrates its probable heritage and ancestry as an established concept at an early period.

Political Tokens

The third strand of origin in concept at least can perhaps be traced back to the enigmatic Thomas Spence, who at one time supplemented his income by issuing political tokens, probably 'between the years 1793–7'.[26] Spence was a radical who has come to be seen as one of the earliest proto-socialists. His ideology was utopian in the mould of Thomas More. He believed in parochial ownership and administration of society, and complete adult suffrage, including women. His ideal societies were eulogised through the fictional societies of Crusonia and Spenconia.[27] He earned his living for some time as a bookseller in London, where he also issued his political tokens, which carried satirical comments on George III and popularised his own convictions. He apparently 'frequently distributed [them] by jerking them from his windows amongst passengers' as well as selling them to collectors, who were around even then![28]

People apparently began to collect industrial trade tokens issued by (especially) the northern industrialists, workhouses and traders during the shortage of small denominational coinage in the late eighteenth and early nineteenth centuries – Spence's tokens got lumped in with them. There was outcry amongst some collectors at the way Spence changed the obverses and reverses and 'muled' (that is, crossed) various dies.[29] To use such tokens as a means of spreading propaganda would probably have been innovative at the time. The various sew-on metal medals or tallies issued throughout the nineteenth century to commemorate the Peterloo massacre and the reform bills amongst other things, which preceded the badge, may have gathered intensity from this point, notwithstanding, as previously mentioned, that commemorative tokens and proto-medals had been issued in Britain since at least the sixteenth century. These three strands then of favours and rosettes, the 'livery' badges and political tokens, would seem to be good reference points for further investigation.

Medals and Medalettes

Rosettes appear to make the most common appearance in processions and would seem to have the strongest continuity and line of descent in the labour movement. Parallel with this however, is the old enamelling trade for more elaborate regalia, which was largely supplanted by the coming of the vitreous enamelling process (see below and Chapter 5). The Royal Foresters (friendly society) for instance in 1780 'wore enamelled medallions with the picture of a forester, with his bow, hunting'.[30] In these early days, friendly and trade societies, were all involved in social and political reform and struck medals to assert the cause. One such is the burgh reform medal dating from 1792, struck by the Glasgow Society Friends of Reform, held by the People's Palace Museum which reads: 'Be unanimous, active and steady in asserting & establishing the rights of man, and be not weary of well doing, for by wisdom, prudence and courage in due time, ye shall reap, if ye faint not.'[31] In other cases, metallic appendages are intermittently mentioned. The London Oddfellows in 1802, were using 'a silver medallion inside a hand-painted emblem on bone covered by glass'.[32] By the nineteenth century, base metal tokens often had holes drilled through them for fixing to clothing. A description of the Tinsmiths Society at the Edinburgh trades demonstration of 1832 states that 'The banner bearers wore tin hats and the whole body carried tin batons and wore medals.'[33]

There is no description of the 'medal', but a 'medal' from the late eighteenth century of the Cork Harbour Labourers Guild of St. Patrick, is kept in the Cork Public Museum in Ireland,[34] and 'medallions' of Guilds predating the metal lapel badges are thought to exist.[35] The Tinsmiths 'medal' may have been of this type, or it may have been a reform token with a hole drilled through it. It may of course, simply have been a plain metal disc, symbolic of the trade, with no design on it at all. However, in 1873 in their demonstration against the Criminal Law Amendment Act, the Tinsmiths committee 'bought three hundred rosettes out of the funds'.[36] This is not to suggest that in 1832 they did not wear rosettes or that in 1873 they did not use 'medals', but rather that the pattern of personalised emblems worn by the individual was not a simple progression from the anonymity of the plain ribbon or rosette to a more articulate and sophisticated form in the shape of the badge. Hobsbawm says that 'rosettes, ribbons and sashes were popular it seems not only among miners, but transport workers and among union officials generally.'[37] In addition, there exist medals of obscure organisations such as the white metal medal of the Whitchurch Tradesmen's Society 'Established March 1st 1788'. This bears the beehive of industry and the union maxim 'united we stand divided we fall'. It appears however, to have been established as a friendly society, 'but in its early days was very much concerned with the working class movement for democracy … 'The Society continued until 1902, by which time it had become very much more "middle-class", at least in its administration.'[38]

At the already mentioned Chesterfield demonstration of the Yorkshire miners, it was said that the New Whittington lodge were especially commented on for their 'beautiful silken rosettes'.[39] At the Derbyshire and Nottinghamshire miners' gala in Ripley three weeks later, lodges wore different coloured rosettes.[40] Although these examples are taken only from the miners, it shows that rosettes and ribbons were popular here at least, and provides evidence for the continuity of such items in labour history whereas other more 'articulate' items, such as tokens, etc. have a more patchy history.

Earlier, the Benevolent Institution of Whitesmiths, in their 1825 rule book, state that a 'medal' was to be awarded annually for the encouragement of industry, to be voted by a ballot of members.[41] A 'medal' of this kind could have been a double-sided token, not designed for wear, as such tokens are often referred to as 'medals'. More significantly perhaps, J. Callahan Junior, secretary of the Society of Brassfounders 'called on all members to provide themselves with a blue favour with ornament to be attached to the left breast … .'[42] This was to be worn on the annual Saint Monday parade of 1828. It is significant because although 'medallic' items may have been around at this time, such instances that are known tend to be vague and intermittent, whereas the above example suggests that the badges were ceremonial medals which were to become more prevalent in the 1890s; being pre-articulated or proto-fashioned, and thus suggest a development in the continuity of the theme of rosettes, etc. It must be said though that the 'ornament' is not described, and the idea may have been given to Callahan Junior by already existing articulated appendages. Favours and fancies had been attached to all kinds of clothing, or even knight's lances in medieval jousts, but here it is made quite clear, that it should be attached to the breast.

Tallies

'Tokens', 'checks', 'metallic tickets', 'passes' and 'tallies' have become the most commonly used terms within paranumismatics (the collection and study of coin-like objects). Prevalent since the early nineteenth century, they 'were very much part of … commercial, domestic and industrial life … during the last two hundred years and in some instances represent the last remaining artefacts of people, organisations and industries which have long since gone'.[43] A study of those issued in Wales over the last two hundred years cover all major industries, plus advertising tickets, barbers' checks, brewery checks, church, choir and Temperance Hall tokens and passes, market traders' tickets, military, refreshment, telephone, tool and pay checks, transport tokens and passes, truck tickets, and of importance here, trade union registration tallies, mainly in the mines (see Chapter 3). They were vital to the pre-Second World War cooperative movement, when each local society issued its own tokens for the dividend, prepayment and mutuality systems before the coming of supermarkets and printed trade stamps, and were used in working men's clubs until decimalisation.[44] Tallies in general ranged in quality from pressed tin to brass, stamped with the relevant number, words or other visual recognition device. Within trade unions they played a parallel role with the medalettes discussed above, though they were mostly used (but not exclusively) in mines and docks (discussed in Chapter 3).

Technology

Hobsbawm, citing Muller, claims that badges and watch chain fobs began to spread from about 1860 onwards.[45] This though is far from certain. Muller makes only a calculated guess without any evidence for the assertion. There is no certain date from which enamel badges were first made, but they were clearly the end result of industrial processes which in common with other developments of the industrial revolution, eclipsed the former handmade products:

> The development in the eighteen forties in Birmingham of the drop stamping machine, enabled dies to be struck with raised retaining lines, in imitation of and far cheaper than the original Cloisonné goods, and resulted in the virtual demise of the Wednesbury hand-painted trade. Badges were not, however, produced in quantity until the latter half of the nineteenth century ... .[46]

Early Examples of the Badge

In 1833, we find an indignant vicar, one Reverend Bywater, lecturing an assembly of Oddfellows Friendly Society members, who in accordance with their rules, had turned out in full regalia to honour the funeral of a deceased member:

> What do you mean by coming here with your badges? ... I care not for your badges; they are emblems of wickedness; and you are worse than devils or infidels; and if you do not forsake your badges you will not only go down to the grave as this man has done, you will sink down to hell eternal.[47]

Certainly by the 1890s, lapel badges were in production. An enamel badge of the Knights of Labor believed to date from 1885–90 is in the possession of one Canadian collector,[48] whilst by 1886:

> ... the list had grown to include gold KOL pins, badges, buttons labels, 'ladies lace pins', collar buttons, books and portraits of Powderly, Stephens and the general officers.

By the decade's end it was possible to buy two different badges, seven varieties of buttons, seven batches of labels, two styles of lace pins and three types of scarf pins.[49]

By 1884, members could buy solid gold badges 'about the size of a penny' for three dollars, whilst a larger badge, mounted to a scroll with gold links was available for nine dollars. There then ensued an 'open season' amongst manufacturers who manufactured spurious KOL badges, and undercut each other without the KOL's sanction. Between 1886 and 1890, one company, C.C. Darling of Providence, offered fourteen different badges and charms of the KOL, and over thirty designs are known to exist.[50] Other badges available were the bronze lapel buttons*, selling for ten cents each or $7.50 a hundred:

About the size of a dime, KOL lapel buttons* employed several bits of familiar imagery – pentagon, globe and triangle – adding an arrow that penetrated the triangle from bottom to top. The exact meaning of this arrangement remains a mystery, but arrows traditionally denote spiritual service to God, a meaning in keeping with KOL ideology.[51]

It is reported that 'in 1891 the Derbyshire [miners'] officials 'wore handsome gilt badges' with the motto 'united we stand, divided we fall' ... .'[52] The Hearts of Oak Benefit Society in 1892, produced a large brass buttonhole-fitting badge for their fiftieth anniversary. Two years earlier, the National Amalgamated Society of Brass Workers had issued a large, brass medal (that is, the non-wearable kind) which commemorated a great strike of 1890 and listed the achievements and history of the union on its reverse. There is record of an even earlier strike 'medal', which belonged to a former collector. This is of the Miners Association, which only existed between 1842 and 1848.[53] An even earlier 'badge' example, of the United Miners Association, is made of lead and dates from 1827 (held in the British Museum's Department of Coins and Medals). There is also reference in the notes made for the British Museum's exhibition *British Trade Union Badges* (see Chapter 6) to a 'badge' issued by Robert Owen in 1834, for his Grand National Consolidated Trades Union. A slightly later piece has a more precise date. This was issued by the Oldham miners and reads 'Oldham Miners – The Labourer Is Worthy of His Hire – Ox Roast, Oldham, November 1858 – Strike'.[54]

In 1891 some of the earliest examples of strike badges were made in the form of watch chain fobs, when the Amalgamated Society of Railway Servants for Scotland issued bronze, silver and gold medallions to commemorate a strike. The strike (which was lost) lasted from December 1890 to January 1891 over a reduction to a ten-hour working day.[55] The medallions were authorised for production in March 1891.[56] The reverse of one reads: 'I Stood Firm To The Last' (see Figure 2.1), a personalisation more commonly found on modern strike commemorative badges (see Chapter 4) and in this sense perhaps unique.

It is a custom with the TUC to issue enamel badges to delegates at each annual congress. The earliest example of this badge in the TUC's collection dates from

Figure 2.1   Enamel and brass watch chain fob of the Amalgamated Society
of Railway Servants For Scotland commemorating the Scottish
Railway Strike of 1890–91. Here we see the pride in independent
trade union principle incorporated into an adornment for a
medium which was regarded as part of the corporate uniform –
the watch chain. This perhaps implies the syndicalist-inspired
concept of industrial unionism which was to come in the early
1900s when 'railway servants' became 'railwaymen'.
Reproduced with permission of North Lanarkshire Leisure Services
Department.

1904, although UNISON (the public sector union) have one from the Swansea congress of 1901 in their collection, which they believe to be the oldest. However, the TUC believes there was one issued in 1898.[57] The Amalgamated Society of Engineers also issued a special badge for delegates to the 1893 TUC congress in Belfast that year.[58]

The oldest dated metal union badges intended for attachment to the lapel yet discovered, are first, that of the Amalgamated Association of Miners, which existed from 1869 to 1875. The obverse of the medal reads: 'Amalgamated Association of Miners Established 1869'. The reverse reads: 'Forest of Dean District 1871'. This is suspended from a white ribbon,[59] presumably for attachment to the lapel. In Australia, 'eight-hour day' commemorative badges are known to date from at least the 1880s, the first annual eight-hour-day parade having taken place in 1856. Other Australian badges such as the gold medallion of the Bendigo Miners Association, can only be approximately dated from between 1872 and 1882, and therefore older ones may well exist. Three other examples come from around this time. First, a shield-shaped, yellow metal watch-chain fob of the Locomotive Steam Enginemen's and Firemen's Society, dating from between 1879 and 1882, being the earliest incarnation of today's Associated Society of Locomotive Engineers and Firemen (ASLEF)[60] (see Figure 2.2). This badge depicts clasped hands, the union's initials and rose, shamrock and thistle design with the owner's initials 'J.S' underneath. The reverse pictures a four-wheeled locomotive and 'G. Stephenson' below.

Second, there is a badge of the Independent Order of Mechanics which was worn at the Preston Guild procession of 1882.[61] This may or may not have been a trade union. No union of this specific title is known. However, an 'Independent Order of Engineers and Machinists Trade and Friendly Society' is recorded as lasting from 1872 to 1893.[62] Finally, there is the badge issued by the Amalgamated Society of Engineers in 1885, for the ceremony to commemorate the commencement of work on the Manchester Ship Canal.[63] Muller wrongly assumed that this item was made to sew directly onto the clothing of the wearer,[64] as the example he illustrates is unmounted.[65] It is in fact a base metal token with holes punched through it, but not for direct attachment to clothing. Rather it is sewn to a hessian-backed red rosette, from which are attached two streamers bearing the name of the union (a copy is held in a British private collection). The hessian has a large pin through it with which to attach it to the clothing, and the whole effect is of a token mounted on a rosette, therefore synthesising the two media to produce a badge.

The putting together of a token (also called a medal) and a rosette, both having been in common use for some years by this time, is perhaps symbolic of a desire to have the durability and resilience of a token incorporated into something eye-catching like a rosette, although it could be speculated in the light of this, that the reform and other tokens issued in the earlier nineteenth century also with holes in them, may have been mounted in a similar way, and that the ASE badge is only a continuation of an already utilised process or tradition.

Figure 2.2   Silver fob of the British Locomotive Steam Enginemen's and Firemen's Society c.1879–82. The initials of the owner are engraved at the bottom, exemplifying the personalised status of this newly emergent iconography within the trade union movement.
Reproduced with permission of Bonham's Auctions, London.

Within five years or so, the enamel badge would amalgamate both durability and attraction. In terms of positive dates then, 1871, 1882 or 1885 as far as can be found, are those from which the first British trade union lapel-orientated badges are known to have been issued. In North America, the Knights of Labor, who operated in the US, Canada and Britain between the 1880s and 1901[66] are known to have issued lapel badges from the 1880s: examples from c. 1886, are in the possession of a Canadian collector, as is a kind of 'rough medallion of uncertain function', issued by the Oshawa branch (Ontario, Canada) dated 1883. We also know of a hall-marked gold and enamel lapel badge of the 'Brotherhood of Railroad Brakemen', established in 1883, issued before 1890 when it changed its name.[67] Badges were being made from various materials,[68] but the two types that have proven to be most popular are the enamel badge, which by the early 1900s was used increasingly, and the tin, or as the Americans call it, 'button' or pin-back badge. The latter is more frequently used to promote campaigns, and usually bear slogans; being far cheaper than the enamel type, they proliferated as much as the enamels.

The Button Badge

Fortunately, far more is known about the origins of this type of badge. The invention of celluloid in the 1870s led to attempts at making campaign badges for the 1876 American presidential campaign. However, the celluloid at this time though was too brittle and was dropped.[69] Nevertheless, small studs for the lapel were made for the 1888 presidential election and pictured the candidates Harrison, Cleveland, Thurman and Fisk.[70] Finally, 'Buttons as we know them today were first patented by the Whitehead and Hoag Co., Newark, New Jersey. Celluloid was used as a thin transparent covering to protect the paper the image was printed on.'[71] Such badges were first issued in 1896, 'production being stimulated by the intensity of the McInley and Bryan presidential campaign battle over the gold and silver coinage ratio'.[72] The button badge was also issued in place of insert cards with sweets and tobacco.[73] The tin badge then, is an American invention and it was not long before they were being imported into Britain. US unions have always used buttons to a far greater extent than enamel badges. The button badge came to Britain via agencies set up in London by Whitehead and Hoag and were used for Queen Victoria's Diamond Jubilee in 1897; further issues pictured Boer War heroes.[74] It is estimated that by 1902, British manufacturers had begun making these badges, and by 1905 imports had all but stopped.[75] White and Lambert by 1908 in Britain were one of the first manufacturers. Production of tin badges, with the image printed directly onto them, began in 1916.[76]

The button badge proved versatile to the unions, substituting for enamel badges during the Second World War, during the metal shortage. They were also utilised, not as advertising devices in the conventional use of the term as many early buttons were, but as actual membership badges of the unions, acting as an advert in a different sense. Good-quality lithographic mass production of the paper insert that formed the design of the badge commended itself to small unions with little finance to expend on iconography, being considerably cheaper than their grander (?) enamel cousins. Many unions though, used both enamel and button membership badges. Whether or not the tin badge was first introduced by a union and later superseded by the enamel as membership, income and confidence grew is not known, but it may have been. The tin badge in the early days was often used by unions as a 'check-off' or 'clearance' badge, which showed that members were clear on the books. It was also used as a straight membership badge. It cannot be proved that the tin badge used in this fashion was a sign of austerity amongst the unions using it, but again it is a point worth considering. Mainly after the early 1900s, the button badge was also of great use to the new and large general unions who could order them in the numbers required for their large memberships, and make great savings in comparison with a similar number of enamel badges. The use of the button badge means that a good number of small unions which are no longer extant, have left a very attractive legacy to labour historians, perhaps in some cases being the only tangible reminder that they ever existed.

The Union Label: The United States

Within the labour movement, the button badge has, if not a direct, at least a tacit connection with a slightly earlier phenomenon, that of the paper insert label.[77] Button badges, it could be fairly said, are one step up from the more ephemeral sticker which within the labour movement has been used for the same purpose, that is, mass publicity for a campaign or cause. The paper insert label is still used in the US today[78] from where it is thought to have originated, where it is promoted as 'the worker's hallmark'. A thorough academic work was published on the use of the insert label in the US, as early as 1910.[79] The earliest example of the union label it seems, dates from 1869. In that year, a carpenters' 'Eight Hour League' was started in San Francisco. They adapted a stamp 'to be used on the products of plaining mills which were run for only eight hours'.[80] By 1875, another recently formed craft union, the Cigar Makers Association of the Pacific Coast, adopted a stamp as their trade mark, and by 1880 the Cigar Makers International Union had written rules into their constitution governing the label's use. There was at this time, in the US, a great deal of resentment at the use of Chinese (and by extension, sweated) labour in the cigar industry, and hence the label. This was printed on white paper and gummed to the cigar box, and read: 'The cigars contained in this box are made by WHITE MEN.'[81] By 1878, over fifty manufacturers were using the label, and two years later, the Cigar Makers International Union, were using an even more reactionary reading label, which asserted that the cigars were made by 'a member of the Cigar Makers International Union of America, an organisation opposed to rat shop, COOLIE, PRISON or FILTHY TENEMENT HOUSE workmanship'.[82] Other than racism, the reason for such an outspoken form of wording is explained in the caption accompanying the label of the Label, Broom and Whisk Makers Union:

> The label of this organization appears upon the handles of brooms close to the end of the same. This label appearing upon a broom or whisk, is an absolute guarantee that the same were not made by contract prison labour, but by union labour receiving a fair rate of wages. A large number of products are being made yearly by contract prison labour. To avoid purchasing this class of goods, insist upon the union label of the broom makers, when making a purchase. The label is printed in black on a blue background. [83]

By 1881, the Detroit branch of the Cigar Makers International Union reported a doubling of membership, attributable solely to the use of the label. The union overall for the period 1880–81 reported the issuing and distribution of over 1,500,000 labels,[84] whilst other unions such as the United Hatters of America, had affixed 95,000,000 individual labels by 1888. A government report from around the same time, stated that 'several cities have gone so far as to pass ordinances requiring all city printing to bear the union label.'[85]

The Knights of Labor began issuing its own labels in 1884, which stated that the goods their label appeared on, were not made by: 'convict, contract or other slave labour'.[86] Weir describes the label used by KOL barrel makers (coopers) as 'a modest slip of green paper five and a half inches long by one and a half inches wide'. It bore upon it the following: 'This stamp is placed on all cooperage made by union men only. It is for the protection of their Trade, Home, Industry and Consumers, from unclean and filthy packages.'[87] KOL labels were soon thereafter issued for specific trades, as well as a generic KOL label; branches lobbied the KOL central office to have their designs accepted. The coopers' label featured a barrel with the KOL's triangle symbol in the centre. When the Federation of Trades and Labor Unions (FOTLU) was formed in 1886, the KOL insisted that it exclude craftsmen (the FOTLU was predominantly a craft-based organisation). This led to rival label campaigns between pro-FOTLU craft workers, especially in the cigar trade, and KOL craftsmen. There followed a war of attrition between the two bodies for supremacy in union label recognition, each boycotting the other's produce. The Cigar Makers International Union (CMIU), which was a FOTLU affiliate, used a blue label, whilst the KOL cigar makers used a white one. As the 'label wars' hotted up, the KOL changed their label to blue. Samuel Gompers, the FOTLU president (later founder of the AFL) called on his audiences to 'crush it when you see it', whilst some six thousand members of the CMIU paraded through New York City 'behind blue satin facsimiles of the CMIU label, and slogans like "Buy Blue Label Cigars"'.[88] The ultimate effect was to strengthen FOTLU, which reconstituted itself as the AFL in 1888, as 'straight ahead trades unionism' and to weaken the KOL, who had a wider vision of cooperative ownership. Not all KOL members were apparently vigilant in their shopping habits. *The National Labor Tribune* in November,1886 was moved to advise 'Watch the Knight of Labor as he goes to purchase goods; he belongs to the K. of L., yet never stops to look after the K. of L. stamps. He buys boots without the label; and his clothes were made in a shop by scab labor; he wears a hat without a union label … .'[89] By 1908, the AFL had issued a general label for unions not issuing their own. This label covered amongst others, the Badge and Lodge Paraphernalia Workers Association! Spedden states that in 1908 'there were affiliated to the AFL, 117 national trade unions. Of this number, 68 unions were using the label in some of its forms. The total membership of the label using unions was 724,200, or approximately 47 percent of the aggregate membership of the AFL.'[90] The American Federation of Labor (AFL) published annual directories of label-using unions, from at least 1911. Some labels were obviously more than paper inserts, such as that of American Wire Weavers Protective Association:

'This label appears on the product of all union made fourdrinier wire cloth. It is worked in gold and blue with the lettering in red.'[91]

Many service sector unions used a shop card to indicate that the establishment was conforming to union rules, prominently displayed in the shops on the walls, or on the counter, etc., such as those of the Meat Cutters and Butcher Workmen's Union and the Journeyman Barbers Union.[92] In the case of the Retail Clerks International Protective Association, potential customers were advised:

> The Retail Clerks Store Card is granted only those merchants entering into trades union agreement with their organization, and the demand for this Card will mean the services of Union Clerks who will advance the sale of label products at every opportunity. Insist upon the display of the Store Card of the Retail Clerks International Protective Association.[93]

> A considerable number of such unions use a button to indicate that the workman performing the service is a member of his union in his trade. The Retail Clerks International Protective Association was the first of these to adopt a button. From 1891 to 1898, the button has become less important than the shop card.[94]

The button badge is still used to a very large extent today in the US. It often bears the label imprint on it somewhere, of the Printers and Novelty Goods Union. It is interesting that Spedden asserts that the Retail Clerks used the button from as early as 1891, as button badges as we know them today were not patented until 1893, and not actually produced commercially until 1896. Therefore, a prototype of some kind must have been used, either this, or Spedden was using the term 'button' too loosely. The earliest use of a lapel badge proper, for campaigning purposes however, may have been the sulphide brooches issued for Martin Van Buren's presidential campaigns during the 1840s.[95] The Journeymen Horseshoers Association was

> ... particular in providing for ownership of the badges or buttons which supplement the label as a mantel of union labour. No local [branch] is allowed to secure more badges than there are members of the local. 'A price not in excess of the cost of the badges (to furnish them) shall be charged to each member, who desires to have the badge in his possession, but this cost price must not be construed as a purchase price, as the badge must always remain the property of the International Union'.[96]

The Union Label: The United Kingdom

There is anecdotal evidence to suggest that prior to 1914, British cigar workers reached agreement with the employers that one cigar in every box should bear a union label. No evidence exists to support this however, although Ben Cooper, general secretary of the Cigar Makers Union, spoke about a Cigar Makers Union label at the 1908 TUC, and which was registered at Stationers Hall, London. Perhaps the greatest use that the label was put to in Britain, was in the campaign to prevent work leaving union shops for 'foul' (that is, non-unionised) shops, by the Felt Hatters Union from the 1890s. The Amalgamated Society of Journeymen Felt Hatters, Felt Hat Trimmers and Wool Formers Unions based in Denton, Lancashire, launched in 1893, a union label campaign for this purpose. The American Felt Hatters Union had begun using the label system from 1885, and their British cousins learned of it from them. The self-adhesive paper labels were attached to the inside of all hats made by union members. The labels pictured the emblem of a beaver chasing a rabbit, and the words: 'This Hat Union Made', and were issued in continuous perforated sheets. The 1893 issue was a largish size, but in 1895 was reduced to postage-stamp size. Men walked the streets of Denton and Manchester carrying sandwich boards advertising the campaign and advertisements were placed in union journals, whilst display boards advertising the campaign were placed in the windows of union shops. By 1895 when the size of the label was reduced, over two million labels had been issued,[97] and 'The practice continued until the 1960s, [when] the hat market collapsed with changes in fashion.' [98] There are several anecdotes relating to the use of the hatters' label, two of which were reported in the August 1911 issue of *The Transport Worker*:

> [There is a] story that a respected member of Liverpool Trades Council tells about himself. One Saturday evening at half past nine he entered a shop in Elliot Street and asked for a trade union hat with the hatters label in it. The tired assistant with gentle irony replied: 'do you think that this is a trade union hour to buy one?'. It was not the purchaser's first offence in this respect, but it has been his last.
>
> When the TUC last met at Liverpool in 1906, seventy delegates sent their hats to be brushed. The assistant who did the brushing was a member of the Hatters Union. He looked for the union label and found that in only three cases out of seventy, had the owners – well known labour leaders – taken the trouble to buy a hat made under trades union conditions.

This, if true (it may be apocryphal) would indicate that the label system, as far as consumers were concerned, was not particularly effective. None the less, it may be that it had more impact on employers, thus causing them to employ only unionised labour. There were strict rules governing access to and distribution of the labels. They were kept in a locked box with only the key holder having access. Rule three stated 'The box must always be kept locked unless the person who has charge of it is present, and the key must not be attached to the box, or left loose about the room, but be kept *strictly* in the *possession* of the person appointed' (original emphasis). There seems to have been an ongoing row in some firms with the union over who should pay for the time spent inserting labels: 'The information was volunteered however, that in one Stockport firm, now closed, the label was inserted by a female employee working in the warehouse. The irony of this, is that neither of the two unions would have allowed this worker to belong to a union!' [99] Peter Carter relates how after seeing Ernest Bevin, leader of the Transport and General Workers Union on film, without a hat:

> ... the union arranged a major presentation to him of free, union made hats, which they publicised under the slogan; 'if you want to get ahead, get a hat'. Other notables in the union and Labour Party world received similar treatment. Imitation being the finest form of flattery, the employers of Atherstone repeated the slogan when they presented a hatless Anthony Eden with a union made hat during the election campaign of 1955![100]

The London Jewish Bakers Union in 1913 issued a paper label pressed into the loaf, in Yiddish, reading 'buy only the bread with the union label'.[101] The union had to strike to implement the system as the employers were against it.[102] The *Daily Herald*, of 10 October 1913, were optimistic about the dispute:

> If trade unionists did their duty, labelling of trade union goods and the boycotting of blackleg goods would be a great power ... there is hardly a trade union leader who inquires whether his clothes are made by a staunch trade unionist or by poor sweated Jews. He's just as indifferent about this as everything he eats or drinks.

The clothing industry saw a number of attempts at implementing the union label scheme in Britain, although some never got off the drawing board: 'The Scottish Operative Tailors and Tailoresses considered resolutions at the 1908 Conference and again in 1911, to set up a union label scheme. No evidence has come to light to show that they were carried or implemented.' [103] Others such as the Garment Workers Trade Union, set up a label scheme in 1907, whilst a Manchester union, the Amalgamated Shirt and Jacket Workers Society had a scheme around the same time, which appeared on the cover of the union's rule book. The Waterproof Garment Workers Trade Union were issuing fabric labels to be sewn into the articles that they made, using two different types of label, one of which bore both union and employers names. The N.U. Boot and Shoe Operatives, also operated a label scheme between 1919 and 1939,[104] and the Typographical Association also used a label prior to the First World War at least.[105] Afterwards, the newly formed National Union of Printing and Paper Workers, in 1921, sought to convince all unions in the printing and paper-making industries to adopt the use of a 'British Paper Trade Unions Label' which would also appear as a watermark on union-made paper. However, a 'meagre' response from other unions to whom a circular was sent with this proposal meant the scheme came to nothing.[106] Larger and with more substance, were the union 'shop signs', which denoted that the shop was staffed by trade union labour. These varied in substance from stiff card to enamel. Signs were used by unions such as Amalgamated Society of Cloggers, The Amalgamated Union of Operative Bakers, The Oldham and District Hairdressers Union and the Birmingham and District Window Cleaners Union.[107]

Even in the 1960s, the National Union of Tailors and Garment Workers unsuccessfully tried to revive the union label, whilst a sad plea, issued by the N.U.

Hosiery and Knitwear Workers in the 1970s in the form of a sticker, urged the consumer to 'Look at the label – save our jobs.'[108] The trade union label, certainly in the first quarter of the twentieth century, articulated a visual call for support and popularised a campaign in the same way as the modern button badge. If not a direct ancestor of the button badge, it makes an interesting comparison, and is derived from the same technological innovations of the late nineteenth century as the button badge, such as offset colour lithography. How successful these campaigns were at the time, we have no real way of knowing. Their artistic and historic legacy however, should be viewed as part of the national heritage and assigned accordingly due importance. Even today, in some casual clothing found in British shops, 'Union Made' labels can still be found sewn into items, such as Lee Jeans.[109]

Stamps and Stickers

Both in the US and Britain, gummed stamps were used extensively in conjunction with badges. The most common were those issued to denote the payment of subscriptions, and bore the name/initials and emblem of the union concerned. Next to these came stamps used to raise a levy for a specific purpose. This might be for political reasons, such as those issued for the election fund of the Fulham branch of the Social Democratic Federation, which bore the words: 'Penny Nails In The Coffin Of Capitalism' and for a 'Surrey – Spain Food Ship 1939'.[110] Others, most especially in the US, were issued as proof of contribution to a strike or fighting/campaign fund.[111] Stickers (or decals as they are known in North America) served a largely propaganda purpose, and date back to at least 1912 in Britain, where 'red spots' as they were called, sporting the slogan 'Socialism means the world for the workers' were advertised in *The Clarion* newspaper at two shillings per thousand or one guinea per twenty thousand![112] In the US, the Industrial Workers of The World (IWW) made great use of such stickers from around 1908 (see Figure 2.3).[113] An IWW handbill from the early 1900s advertising its 'stickerettes' refers to them as 'silent agitators':

> ONE BIG UNION propaganda with the hot air taken out and a kick added. Designed especially for use on the job and on the road. Publicity agents that work everywhere and all the time.
> Just the thing to wise up the slave. Jolt the Scissor Bill and throw the fear of the O.B.U into the boss.
> Eleven different designs printed in black and red.
> Price. One envelope containing 150 stickerettes 25c or one box of 10 envelopes (1,500 stickerettes) $1.50 post paid.[114]

This purpose has sometimes been transposed to stamps, or 'Cinderellas' as philatelists know them. That is, stamps with a purpose other than a prepayment of postage or tax (fiscal) purpose. The Canadian Postal Workers Union most recently

Figure 2.3   Paper sticker or decal of the Industrial Workers of the World (IWW) c.1908. The 'stickyback' as it has sometimes been known, has been used over many years by trade unions, political and radical groups. It has a very public form of history, being as it has, surreptitiously attached to lampposts, subway billboards and public buildings, etc.
Paul Cosgrove collection.

used Cinderella stamps featuring slogans such as 'preserve our public pensions' for use in conjunction with ordinary stamps on envelopes.[115] The sticker is of course still an immediate and effective tool in labour disputes and campaigns, with the button badge making that much more useful.

Reading the Badge

Although this book is concerned with trade union badges, it is worth mentioning that the era in which the badge first became prominent was an age of social organisations, and every conceivable society and organisation was issuing badges and regalia. Ceremonial badges and regalia were being turned out for unions, friendly societies, temperance societies, orange lodges, Sunday schools, political and religious groups, charities, etc. The temperance societies had been issuing base metal medals since the 1860s at least. Friendly societies were and still are great wearers of regalia, and badges added to their considerable armoury of iconography, especially amongst such societies as the Oddfellows, Foresters and Rechabites. In the widest context then, badges were ordered and made in conjunction with and as a complement to the banners and emblems that are now so loved by labour historians, and the unions were at the forefront of this outburst.

The reverse of (especially) the older badges are important. As was once common, the badge was worn in the buttonhole of the jacket, and many of the older badges are made with button* fixings. However, if a union had female members it had to facilitate them with a badge that could be worn in something other than a buttonhole and therefore pins were used. The social relevance of the fixing of a badge even today is seen when it is asserted that

> Buttons* and studs were replaced by catches and pins. Long needle type pins, pins with separate screws and the modern preference for brooch style fittings. Such changes are part fashion, part new production techniques, and part the need to cater for the dress habits of a membership increasingly white collar and female.[116]

Though some badges seem to have been issued without much thought to the design and appear ostensibly simplistic or irrelevant, it would be wrong to assume so. The Knights of Labor's most often used and most visible design was a triangle enclosed in a circle, of which, its leader, Terence Powderly noted:

> … the circle which binds together the ends of the lines of the triangle indicates that the bond of unity by which the membership is bound together should be without end; placed on the outside of the triangle it also indicates that all of the business of the assembly should be transacted among members and for humanity. This circle can be broken from the inside very easily, but from the outside never.[117]

This itself was a simplification both of image and wording, of a far more elaborate meaning conceived for the KOL's great seal.[118] The six-pointed star-shaped badge of the Australian Railways Union, issued between the 1930s and 1980s, had specific meaning:'The six pointed star represents the six states of Australia, the six hour day, and in the 1930s, the basic wage of six pounds.' The blue, red and white, seven-pointed star-shaped badge of the Australian Printing and Kindred Industries Union was 'first issued in September 1967 and sold to members for thirty cents each. The seven pointed star represents each state and the Australian Council of Trades Unions. The colours are the primary colours used in printing.'[119] The 1970s badge of the Irish Post Office Workers Union is a very small triangle, with initials and harp design in the centre, in red and blue. In the welcoming note to new members it is stated that 'Its three sides represent the three main branches of the postal and telecommunications service. The harp is the traditional national heraldic symbol. Red is the traditional colour of the workers movement, and the blue represents the faith in the cause of the workers.' [120] The (British) Union of Communication Workers (UCW), go so far as to provide an A4 sheet to members, which provides the history (from Roman times), interpretation and relevance to it of its badge design: 'the winged staff of Mercury' (1921) or caduceus (1986), which it first issued in 1921.[121] The Irish Customs and Excise Union positively revel in the description of their union's symbol, the griffin, which in mythology, aptly kept watch over hidden wealth:

> The body is that of a lion, and its claws, head and wings, that of a powerful eagle. This emblem was first used by the union in 1971. The Griffin is the emblem of watchfulness, courage, perseverance and rapidity of execution and, as such, is considered very appropriate to represent the ICEU.[122]

Colour can be important. The enamel badge of the Northern Carpets Trades Union, issued in the 1980s, was initially made with a blue border. It is rumoured that the union's activists however, rejected this as 'a tory colour', and the badge had to be restruck in red!

The watch chain fobs were more the prerogative of the skilled artisan, and probably appeared around the same time as the enamel badge. For the part of the Amalgamated Society of Engineers:

> The Victorian craftsman wore his watch chain like a badge of office, and on it hung his ASE fob, It was available in three grades; 1. white silver at 2/-; 2. solid silver at 4/6d; and 3. gold at 25/-. The gold pendant represented the best part of a week's wage.[123]

An even more elaborate range of devices was available to members of the British Steel Smelters, Mill and Tinplate Workers Association:

> ... in April 1905 the union began selling solid gold and silver badges; there was a wide variety to choose from in order to suit all tastes and pockets. Fourteen gold badges were offered for sale ranging from a 9 carat, 5 dwts at 18s. each to a 15 carat, 10 dwts selling at 49s. each. For those who preferred hall marked silver they could choose from six values starting at 3s.6d. and going up to: "silver, richly fire gilt, everlasting wear" badge retailing at 6s.3d each.' ... 'Gold and silver badges could be supplied as a brooch, or with a hook for the button hole or with a ring for the watch chain. member's names could be engraved on the back at 1d per letter or monograms at 1s.3d. Within one month of offering the badges the monthly report of the Steel Smelters was claiming that members had ordered 53 gold and 197 silver badges. Members of the Motherwell branch of the union had purchased 54 gold union brooches for their wives by the end of 1905; the total membership of the branch was less than 200.[124]

It is worth noting by way of comparison, that the giving of 'sweetheart' brooches by the armed forces to their womenfolk is a long practised tradition, and here it seems to have spread to trade unions. Members of the Printing Industries Employees Union of Australia, in 1929, could buy fobs in fifteen-carat gold for twenty-two shillings and sixpence; nineteen-carat gold for seventeen shillings and sixpence or gilt metal for one shilling.[125] In 1904, members of the Federated Railway Locomotive Enginemens Association of Australaisia could buy a union fob in bronze for one shilling; in silver for two shillings; in nine-carat gold for twenty-one shillings, and in fifteen-carat gold for twenty-eight shillings and sixpence.[126] The gold medal of the Australasian Institute of Marine Engineers (Employees), made between 1881 and 1922, featured a ship's propeller as the central design, in the centre of which was mounted a ruby! The Amalgamated Society of Railway Servants were not such a craft union, but they were considered to be so in some respects by the General Railway Workers Union, who were formed in 1889 to cater for all grades of railway workers including those refused admission to the ASRS. A railway porter or station master would often check the station clock with his own watch, and so in such a time-sensitive occupation, it would be only natural that he should have a watch chain to which the fob gave added prestige. The railwaymen in fact seem to have issued more of these than any other union, if people's collections are anything to go by. The watch fob however, was normally worn by skilled artisans such as the Steam Engine Makers Society, and were often issued in precious metal such as the ASE fobs. This was perhaps to signify some material or craft status superiority over the mere badge wearer. However, the majority of fob-issuing unions also issued the fob in lapel form or offered a badge alternative. New members of the National Union of Railwaymen of Australia were from 1936, charged one shilling for a membership badge.[127]

The designs, maxims and mottoes, etc. that appeared on the early badges, were largely adaptations of banner and emblem designs. This tends to reinforce the proposition that the members wanted their banners and emblems on their lapels as it were. The Angel made famous by Walter Crane in the 1880s was adopted by the Electrical Trades Union, with the motto 'Light and liberty'. The NUR adopted the Marxist slogan, 'Workers of the world unite', a motto they were using even when known as the ASRS (prior to 1913). Such a militant slogan for a union with such a servile title as 'Railway Servants' is perhaps a little surprising. Their earlier fobs however, bore the more passive legend 'Help one another', emphasising the friendly society aspect of the union, for which they were much derided by the GRWU. In the period of 'the great unrest' and syndicalist ideas before the First World War, this perhaps demonstrates a hardening of ideas and attitudes after the 1911 railway strike, an example of each type making an interesting social comment.

Many unions used the clasped handshake symbol and the motto 'Unity is strength'. The globe was a common symbol, especially amongst craft unions. This often signified that these unions would have branches in other parts of the world. Craftsmen emigrated to South Africa, Australia, Canada, New Zealand, the US, and in the case of the Operative Plumbers Society at least, a branch was sanctioned in Buenos Aires.[128] A personalised commemorative medal from the 1911 ASRS strike, awarded to A.E. Rochester of the Frome Branch, for 'Playing The Man',[129] was picked up by a collector in a shop in Victoria, British Columbia in Canada![130] Presumably 'A.E. Rochester' subsequently became an émigré, perhaps through blacklisting by the railway companies for 'Playing the Man'. Indeed, the Australian branch of the

British Amalgamated Society of Engineers did not become an independent trade union in its own right until 1972.[131] One of the most evocative legends used on a badge was that of the National Federation of Women Workers, whose legend was 'To Fight, To Struggle, To Right The Wrong'. Another common symbol was the tied bundle of sticks, from the fable of the faggots which were symbolic of unity mentioned in Chapter One. The crossed keys of knowledge and the beehive of industry also make appearances. The proposition in Chapter 1, that badge designs were synopses of banner designs, is almost certainly true. It may however be reasonable to assume that in some cases, the banner would be a grand enlargement of a badge design. Given Tutill's near monopoly of the banner trade, and the increasing cost of having them made, a badge would be a good form of union identification. This would give members something to have that represented the union, which at the same time would act as a miniature billboard or advertising hoarding to non-members, without incurring the extravagant expense of a full banner.

Many of the early lapel badges feature the clasped hands and the tied bundle, perhaps copied from each other with their own union name added, in the same way that Tutill's banner designs were.[132] Having discussed the origins and early examples of the union badge, we will next look at the importance of the badge to members and officials and the struggles for their right to wear it, incorporated within the wider struggle for union recognition.

Notes

1   J.E. Williams, *The Derbyshire Miners*, London, George, Allen & Unwin, 1961, p. 144.
2   Weir, *Beyond Labor's Veil*, p. 231.
3   H. Jefferson, *The Platform (Volume One)*, London, MacMillan, 1892, p. 122.
4   A. Godwin, *The Friends Of Liberty*, London, Hutchinson, 1979, p. 180.
5   R.A. Leeson, *Travelling Brothers: The Six Centuries Road From Craft Fellowship to Trade Unionism*, London, George Allen & Unwin, 1979, p. 101.
6   J.R.S. Whiting, *Commemorative Medals*, Bath, David & Charles, 1972, p. 15; p. 24.
7   C. Brunel and P. M. Jackson, 'Notes on tokens as a source of information on the history of the labour and radical movement, part one', *Journal of the Society For The Study of Labour History*, No. 13, Autumn, 1966, pp. 26–36; O. Rudkin, *Thomas Spence And His Connections*, London, George, Allen & Unwin, 1927, pp. 90–94; M. Beer, *A History Of British Socialism* (illustrated), London, Spokesman, 1984, pp. 86–89, 103.
8   Muller, *James Sharples*, pp. 140–141.
9   Rubenstein, 'Symbols and Images of American Labour: Badges of Pride', pp. 36–51, p. 43; D. Yorke, 'Union "Lodge Ribbons" In America', *Trade Union Badge Collectors' Newsletter*, No. 67, Spring, 1999, pp. 18–21.
10 J. Sage, *Memoirs of Josiah Sage*, London, Lawrence & Wishart, 1951, pp. 16–17. See also *Trade Union Badge Collectors' Newsetter*, No. 68, Summer, 1999 for illustrations of early British trade union ribbons worn at funerals..

11 Weir, *Beyond Labor's Veil*, p. 237.
12 Smith, *Emblems Of Unity*, p. 228.
13 Smith, *Emblems Of Unity*, p. 16.
14 In the possession of the Working Class Movement Library, Manchester, reproduced in *Trade Union Badge Collectors' Newsletter*, No. 69, Autumn, 1999.
15 Sequin, *The Graphic Art Of The Enamel Badge*, p. 6.
16 Cited in Durr MS, p. 7.
17 F.H. Radford, *Fetch The Engine*, London, Fire Brigades Union, 1951, p. 16.
18 Ibid.
19 Ibid.
20 Muller, *James Sharples*, pp. 140–141.
21 Muller, *James Sharples*, pp. 140–141. For the practice of craft traditions and the evolution of Journeyman organisations from the guilds, see the following: D. Knoop and G.P. Jones, *The Medieval Mason: An Economic History of English Stone Building in the Later Middle Ages and Early Modern Times*, Manchester, Manchester University Press, 1933; J.R. Kellet, 'The Breakdown of Guild and Corporation Control Over the Handicraft and Retail Trade in London', *Economic History Review*, second series, Vol. 10, pp. 381–394; Leeson, *Travelling Brothers*; R.A. Leeson and C.R. Dobson, *Masters and Journeymen: A Prehistory of Industrial Relations 1717–1800*, London, Croom Helm, 1980.
22 Brake, *Men Of Good Character*, p. 36.
23 Muller, *James Sharples*, pp. 140–141.
24 P.M. Chaplin, *The Thames From Source To Tideway*, London, Whittel, 1982, pp. 131–132. Sequin, *The Graphic Art of the Enamel Badge*, p. 6, pictures a round brass badge of the Thames Guild of Free Watermen, dating from the late eighteenth century.
25 H. Pelling, *A History of British Trade Unionism*, London, MacMillan, 1963, p. 95.
26 Brunel and Jackson, 'Notes on tokens', p. 27.
27 Rudkin, *Thomas Spence* , pp. 46–48, 68–70; P.M. Kemp-Ashraf, *The Life and Times of Thomas Spence*, Newcastle-Upon-Tyne, Frank Graham, 1984.
28 Brunel & Jackson, 'Notes on tokens', p. 27; see also Rudkin, *Thomas Spence*, p. 91.
29 Brunel & Jackson, 'Notes on tokens', p. 27.
30 Durr MS, p. 24.
31 E. King, *The People's Palace and Glasgow Green,* Glasgow, Richard Drew, 1988.
32 Durr MS, p. 22.
33 Brake, *Men Of Good Character*, p. 87.
34 B. Loftus, *Marching Workers*, Arts Council of Ireland, 1978, p. 77.
35 Smethurst and Devine, 'Trade Union Badges', p. 94, n.14.
36 Brake, *Men of Good Character*, p. 157.
37 E.J. Hobsbawm, *Worlds of Labour*, London, Weidenfeld & Nicholson, 1984, p. 72.
38 J. Barton, Whitchurch History and Archaeology Group, personal communication to J. Fleming, London, 22 September 1996. A pencil rubbing and written description of the medal appears in *Trade Union Badge Collectors' Newsletter*, No. 55, August, 1996.
39 Williams, *The Derbyshire Miners*, p. 144.
40 Ibid., p. 145.
41 Brake, *Men of Good Character* op. cit., p. 321.
42 Ibid., p. 84.

43 Cox and Cox, *Tokens, Checks, Metalic Tickets*, p. 1.

44 See ibid., pp. 260–262, 218.

45 Hobsbawm, *Worlds of Labour*, p. 72, citing Muller, *James Sharples*, p. 141.

46 R.E.V.Gomm, information leaflet, undated.

47 R.H. Moffrey, *A Century Of Oddfellowship: being a brief record of the rise and progress of the Manchester Unity of Independent Order of Oddfellows*, Manchester, G.M. and Board of Directors IOOF, 1910, pp. 43–44.

48 D.Yorke, personal communication, 1998.

49 Weir, *Beyond Labor's Veil* , p. 240.

50 Ibid., pp. 244–245.

51 Ibid., p. 245.

52 Hobsbawm, *Worlds Of Labour*, p. 73.

53 H. Hawkes, 'Union history under the hammer', *Birmingham Evening Mail*, 22 September 1990.

54 J. Hammond, *Trade Union Badges* (first edition), Worthing, Private publication, 1991, p. 57.

55 P. S. Bagwell, *The Railwaymen: the history of the National Union of Railwaymen*, London, George, Allen & Unwin, 1963, pp. 139–149.

56 Bagwell, *The Railwaymen*, p. 147; F. Little, 'Summerlee Heritage Trust and the Scottish Railway Strike 1890–1891', *Scottish Labour History Review*, No. 5, Winter 1991/Spring 1992, pp. 12–13 which includes illustrations.

57 Christine Coates, TUC librarian, personal communication, 30 January 1987.

58 F. Devine, 'Who Dares Wear The Red Hand Badge?, *Liberty*, Journal of the Irish Transport and General Workers' Union, June, 1984.

59 Hammond, *Trade Union Badges*, p. 53.

60 Bonham's Auctions, *Posters, Live Steam Models, Transport Memorabilia And Toys*, 23 July 1997, p. 56, Lot 318a.

61 Muller, *James Sharples*, p. 14.

62 A. Marsh and V. Ryan, *Historical Directory of Trade Unions, Volume 2*, Hampshire, Gower, 1984, p. 39.

63 See Sir Bosdin Leech *The History of The Manchester Ship Canal*, London, Sherriton & Hughs, 1907, pp. 265–266 for a description of this ceremony.

64 Muller, *James Sharples*, p. 141.

65 Ibid., p. 264.

66 See E. J. Hobsbawm, 'General Labour Unions In Britain 1884–1914', *Economic History Review*, second series, No. 1, 1949, pp. 123–142; H. Pelling, 'The Knights of Labor In Britain 1880–1901', *Economic History Review*, second series, Vol. IX, Numbers 1, 2 and 3 1956–1957, 1956, pp. 313–331.

67 D. Yorke, personal communication, 1998.

68 An example of other materials used to make badges with is that of the 1905 TUC delegates' badge. Congress in this year was held in Hanley, Stoke-on-Trent, in the heart of the English potteries. To commemorate this, the congress badge was made in porcelain. James Sexton of the National Union of Dock Labourers was president (an example of the badge is to be found in the Unison collection, London). Leather was also utilised to make badges, sometimes carrying adverts for the manufacturers on the reverse. Usually, a strong adhesive backing would be put over a safety pin in order to enable it to be worn. The front of such badges are usually of gold block stamped into

leather. These badges were certainly around in the 1890s and probably predate both enamels and buttons. In 1986, a strike badge was even made of slate, commemorating the North Wales slate quarry strike of 1985/6, see Blaenau Ffestiniog Women's Support Group, *We Stand Together: Blaenau Ffestiniog 1985–1986 – seven months on the slate,* Wales, Blaenau Ffestiniog Women's Support Group, 1986, p. 55. See also Setchfield, *The Official Badge Collectors' Guide,* pp. 18–21 for recent examples of badges generally made from various materials.

69 T. Hake, *The Button Book,* New York, Daffran House, 1972, p. 14.

70 Ibid.

71 Ibid.

72 Ibid., p. 15.

73 Ibid.

74 Setchfield, *The Official Badge Collectors' Guide,* p. 3.

75 Ibid., p. 4.

76 Ibid.

77 See E.R. Spedden, *The Trade Union Label,* Baltimore, John Hopkins University Press, 1910; P. S. Foner and R. Schultz, *Das Andere Amerika,* Berlin, Elefanten Press, 1986, p. 113.

78 The American Federation of Labor and Congress of Industrial Organisations (AFL-CIO), the American equivalent of the British TUC, established the 'Union Label and Service Trades Department' in 1909 and it still flourishes today. It states its purposes as: 1) to advertise union label products, 2) publicise and encourage support of AFL-CIO-endorsed boycotts, 3) educate members of trade unions, their families and the general public (C.E. Mercer, President, American Federation of Labor and Congress of Industrial Organisations, personal communication, 2 March 1998). It runs an annual 'union label' week, to promote awareness of the union label. It also publishes a bimonthly newsletter, *Label Letter.* This lists companies who readers are encouraged to buy from and those who are blacklisted, as well as fictionally demonstrating how the label affects people on a daily basis. This is capped by the annual AFL-CIO Industries show, held each year since 1938 (other than during the Second World War), which is 'an annual union label trade show with over 300 exhibits including AFL-CIO National and International Unions, as well as companies that employ union members' (Mercer, personal communication, 1998). There is a history of counterfeit labels in the US, the AFL-CIO prosecute these vigorously where they are discovered (American Federation of Labor and Congress of Industrial Organisations, *The Union Label: An Historic Overview,* undated c.1980s, Washington, DC, p. 3). In 1999, the AFL-CIO were also running an information website on the contemporary use of union labels and the lastest issues involving them on <http:\www.unionlabel.org>

79 Spedden, *The Trade Union Label.*

80 Ibid., p. 10, n.2.

81 Ibid., p. 10.

82 Ibid., pp. 14–15.

83 American Federation of Labour, *Trade Union Labels Directory,* 1911, p. 17.

84 Spedden, *The Trade Union Label,* p. 16.

85 American Federation of Labor and Congress of Industrial Organisations, *The Union Label: An Historic Overview,* p. 3.

86 Spedden, *The Trade Union Label,* p. 17.

87   Weir, *Beyond Labor's Veil*, p. 252.
88   Ibid., pp. 255–260.
89   Cited in Ibid., p. 57.
90   Spedden, *The Trade Union Label*, p. 22.
91   AFL, *The Trade Union Label Directory*, p. 61.
92   Ibid., p. 62.
93   Ibid., p. 63.
94   Spedden, *The Trade Union Label* , p. 30.
95   T. Hake, *Political Buttons, Book III 1789–1916*, Pennsylvania, Hakes Americana and Collectible Press, 1987, p. 21.
96   Spedden, *The Trade Union Label*, p. 44.
97   J.R. Smith, *The Hatters*, Denton, Amalgamated Journeymen Felt Hatters, Felt Hat Trimmers & Wool Formers Societies, 1970, p. 15.
98   P. Carter, 'The Union Label – A Collectors Guide', *Trade Union Badge Collectors' Newletter*, No. 47, February, 1995b, pp. 7–17, p. 7.
99   P. Carter, 'Beware Foul Made Hats: Felt Hatting and the Union Label', *Bulletin of the Working Class Movement Library*, Manchester, 1995, p. 26.
100 Carter, 'Beware Foul Hats', p. 22.
101 Carter, 'The Union Label', p. 8.
102 Gorman, *Banner Bright*, p. 170.
103 Carter, 'The Union Label', p. 9.
104 Ibid., p. 8.
105 J. Hammond, 'Rare Trade Union Label', *Trade Union Badge Collectors' Newsletter*, No. 55, August, 1996, pp. 1, 9.
106 C.J. Bundock, *The Story of the National Union of Printing, Bookbinding and Paper Workers*, Oxford University Press, 1959, pp. 184–185.
107 Carter, 'The Union Label', pp. 8–9.
108 Ibid., p. 10.
109 A. Redpath, 'Lee Jeans Union Made Labels', *Trade Union Badge Collectors' Newsletter*, No. 65, Autumn, 1998, p. 18.
110 Gorman, *Images of Labour*, pp. 114, 116.
111 D. Yorke, '"I Helped": Union Assessment Stamps In America', *Trade Union Badge Collectors' Newsletter*, No. 63, April, 1998.
112 Gorman, *Images Of Labour*, frontispiece.
113 e.g. see G.M. Smith, *Joe Hill*, Salt Lake City, University Of Utah Press, 1969, pp. 8, 17, 34.
114 Reproduced in Smith, *Joe Hill*, p. 34.
115 *Trade Union Badge Collectors' Newsletter*, No. 63, April, 1998.
116 Smethurst and Devine, 'Trade Union Badges …'.
117 Cited in Weir, *Beyond Labor's Veil* op. cit., p. 232.
118 See ibid., pp. 237–239.
119 Smith, *Emblems Of Unity*, pp. 71, 208.
120 Smethurst and Devine, 'Trade Union Badges', p. 91.
121 *The Post*, April, 1921; Union of Communication Workers, London,1986.
122 McDonald, M., General Secretary Irish Customs and Excise Union, personal communication, 12 October 1987.

123   E. Frow and R. Frow, 'Badges of The Engineers', *AUEW Journal*, August, 1980, p. 17.
124   'Gold, Silver And Silk Badges For Steelworkers', p. 172.
125   Smith, *Emblems Of Unity*, p. 207.
126   Ibid., p. 134.
127   Ibid., p. 189.
128   J.O. French, *Plumbers In Unity*, London, Plumbers Trade Union, 1965, p. 53.
129   'Playing the Man' means 'to do the decent thing', in this case, to stand by the union.
130   D. Yorke, 'ASRS 1911 strike badge', *Trade Union Badge Collectors' Newsletter*, No. 57, December, 1996, p. 1.
131   Personal Communication, AEU, 1987.
132   See W. Moyes, *The Banner Book*, Newcastle upon Tyne, Frank Graham, 1974.

Chapter 3

To Fight, to Struggle, to Right the Wrong: The Badge and the Struggle for Union Recognition

> We had a hard struggle before the employers would recognise the 'docker's button'* – an
> ingenious badge designed by McGhee after he became our president.[1]

So far the badge has been discussed in relation to other forms of iconography, and
we have also explored its possible origins. In this chapter, we look at the badge in
the context of those who wore it, and the sentiments and importance attached to it
by members and officials alike. The significance of the badge in the wider struggle
for union recognition will now be discussed.

In so doing it is attempted to portray the union badge as essentially a piece of
working iconography of the rank and file, material culture in action, not just a
decorative accoutrement. Banners and emblems had their aesthetic and morale-
boosting elements, but mounted on walls or paraded in galas they were altars to be
worshipped. The badge on the other hand, had far wider implications: it was worn
by the member, if they so chose, at the work place as well as away from it, and was
a more permanent and publicly viewed proclamation of a member's convictions. As
such, it laid the member open to suspicion from ambivalent employers as to their
true loyalties, and led to victimisation. On the other hand, it could lead to friendly
enquiries from potential members. It signified that the wearer would have a point of
contact with the union, and could be discreetly approached for information without
declaring their intentions openly in a situation where the very mention of the union
could often lead to dismissal.

Dock and Waterside Workers

Richard McGhee was president of the National Union of Dock Labourers[2] between
its formation in 1889 and 1893. Both he and the union's general secretary, James
Sexton had been sometime members of the Knights Of Labor in the 1880s in
Liverpool and Glasgow.[3] The 'quarter badge', as it was known, was in operation
from 1890. Sexton describes the badge:

49

It was changed quarterly, and was issued only to members who were not in arrears with their subscriptions. It bore on its face the figure noting its date, with another which was the wearer's number on the branch roll, and a third figure – this one on the back – indicated the branch to which he belonged. The shape and colour of the badge were changed each quarter.[4]

It is still unclear how or where the quarter badge system originated, but is likely to have been in the US. The historian of the International Longshoremans Association (that is, the American dockers' union), Maud Russell, tells how by 1886 at least ten thousand longshoremen on the US eastern seaboard were wearing white metal union badges during working hours. The badge was a 'shield, half moon, heart and shamrock [which was] replaced quarterly'. These were later replaced by the ubiquitous (in the US) button badge worn in members' hats and lapels.[5] Even earlier, Russell tells of a woefully unsuccessful longshoremen's strike in 1874 in which 'Workmen of other trades – teamsters, riggers, sailors – continued to service the struck wharves, even though many of them wore shiny new union buttons … Some strikers surrendered earlier than others – throwing away their gold union badges and shamefacedly reporting – indeed, begging – for work at 30c an hour.' [6] Therefore, the use of badges in some form by US dockside workers pre-dates their implementation in Britain.

Both McGhee and the NUDL's first general secretary Edward McHugh acted as KOL organisers at some point and it is probable that the adoption of the system was initiated either by contact with sister unions such as the ILA's earlier incarnation, the Longshoremans United Protective Association in America or through its implementation by visiting KOL organisers during the 1880s. As we have seen in Chapter 2, the use by the British Felt Hatters of the union label was so transmitted from the US.

As used in Liverpool, the quarter badge conveyed, Sexton says, 'quite a lot of information to all those who could understand it'.[7] The Mersey Quay & Railway Carters Union (MQ&RCU) also used the system. At first they merely copied the NUDL in issuing badges numbered 1–4 to indicate the relevant quarter. However, by 1910 they had apparently refined the system. Their badges were differentiated by shape and design, but varied also according to rank and seniority.[8] They also decided to issue them half-yearly rather than quarterly and number them.[9] The MQ&RCU, established in 1889, became in 1918 the Liverpool & District Carters & Motormen's Union (L&DC&MU), until its amalgamation in 1947 with the Transport and General Workers Union (TGWU).[10] Between 1918 and 1947, 'the exact period that the badge covered would in future appear on the badge itself … either April–September or October to March … During the 1939/45 war badges were produced without enamel.' [11] The reason for the introduction of the quarter-badge system was to attempt to gain preferential treatment for union members, and to induce non-members to join. It was also to speed up the system and overcome the difficulties of administering receipts by card-marking money stewards.[12] The wearing of the badge also had the obvious advantage of members being able to recognise each other. The importance of the quarter badge cannot be overestimated. An NUDL circular of February 1890 says that union men can only be distinguished by their badges, and further that:

> ... we wish to impress upon you that the wearing of a badge is not only an essential duty to yourselves and your fellow workmen, but that it should be felt to be what it really is, a badge of nobility, for it is at the present the only sign a working man can show that he wishes to better his own condition.[13]

The same article asserts that Liverpool is the only port in the UK where the badge is not displayed. This is probably a reference to the normal membership badge, as until recently (see below) the London dockers are not known to have used the quarter-badge system. The Dock, Wharf, Riverside & General Workers Union (DWR&GWU), the main London dockers' union, issued various badges which were presumably worn at work. They also undoubtedly suffered from the same tyranny as their Liverpool comrades and showed the same caution when wearing badges at work. The nearest thing to the quarter badge that has so far been found of the DWR&GWU, is a button badge, an example of which is in the TUC's collection in London. It pictures in bright allegorical colour two dockers, surrounded by various maxims and proclamations of unity. The buttonhole fitting on the reverse however, rather than being a straightforward stud, is made of bronze, and is shaped like a small star. It depicts two clasped hands in the centre, and has the union's initials around the points of the star. This being an unusual type of fitting, it could mean that members wearing it in the docks or wharfs owned by belligerent employers, could wear it with the lithographed face of the badge facing inwards, with the star shaped stud outwards. As the stud is small and dark in colour, this would largely escape the notice of employers and yet still acknowledge recognition to fellow members who would presumably know what to look for.

The International Federation of Ship, Dock and Riverside Workers

Recently, a six-pointed, star-shaped lapel badge picturing clasped hands and the initials IFSDRW has been discovered.[14] On its reverse, it reads 'Registered 4', indicating its status as a quarter badge. The initials stand for the International Federation of Ship Dock and Riverside Workers, established in 1896, and just three years later became the more familiar International Transport Workers Federation. The IFSDRW was set up largely due to the efforts of Ben Tillet and the DWR&GWU, after his failure to amalgamate successfully his union with the South Side Labour Protection League and the National Union of Dock Labourers in 1895,[15] and so by proxy at least, London dockers employed the quarter-badge system.[16] In 1897 a report of the Federation listed fourteen countries in which it organised, but mentions only Britain and Sweden as utilising the quarter-badge system.[17] A Swedish dockers' belt bearing badges with 'ITWFS' on them (the 'S' standing for Sweden) is extant.[18] Apparently the Swedes persisted after the discontinuation of the system by the Federation in Britain.

The IFSD&RW in fact, suffered from a similar campaign of oppression from London dock owners as did the Liverpool men. In a leaflet (No. 3) 'The Federation Button' dated October 1896, an anonymous writer (probably Tillett or Mann) berates the employers for circulating a 'stupidly worded leaflet' headed 'Skulkers' Button'*, which apparently made 'wickedly false misrepresentation as to what the Button* – meaning the Federation button – really indicates'. The memory of the great dock strike of 1889 was still fresh at this time, and the symbolic attack on the badge would be obviously seen as an attempt to break the union. The leaflet concludes 'the loyal wearing of the Button*, which every man in Great Britain has a right to do if he thinks well, will materially help on the organisation and the spirit necessary to enable us to overcome all difficulties.'

This would, however, seem to be the only instance of a quarter-badge system in the London docks, and was discontinued after 1897. John Lovell gives evidence that, with the London Stevedores at least, the quarter-badge system was not utilised when he says 'The inspection of cards at the place of call however was an instrument that could be used to maintain the level of financial membership, for union cards were issued quarterly and differed in colour from one quarter to the next.' [19] Thus the membership card was used here on the same basis as the Liverpool badge system. It would though perhaps be hard to recognise a well-thumbed membership card, and one has to ponder how such a comparatively flimsy item as a membership card ever remained intact in the rigours of dock work.[20]

Liverpool

The Liverpool dock strike of February – March 1890 gained a nine-hour night shift and a wage increase, but failed to realise the closed shop which was the key objective of the strike. During the strike, the NUDL also had to contend with a local assembly of the Knights of Labor, which organised the stevedores and which did not support the strike.[21] By March 1890, a closed shop was felt to be impractical and so the quarter-badge system was utilised instead.[22] An NUDL handbill was circulated on 3 March 1890 stating that 'Official badges of membership were now being distributed at the offices and that on and after March 3rd, it would be essential for every member when seeking work, to have his badge prominently displayed in his coat buttonhole'.[23] The badge though, was soon recognised for the valuable weapon it was by the employers and was consequently widely suppressed, the repercussions of which are discussed later in this chapter. Specific rules were drawn up relating to the badge, and stiff penalties imposed on deviators. The NUDL rule book of 1901, p. 18, rule 12 states 'Each member shall be supplied with a badge. He shall when seeking employment prominently exhibit his badge and on demand of any member of the branch or district produce it for inspection.'

Throughout the 1890s, in Liverpool, the docker's button* was recognised by some of the master stevedores and porters in the south docks, but the employers in the north docks led a concerted campaign of repression against the badge system.[24] The 1905 rule book of the MQ&RCU, p. 3, rule 19 states 'Each member shall wear his badge in a conspicuous place when on the stand or at work and shall when asked by the delegate produce his badge.' The same rule book also states if any member refused to display his badge that 'The delegate shall report the same to the committee and shall be dealt with as the committee shall from time to time decide.'

The 1901 NUDL rule book does make exceptions to the compulsory showing of the badge in cases where the branch is too weak for the rule to be safely enforced, but if a branch adopted the clause it was binding (p.18). The badges were effectively on loan to the members from the union as it is stated that the badge remains the property of the union during the current quarter, and all old badges were to be surrendered to the branch at the end of each quarter.[25] The MQ&RCU stated that any member found lending or pledging his badge would be fined: 'For the first offence any sum not exceeding £1.00 and for any future offence any sum not exceeding £5.00, or the option of the committee may be suspension or expulsion.'[26] Rules 28 and 29 of the 1905 rule book as above, were still present in the 1946 rule book, with the sums of money allowable in fines unchanged (p. 28). Members could also be fined up to 5 shillings for failing to display the current badge if requested to do so, and a charge of 4 pence was made to all members on the changing of badges. Members losing their badge could obtain a replacement for 6 pence (p. 28). Junior members were to have a badge of a different shape. Junior members were those aged under 18, at which point they went on to full rates. Their badges had 'either a large "J" or the word "Junior" incorporated into the design of the badge'.[27] Officials had a special badge which pictured a horse's head and a motor van. This badge 'under the rules of the LDC&MU gave him the right to challenge any man not wearing the current badge'. This included funeral staff![28] The L&DC&MU never developed a shop steward system 'preferring instead to have a relatively large number of full time officers, all of whom had a street patrolling function'.[29] 'Walking Delegates' as these officials were often known, must have had a comprehensive knowledge of all the different shapes, colours and numbers on the badges which would need regularly updating. In fact, they were responsible for delivering the circulars by hand, to the garages and stables, notifying members of the change of badge every quarter:

From 1918, members were organised into branches – the union was growing! Badges can be found with C, N, W, E, S as a prefix to the number. Central branch, C was based at Scotland Road; North N covered Bootle; West W, was Birkenhead and Wallasey; East, E was the office at Low Hill, Edge Lane, and finally South, S meant that the member was in the branch that had an office plus officials based at Upper Warwick Street, Park Road.[30]

Sexton says that the badge was 'a really formidable weapon, though the employers did not realise this for some time.'[31] Once they did however, they were quick to act. They placed advertisements in the local press and stuck posters both inside and outside the docks all along the walls, stating that from that time onwards, no man wearing the badge would be hired at the docks.[32] George Milligan, a district secretary of the NUDL, recalled that organisation in the Liverpool docks suffered a severe blow after the banning of the badge between 1890 and 1911. He says foremen were encouraged to bullying, and the stands were open to anyone, 'but there still plastered on the walls of the sheds was the ominous notice; "men wearing union badges will be immediately dismissed".'[33] Sexton estimated that the NUDL suffered a 50 per cent drop in membership as a result. Members were told that they would no longer be required to wear the union badge, but were told to be able to produce it at any moment if required. Sexton regarded this as 'weak-kneed' and 'wishy-washy', and states that many members left in disgust at 'this gutless decision'[34] (see Figure 3.1).

The system of the quarter badge is then shown to be a most effective means of membership control, but like everything else was susceptible to the tyranny of the employer if the opportunity presented itself. The importance of the quarter badge to the dockers is well illustrated in the following reminiscence of Phillip Roach, a retired docker from Liverpool:

> When I transferred from Liverpool South to Birkenhead, the first job I had was down below in a Bibby boat. And when I got below, the other seven men weighed me up for a minute or two, and then one man took off his cap and put his union button* in it, the others followed suit. This was done without a word being spoken. It was only when I put my button* in my cap that anybody would speak to me.[35]

Wearing the Union's Badge and the Employer's Tally

The badges during the years of oppression were worn with the stud facing outwards in order to attract less attention.[36] It would appear that the effective implementation of the badge system, certainly within the L&DC&MU, enabled it to survive the 1930s with a relatively small drop in membership. Membership in 1930 stood at 8,980 and in 1939 7,827.[37] There also seems to have been a custom probably originating in the 1890–1911 period, of wearing the badge in the belt rather than the lapel, being less conspicuous there. Sexton, writing under the pseudonym 'Citizen' in the *Liverpool Labour Chronicle*, describes an element of the dispute at the Manchester Ship Canal in 1895, which gives some evidence for this custom: 'The cause of all the trouble in Manchester was the refusal of the ship canal company to allow our members [the NUDL] to proclaim themselves trade unionists by wearing the badge, and as the men refused to deny their colours, they were locked out.'[38] There was apparently no objection to non-union labour, but union

Figure 3.1 Various quarter badges of British trade unions c.1890s–1940s. L–R: National Union of Dock, Riverside and General Workers; Ship Constructors & Shipwrights Association; Irish Transport and General Workers Union; the Amalgamated Carters and Lorrymen's Union; North Stafford-shire Miners Federation; Liverpool & District Carters & Motormen's Section of the Transport and General Workers Union; Liverpool & District Carters & Motormen's Union Official's badge; Nottinghamshire Miners Association.

Author's Collection.

55

men merely claimed the right to belong to a union, signified by the badge. Sexton continues: 'When the dispute was over, the men went back to work wearing their badges in their belts instead of their buttonholes so that the poor terrorised free (?) labourers should not be intimidated against their will to join the union.'[39] A further theory for the wearing of the badge in the belt was put forward: 'Coats could be lost or stolen as they were removed at work, whereas the belt was an essential item not merely to hold up the trousers, but to support the small of the back.'[40] In addition, 'Glasgow dockers maintained the same tradition, handing down studded belts within dock front families.'[41] The NUDL gained recognition in the south end of the Liverpool docks from 1890, and preference was given to badge wearers at the stands, but once inside the docks, they 'had to remove the all-important button*'.[42] If so, the belt would be as good a place as anywhere. A member would be able to cover it less conspicuously than if it were in his jacket, if need be. The quarter badge, although designed to recognise and recruit members, seems to have suffered from an element of militant particularism. The Irish Transport and General Workers Union in the 1940s, seems to have displayed this. First-preference men wore a white diamond-shaped badge, whilst second-preference men wore shields of various colours according to the year, and it was said that 'any shield wearing man being taken ahead of first preference men, would produce an angry reminder that "diamonds are trumps today".'[43]

The quarter badge having been introduced to distinguish union from non-union members had, later at least, resulted in distinguishing more favoured from less favoured union members, and was perhaps in danger of becoming a little too incestuous to serve the purpose for which it was originally intended. In 1911, the seamen's strike in which the NUDL were involved, restored the right to wear the union badge freely: 'Men were allowed to wear the union button* on the stands and the employers undertook "not to discriminate in favour of non-union labour".[44] Furthermore 'there would be no victimisation of union men and that the union badge would be recognised.'[45] None the less, it was still felt necessary as late as the 1930s, for the union to insist on the badge being worn the right side up, otherwise 'the member will be regarded as a non-unionist.'[46] Even as late as 1945, a circular from the L&DC&MU, dated 9 July, states that badges 'must be worn right side up, in a conspicuous place'. The display of the badge did not always mean employment, but in its best years helped to gain preference. A telephone system between stands, agitated for by Sexton, helped to increase union employment. The quarter badge, though, could also lead to inter-union conflict. At Hull, in 1923, the newly formed Transport and General Workers Union (TGWU), signed an agreement with the port employers, that only TGWU members be engaged for work. This would be effected by the TGWU operating the quarter-badge system. Hull had never been organised by one union, and competing unions immediately protested. Disgruntled members of the TGWU had been poached by the Workers Union,[47] and the quarter-badge scheme was designed both to get them back and to stabilise the TGWU's organisation in the Hull docks. The Workers Union staged a two-hour strike in protest, and were successful in having the badge agreement withdrawn. As a Mr L.M. Worsnop, of the Workers Union, reported to the TUC annual conference in 1923: 'They [the TGWU] have flirted with Havelock Wilson and tried to copy his PC5 methods. What happened? We had a strike in Hull last Easter to break the badge agreement. It lasted less than two hours and the agreement was smashed.'[48]

The employers gave out tallies to their own preferred men, imitating the dockers' system to their own advantage. One such system, instituted in the Bristol docks in 1919, was the subject of a Transport Workers Court of Enquiry in 1920. Under this system, a Port Labour Committee, consisting of five employers and five representatives of the dockers' union (DWR&GWU), administered the tallies. Tallies issued to dock labourers were round and square, marked 'D', whilst all carters, warehousemen and permanent loaders tallies, were triangular or oval and marked 'C'. The tally was a form of registration and no man could be engaged without his tally. When asked by the Court of Enquiry, 'who really has the control of the issuing of the tallies?', the general manager of Bristol docks replied: 'The control of the issuing of the tallies to the casuals is done entirely by the Union officials',[49] thus only partially answering the question.[50] In Glasgow at least, in 1936, this led to a battle of wills between the National Port Employers and the Scottish Transport and General Workers Union, a 1932 breakaway from the British TGWU. The breakaway resulted from the interpretation of the nature of the special preference, which was accepted by the TGWU in 1932 and which lasted right up to the 1960s. This operated, in Belfast for instance as follows:

> ... the new category of preference men were issued with a badge with the initials 'S.P.'. The dockers called this the sacking preference badge. It probably stood for Special Preference. It meant that the particular worker was both skilled and reliable, and would be given employment preference – first to be hired, last to be laid off.[51]

The Glasgow dockers conversely wanted to implement their quarter-badge system as a means of special preference, rather than the employer's tally system, that is, to give preference to union members, identified by wearing the relevant quarter badge. This was accepted by the employers in an agreement of 1936: 'The Glasgow men also felt that their scheme took power out of the hands of some remote employer dominated National Council and placed the power of deciding about employment preference into the hands of the union branch.'[52] Effectively, non-union men were only hired when there were no union men left in need of work. Under the 1936 agreement, foremen were required to observe this rule, any ignoring of which, would require explanation to the branch committee or be reported to their employer. This thus implies that the union had the right to discipline a foreman.[53] It is posited that the STGWU (which eventually re-amalgamated with the TGWU in 1972) controlled labour supply in the Glasgow docks by 'closing the books'; that is, by refusing to admit any new members in times of work shortage. As work was conditional on being a member of the union, excess labour and thus the lowering of pay rates was avoided in this way.[54] Therefore, in Glasgow at least, the quarter badge is revealed as pivotal in the struggle for the control and regulation of union membership, labour supply and the organisational structure of carrying out the work itself.

One ex-full-time officer of the L&DC&MU, Harold Bates, spent three days in Scotland Road and three in Birkenhead. He would patrol the stands checking the badges had the right numbers. Any worker not wearing it would be asked to pay up, and on refusal, his employer would be faced with a walk out by his unionised employees.[55] The badge also served as a way of preventing company spies from getting into union meetings. After the 1890 dock strike it was reported that 'meetings are conducted in private and none but those who can produce the union badge are admitted to them.'[56]

The National Warehouse and General Workers Union, which was established in 1911 as a result of the seamen's strike that year and based in Liverpool, also employed the system:

> The warehouse workers at the docks seemed to have adopted the quarterly badge system, perhaps taking a lead from the dockers themselves. The difference was however, that the NWGWU did not number their badges, i.e. 1,2,3,4, to represent quarters, but simply issued a different shape (and a different metal?) for each quarter. Whatever shape or substance of the badge, it always depicted the union's national logo of handshake across the globe.[57]

There are also examples extant which are attributed to the Liverpool South Side Dock Labourers Association, bearing the initials 'LSDLA', the quarter '4' and the wearer's number on the branch role '553'. The red hand badge of the Irish Transport & General Workers Union, dated 1913, became the emblem of resistance in the Dublin lockout of that year, and was apparently later adopted as a cap badge of the Irish Citizens Army: 'Members wore the badge in defiance of the challenge to the right to organise. It was a symbol of the legend of 1913, a hallmark to the integrity and courage of the bearer.'[58] It also makes a literary appearance in James Plunkett's 1969 novel based on the 1913 strike, *Strumpet City*. The TGWU continued to issue quarter badges after absorbing the majority of waterfront unions in the inter-war period, and issued some in 1947 after absorbing the L&DC&MU. With dock registration and the closed shop, the need for the quarter badge stopped, although occasional instances are known where they were later issued as a clearance symbol. The TGWU 11/3 branch issued one for the whole of 1953. There are also circulars distributed from the Liverpool offices of the TGWU dated 2 April 1962 and 19 April 1962 which refer to the use of membership cards as a means of control. Possibly these replaced the badge system there, as the last known issue in Liverpool of a control badge is one issued for the whole of Liverpool and Birkenhead in 1961. During the 1950s at least, the TGWU was known as the 'white union' and the Stevedores and Dockers Union as the 'blue union', because of the colour of their membership cards.[59]

Australia

In Australia, 'financial member' badges continued for much longer, although they tended to be issued annually rather than quarterly[60] from the 1940s onwards. A badge of the Federated Clerks Union of Australia, Shipping Clerks Division exemplifies this. Issued by the New South Wales (NSW) branch for 1944, it bears the member's number on the reverse, and is 'designed for a date clip to be attached to the top lug',[61] which means the same badge could be reused on an annual basis, with only the date clip being regulated for distribution.[62] The NSW branch of the Federated Storemen and Packers Union, issued dated enamel lapel badges every year beginning in 1937–38 through to 1965–66, but 'from 1966 the union issued a card to members instead of a badge each year.' [63] Similarly, the NSW branch of the Municipal and Shire Employees Association, established in 1903, issued annual dated enamel badges from 1930 to 1954: 'This was the last year that a dated badge was issued and it was designed to have a date clip attached for subsequent years',[64] although some unions such as the Sydney branch of the Waterside Workers Union, established in 1902, discontinued the issuing of annually dated badges in 1948,[65] around the same time as in Britain. Presumably, technical innovation provided the 'date clips' in the 1950s, thus allowing unions to reduce costs of having new badges issued each year. Certainly the Australian Workers Union issued annual financial button badges from 1938 to 1962, opting for an enamel badge with date clip in 1962–63,[66] whilst the Shop Assistants Union issued annual enamel badges with the date engraved and member's registration number stamped on the front between the 1920s and 1960s, with the colour combination of the enamel being changed each year.[67] The Transport Workers Union of Australia is perhaps the union which has perpetuated this system the longest. Beginning in 1943, both the New South Wales and Tasmanian branches at least have issued enamel financial year badges and fobs ever since.[68]

In Britain, the National Union of Distributive & Allied Workers (NUDAW) issued a quarter badge in the early 1920s, but no other examples are known within this union. It is thought that it may have been issued to the union's membership in dockside warehouses, where the National Warehouse and General Workers Union, based in Liverpool, helped form NUDAW in 1922.[69] The Shipwrights and Ship Constructors Association (SW&SCA) used the system. Although little is known about the origins of the system within the Association, it was believed by the late Harry Murt, a former full-time official with the Association in Liverpool, to have arisen in his area out of a dispute between the SC&SWA and the Liverpool Shipwrights Association (LSA). The oldest examples of the badge in his collection date from 1923 and continue to 1950.[70] They were used in the same way as the Liverpool docker's badges. All these badges were made of metal except those for the war years when they were made of tin; very useful at a time when people's garden gates were being collected for war materials!

Mine Workers

Next to the waterfront workers, the miners were those who most used the quarter-badge system. Their badges were in the form of brass sew-on tallies which were sewn to their caps and jackets. At least one example is known to date from the 1860s or 1870s. This is a brass tally of the Church Lane lodge (No. 27) of the South Yorkshire Miners Association, which existed from 1858 to 1881.[71] It pictures a colliery pit head scene on the reverse and the name on the obverse. However, it does not bear any indication (that is, A–D or 1–4) that it was used as the quarter-badge system was, and may have been used simply as a means of membership identification. It is not until a few years later that we find more detail of the system: 'In June 1889, the Derbyshire Miners Council decided to purchase six thousand medals [tallies] which were to be sold at a penny each.'[72] These tallies were issued to members in the coalfields across the country, usually on a quarterly basis, especially during recruitment campaigns: 'Members were asked not to ride the shaft with men not wearing a current badge [tally] on their caps or lapels. This idea was revived during the "back to the union" campaign which opened in 1922.'[73] The quarter on the badge was defined, either by number (1–4) or letter (A–D). In Derbyshire, the size of the tallies was reduced and they were worn specifically on the lapel rather than the cap, and were varied in shape and design.[74] North Gawber and South Kirby of the Yorkshire Miners Association had six and eight respectively different designs of tally during their 100 per cent (membership) campaign of the 1930s.[75] The gravity with which these tallies were viewed is expressed by the executive of the Derbyshire Miners Association, who in 1891 stated 'Members are desired to wear the medals [tallies] as the surest way to detect those unprincipled men who profess to be in the union here and there, but in reality are nowhere.'[76] If the membership shared the same sentiments as the executive, it would be safe to assume that the tally system was taken very seriously, as the Executive Committee go on to say that non-members who pretend to be members: 'cannot be tolerated with the same freedom and be looked upon in the same way as men who are doing their duty to their class'.[77]

During the 100 per cent (membership) campaign of 1910–14, the Lancashire and Cheshire miners issued tallies for January, April, July and October. Such campaigns were common across the coal fields, suggesting widespread use of the system.[78] Tallies were also used extensively in the Australian docks. The 1903 example of the Sydney Wharf Labourers Union is not only stamped with the member's registration number and the date, but the monogrammed initials 'WMH'. These were the initials of the secretary, William M. Hughes! Although seemingly most popular with dockers and miners, the quarter-badge system was used elsewhere as well. The Bolton & District Carters Association used the system from 1890, expanding when amalgamating with surrounding unions in other parts of Lancashire to become the Amalgamated Union of Carters and Lurrymen [sic].[79]

The Use of the Quarter Badge Elsewhere

Although Sexton's assertion was that McGhee, the NUDL president, had invented the quarter-badge system in 1890, there are possibly other, older precedents. The London Mariners and Riggers Union issued a token, the size of an old halfpenny, which now resides in the collections of the National Museum of Labour History (NMLH) in Manchester. On its obverse it pictures Britannia and the date 1866. The reverse is divided into four, and bears a stamped 'v' for each halfpenny paid.[80] The LM&RU was established in 1866, so whether the date refers to the union's establishment or the year for which the token was valid is unclear. However, it does seem to synthesise both the membership card and the later quarter badge, and thus illustrates how the organisation and retention of members was developing at the time. One researcher, John Smethurst, suggests that earlier prototype control tallies can be located amongst pre- and proto-trade union seamen's organisations such as friendly and benevolent societies in the early and mid-nineteenth century.[81] The quarter-badge system amongst waterfront workers in Scotland presumably arose from the NUDL who originated and organised there. The system is also known to have been used in Scotland by the Scottish National Horsemen's Association and the Amalgamated Carters Society of Glasgow. It is however, also noted that Hugh Lyon of the Scottish Horse and Motormen's Association (SH&MA) had written to 'the Amalgamated Carters, Lurrymen and Motormen, whose headquarters were in Bolton'[82] about their means of collecting union dues in 1905. The Bolton union used the quarter-badge system, but it is not mentioned if they referred their system to the Scottish Motormen, but could have led to the spread of the system in Scotland if they did. Even if the SH&MS did not use the quarter-badge system, there is evidence that they viewed their ordinary membership badge as a recruitment tool. Hugh Lyon, the general secretary, stated in 1911:

> We have also issued badges for our members to wear, which I trust will be the means of bringing or forcing those who are prepared to share the victories of our members within the pale of our union, so that we may be able in the near future to see every carter earning at least thirty shillings per week [83]

In Ireland, the quarter badge probably dates from the time that the NUDL first introduced it there in the 1890s. However, on the reverse of the previously mentioned medallion of the Cork Harbour Labourers, dating from the late eighteenth century, 'the number 56 has been incised in the centre.' [84] This arguably may indicate a membership or control number, which would then make the system significantly older. However, the Guild of St Patrick may simply have been a religious or benevolent order to which the labourers belonged. The first known Irish quarter badges proper were those of the Irish Transport Workers Union (ITWU, later to add 'and General') from 1909 onwards. The badge-studded belt of one Myles Kinsella, a Dublin docker, displays the last quarter

badges of the NUDL made before the ITWU, which are also featured.[85] C.
Desmond Greaves also cites the instance of a meeting at which James Sexton was
due to speak on 12 January 1909 in Belfast, when James Larkin's star was rising
in Ireland. The meeting is reported to have broken up in confusion 'in which the
platform received a hail of discarded NUDL badges'.[86] Outside the docks, the
system was used by the Tipperary Workingmen's Protective and Benefit Society,
dating from 1912. They are the button type and picture the general secretary,
Michael Callahan and the numbers 1–4. The society amalgamated with the ITGWU
in 1943.[87] In Australia, there was also a system of annual, as well as quarter
badges, such as those issued by the Amalgamated Road Transport Workers Union
of Australia, NSW Branch in the 1930s and 1940s at least. A new enamel badge
was issued each year, with a different colour for easier identification. Interestingly, they were normally worn on the hat band rather than the lapel.[88] The
British NUR also issued special badges of the button type. They appear sometimes dated, sometimes not, and some bear pictures of trains. (see see Figure 3.2)
It is believed they were issued for specific recruitment campaigns. It is further
believed that they would have been worn on a designated day, in a prearranged
colour or design by members. Anyone on that day not seen wearing the badge
would be assumed not to be a member, and would be approached to join.[89] They
were seemingly issued in the 1930s, and have around the lip of the badge in some
cases 'property of the NUR, returnable'. It is also felt that they may have been
originally issued as a way of distinguishing NUR signalmen from members of the
breakaway Union of Railway Signalmen.[90] Interestingly, the Australian railway
unions also issued badges which stated on the reverse or in the rules, that they
remained the property of the union.

As long ago as 1892, the New South Wales Loco Engine Drivers, Firemen and
Cleaners Association issued a watch chain fob in three grades – gilt, bronze and
silver – which stated this on the reverse. The Federal Electrical Trades Union of
Australia, also stamped 'Property of the FETUA' on the reverse of their badges.[91]
Examples of badges issued by the National Union of General & Municipal Workers
in the 1920s and 1930s with the words 'Fish Bobber', are known. These are round,
white enamel badges with either a large red number '1' or '2' on them. These are
believed to have been used on the east coast fishing ports, although the purpose of
the numbers and the organisation of the members of the union who wore them,
remains obscure.[92] Even today, in Australia 'badge-show days' are organised by the
Barrier Industrial Council (BIC):

> Each quarter of the year, on the second Tuesday of the middle month, all unionists have
> to wear a specially struck badge to prove financial membership of a union. Different
> badges are issued for each shift in the mines and for town workers. Anyone not wearing
> a badge is not allowed to work, and has to pay a fine to the Barrier Industrial Council
> equal to a day's pay [93]

Figure 3.2   Lithograph, celluloid and tin (button) badges of the National Union of Railwaymen c.1930–1940, each 25 mm. Worn on designated 'recognition days', these once purely functional badges now convey strong images of nostalgia for a lost golden age of public transport which mask the long hours and dangerous nature of working on Britain's railways at the time.
Joe Fleming collection, photograph Dean Bennett.

One example of these BIC badges was issued by the Workers Industrial Union, formed in 1918 on the industrial 'OBU' (One Big Union) ideal. It dates from 1937 and pictures Tom Mann, an engineer, who after founding the Workers Union in Britain in 1898, had gone to Australia, to spread the word on industrial syndicalism:

> Tom Mann was a British unionist who was invited to Broken Hill in 1908, to assist in organising the mining unions and to increase membership. He was actively involved in the 1909 lockout, and was arrested along with other strike leaders. He was acquitted and became an advocate of the resumption of work after the strike entered its fifth month, and it was clear that the miners could not win their objectives.[94]

Mann returned to England, and was elected as the first General Secretary of the newly formed Amalgamated Engineering Union in 1920.

The badge itself was no mere throwaway gimmick. The ITGWU states in Rule 4 of their 1915 rule book that 3 pence will be charged for a badge of the union.[95] The 1918 rules of the Irish Automobile Drivers and Mechanics Trade Union stated 'A member can hire a badge of the union for which he will pay 2/6d. The committee can at any time call on a member to hand up same.' [96] In Australia, Rule 23 of the Sydney Coal Lumpers Union in 1950, stated 'Medals shall be worn by members while at work and shall be produced when requested to do so by an officer of the union. Any member losing his shall report same to the Secretary, who shall issue another medal upon payment of 5/-.' [97] The rule book of the United Commercial Travellers Association of Australia further stated 'A uniform badge should be carried by the members of each affiliated Association. In the event of retirement of a member, he shall surrender the badge to the Association [to which] he belongs.' [98] Rule 23 of the Australian United Labourers Association 1912 rule book states that:

> a). That the national badge be the letters ULU in silver on a blue background. b) That the badge be supplied to members at 2/- each on the understanding that in the event of any member becoming unfinancial or being guilty of conduct unworthy of a member, the union shall retain the right to recall the union badge and return the member his money.[99]

The systems used on opposite sides of the world therefore can be seen to be remarkably similar.

The quarter-badge system was clearly a developing one. It was more complicated than a mere check-off system. The differentiation by colour, shape, design, lettering and numbering was constantly being revised for efficiency and protection from fraudulent use. Regional and local particularism can be detected in the issuing and wearing of badges, which, as will be discussed in Chapter 4, in more recent times, has iconographically and otherwise been far more in evidence. Over time therefore, the use of the badge in the trade union can be seen as illustrative of a process of devolution as designs for and the issuing of badges became a local rather than (or as well as) a national undertaking within the union concerned. The emphasis on the badge as remaining the union's property in many rule books, highlights the concern with an attempt to inculcate respect for the symbolic nature of the badge, as well as an exercise in precaution and control. Outside the quarter-badge system there are other instances of struggle for union recognition, in which the badge played a key role. Cases of petty tyranny were common in the early days of the movement, and several cases of such petty-mindedness will now be examined in the context of the ordinary membership badge, all three of which involve uniformed workers.

The London and Provincial Union of Licensed Vehicle Workers, 1913

The London and Provincial Union of Licensed Vehicle Workers (LPULVW) was formed in 1913 out of the London Cab Drivers Trade Union, and in the same year faced a dispute over its ornate membership badge. The Tillings bus company in September 1913, suspended twelve men who refused to remove the LPULVW membership badge or the 'red button'* as it was known, from their uniform.[100] This led to an all-out strike by the LPULVW, the Acton (London) branch of which had a banner made proclaiming: 'No Badge, No Bus'[101] (see Figure 3.3). The company refused to see a delegation from the union, although it denied having any objection to union membership[102] The matter was settled when both sides accepted arbitration and the LPULVW was granted full recognition by Tillings. The LPULVW issued a strike badge which pictured the clasped hands of unity and bears the inscription 'London and Provincial Union of Licensed Vehicle Workers – Victory – 1913'.[103]

It is also worth noting that badges played a distinguishing role between the LPULVW and its more moderate Manchester-based rival, the Amalgamated Association of Tramway & Vehicle Workers (AATVW). Bus workers' union historian Ken Fuller writes:

> During the few years of its existence, the LPU became known as the 'red button union'* and the AATVW as the 'blue button union'*. Although these labels had their origins in the colours of the two unions' badges, they were not without their political significance.[104]

In 1915, in the London tram strike, the LPULVW struck over the length of spread over (the time from signing on to signing off a shift) against the London County Council (LCC). The AATVW were loathe to support it, but their members came out in support anyway. The AATVW dragged its heels and a drift back to work brought about an organised return. Archie Henderson, an AATVW organiser, left the union, joined the LPULVW, and urged all AATVW members to 'put on the red button'*.[105] When the LPULVW and the AATVW amalgamated to form the United Vehicle Workers (UVW) in 1919, the secretary of the new amalgamation, Stanley Hirst, is reported as saying: 'Occasionally I have found to my regret that although we are now one union, there is still a tendency to discuss certain matters in terms of 'reds' and 'blues'.[106] It is notable, that the AATVW also issued a badge with red in it.[107] Perhaps this was to allay the dishonourable or moderate label they may have been branded with through their blue badge.

Amalgamated Tramways Employees Association

A tramways employees strike in Brisbane, Australia, in 1912, was sparked off by the banning of the wearing of the union badge whilst on duty. The strike eventually

Figure 3.3   Obverse side of the Acton branch banner of the London and Provincial Union of Licensed Vehicle Workers. Proclaiming 'Victory 1913. No Badge No Bus', the pivotal nature that the lapel badge played in early struggles for union recognition is here evocatively recognised.
Reproduced by permission of the National Museum of Labour History, Manchester.

involved forty-three unions![108] The Brisbane Tramway Company refused to recognise, and tried to break, the Australian Tramway Employees Association (ATEA), which had been formed by amalgamation of organisations from Victoria, South and Western Australia, in 1910:

> In an attempt to force recognition, the union instructed its members to wear their union badge while at work as from 11 am, Thursday 18th January 1912. When the company dismissed the men for wearing badges, forty-three unions went on strike in support of the Tramway Union on 13th January 1912. While this strike was not wholly successful, the tramwaymen did win the right to wear their union badge.[109]

Therefore, we can see how the badge played a pivotal role in deciding grave action by both employers and unions. The visual assertion of belonging to an organisation, other than the one represented by the uniform, implies that employees could think and act for themselves, and were not mere 'servants' of the company.

Interestingly, a silver Australian medal of the New South Wales Government Tramways Employees Union, from probably a slightly earlier period, was also issued both with and without the word 'union' on it.[110] Perhaps the latter was for wear in situations where such open proclamation of union membership would lead to dismissal. Without the word 'union', it is simply a statement of who one worked for. This union, formed in 1902, became the NSW branch of the ATEA. It therefore implies that organisation in the Brisbane Tramway system had encountered similar resistance before 1912.

New South Wales Transport Strike, 1917

The reintroduction of Taylorism (time and motion study) in some Australian workshops, in 1917, led to a two-month strike by transport workers, predominantly railway workers. The main unions involved were the Amalgamated Rail and Tramway Service Association,[111] Trolly Draymen and Carters Union, Waterside Workers Federation of Australia, Miners Federation and Seamen's Union of Australasia. The NSW government raised a volunteer labour force of seven thousand, with the wage inducement of twelve shillings a day. The volunteers (mainly from country areas) supplemented those workers who had not joined the strike, and maintained a skeleton service throughout the strike. Eventually, the strike was broken. As a result, twenty unions were deregistered: 'This cleared the way for pro-government loyalist unions to be established in the railways and on the waterfront.'[112] Despite promises of no victimisation for an orderly return to work, three thousand men were not rehired, whilst others lost seniority. A number of badges were issued to commemorate the strike, but two are of primary interest. The first was issued by an organisation known as the 'Lilywhites' formed in 1918: 'The unionists who remained on strike to the end formed an association known as the Lilywhites. This was a secret organisation and very little is known of its organisation. The future Prime Minister of Australia, J.B. (Ben) Chifley (1945–49) was known to have been a member.'[113] Moreover, 'Membership was open only to those men who did not go back to work until the strike had ended.'[114]

The fob was struck in silver, in the shape of an inverted horseshoe, with a lily in the centre and the words 'In Commemoration of 1917'. The volunteers and those who stayed at work, were awarded a badge by the NSW government, picturing the Australian coat of arms and the words: 'Loyal Workers Industrial Crisis 1917':

> The badge given to the loyalists by the authorities is very rare. As no man would have dared wear this badge in public without experiencing verbal or physical abuse, it is reasonable to assume that their rarity is due to most being discarded shortly after use.[115]

The badges are comparable to those issued during 1926 in Britain, when the railway companies gave out 'loyalty' medals to volunteers who worked a skeleton train service throughout the 'industrial crisis' or general strike. The consequences were also similar to those in the British coal fields after November 1926. Legitimate unions were derecognised and 'moderate' unions were given preference, a position which took years to overcome.

The Postmen's Federation, 1913–18

As if to underline the Tillings/LPULUW dispute and the wearing of the union badge on uniforms, it is mentioned again in the correspondence between the Postmen's Federation (PF) and the GPO, in relation to the PF badge. The following would seem to be the opening salvo: 'With the settlement of the London bus dispute we have not seen the last of the badge trouble it seems. That particular politician who is credited with running the post office has issued a ukase forbidding Croydon postmen to wear badges of their Federation.'[116] Because both occupations involved uniformed workers, there was perhaps a certain empathy between them, and they saw the refusal to be allowed to wear a union badge as an aspersion on their supposed status. Postmen, bus drivers and railway workers incidentally are amongst those workers who these days seem to wear the most badges of all. *The Postmen's Gazette*, by 1897 at least, was openly advertising various pendants, watch chain fobs, sleeve links, scarf pins, fancy laurel wreaths, and even officers' pendants of the Postmen's Federation for sale by the firm of 'Masters' in Rye, Sussex. Therefore a certain pride in wearing them can be assumed. The ensuing correspondence is inconclusive, but worthy of examining. The Federation, in the *Postmen's Gazette* for 21 February 1914, p. 82 states 'Recently a number of applications have been received for facilities to wear a Federation badge. Committee considered the matter and decided to make applications to the Post Master General for permission to do so. Reply has been received refusing application.' The correspondence between the PF and the Post Master General (PMG) running from October 1913 to January 1914 is published in the *Postmen's Gazette* of 21 February 1914, beginning with correspondence to the PMG of 7 October 1913 in which the Federation asks for the recision of the ban, asserting that the wearing of union badges is now 'practically universal'.[117] The Federation call the ban unfair as the wearing of temperance ribbons is permissible on uniforms. It concludes by assuring the PMG that it would ensure that the badge would be worn in such a manner as not to obscure any 'distinctive marks' on the uniform.[118]

There is then a brief reply from the GPO reiterating the original decision to ban the Federation badge on duty, dated 16 December 1913. The Federation then asks for reasons why the badge could not be worn. It is argued that the refusal can only be construed as 'a disparagement of trade organisations', as it is said that 'you are aware naval and military medals, ambulance decorations and temperance ribbons are allowed to be worn.'[119] The Federation continues that the right to wear the badge had been conceded by many companies who employ uniformed men, and also corporations. They then make a reference to the Tillings dispute: 'I am also to remind the PMG that a short time ago Msrs. Tillings declined to allow their men to wear a union badge and that their action was the subject of the general publics condemnation. Msrs. Tilling gave way in the matter … .'[120]

The Federation asks for further consideration of the matter in a letter dated 3 January 1914. In a reply dated 14 January 1914, which is a little more forthcoming, the GPO try to legitimise the ban by saying that the PMG does not generally 'view with favour' the wearing of 'private badges on uniform' and that the Federation's request will not be reconsidered. Furthermore, medals and badges earned in service to the state or society are of a different kind to 'private badges', and that is why such badges are allowed on uniform. Although an exception was made for temperance ribbons, no further exceptions are contemplated. The GPO state that they cannot be guided by the practice of private employers. A more telling passage is when the GPO states:

> It is in his [the PMG's] view undesirable that a uniform wearing civil servant whose duty brings him into constant contact with the public, should bear upon his uniform evidence of the fact that he is a member of some particular organisation – a fact which in no way concerns the public … .[121]

This is the last correspondence that is noted and the result is left in abeyance. All that is noted is the fact that ex-army and navy men are allowed to wear their association's badges on uniform officially and on this basis, the general purposes committee will reconsider the question. The last correspondence from the GPO is dated 14 January 1914. The matter was eventually resolved when a GPO circular from 3 July 1917 lifts the ban. Staff Rule No. 14 states that:

> The Postmaster General has had under consideration the rule forbidding the wearing of private badges on official uniforms or whilst officers are on duty, whether in uniform or

not; and has decided that the prohibition should not in future apply to the badge of the trade union to which an officer belongs.

The current ruling on the wearing of the union badge is that it is the only non-uniform badge allowed on uniform other than those of charities and flag days, etc. provided they are not obtrusive.[122] This recalls the PMG's attitude to the allowing of temperance medals, etc. on uniform, and perhaps helps to explain why the Communication Workers Union badge is so small, so as not to be obtrusive. Postmen are rarely seen these days without their union badge on their uniform, to the extent that it has become almost part of their uniform.

From the foregoing it is interesting to note that in the early years of the twentieth century, lapel badges had become widespread. Mention is made of several organisations having issued badges, and with the increasing use of badges in a wide cross-section of society, the starchy excuses for not allowing trade unionists to wear badges were becoming less and less convincing. One reason it would be argued that uniformed workers seem to wear badges to a large extent is because it asserts a loyalty deeper to the union than to the employer, or asserts an identity above that of the uniform. It was no doubt to this reason as much as any other, that the PMG's obstinacy can be attributed. The Federation badge was perhaps perceived as symbolic of some undefined subversion of the assumed pride in the uniform and job that postmen and uniformed workers were supposed to have, despite their poor pay and conditions.

The references to the Tillings dispute are interesting, as it was obviously of enough consequence to have been noticed, and its cause to have been linked with that of the postmen's. Especially in relation to the Tillings dispute, in 1986 it was noted that:

> An attempt to ban staff from wearing union badges on their uniforms by London Regional Transport, the body appointed by the government to run London's buses and underground trains, in place of local government controlled London Transport, has been abandoned following strong protests from the trade unions concerned.[123]

Additionally, there was a move in 1991 by British Rail to 'curtail the wearing of badges – though one unobtrusive membership badge will still be allowed'.[124] This was presumably designed to assert the uniform of the company above the insignia of the union. A year earlier, the British Railways Board (BRB) had objected to ASLEF, the National Union of Railwaymen (NUR) and Transport Salaried Staffs Association's (TSSA) desire for their members to be able to wear the prescribed 'unobtrusive membership badge' on the then new InterCity service uniform. The NUR and TSSA representatives at a meeting with the BRB

> ... contended that the wearing of trade union badges indicated loyalty to both union and employer. The Railway representatives stated that the prime objectives of the new uniform clothing arrangements was to provide a smart appearance by the board's staff

and the appendage of numerous badges did nothing to enhance the image that the board wished to project.[125]

The previous position that the one small union badge could be worn, other than on the new InterCity uniform, was restated, but with the proviso that the unions encourage the wearing of BRB badges bearing the wearer's name. There were strong concerns presented by the unions that the wearing of such badges laid the privacy and safety of the wearer open to possible unwanted attention by the public, and some cases of this were cited. However, the BRB insisted that the practice was 'no different to that of several other organisations in the transport, retail and service sectors, and this is seen as an integral part of our customer care and service quality objectives.'[126]

Therefore, whilst insisting on larger more obtrusive company name badges, the BRB balked at anything more than the smallest unobtrusive union badges, thus keeping the union identity to a minimum. In 1998 after privatisation, the position remained the same, except at Great North Eastern Railways (GNER), a former InterCity company where 'Discussions are taking place on reaching an agreement to allow Trade Union badges to be worn.'[127]

The National Asylum Workers Union, 1918

Another incident in which the badge figured prominently in the struggle for recognition occurred at Bodmin Asylum in Cornwall in October 1918. This time it involved the eight-year-old National Asylum Workers Union (NAWU). Discontent with petty tyranny, excessive hours and bad conditions was brought to a head by the initial suspension and then dismissal of five nurses for wearing the NAWU badge on duty.[128] The NAWU badge certainly had all the iconography of solidarity on it. As well as the union name, it bore the inscription 'all for one and one for all', the clasped hands of unity, the scales of justice, a lath bundle, symbolic of strength through unity, and an all-seeing eye representing wisdom (see Figure 3.4).

The design had been submitted for approval of the membership in the March 1914 issue of the *National Asylum Workers Union Magazine*, with recommendation of its acceptance. One objection to its introduction by some members was that 'the authorities would not allow them to be worn', to which the union executive replied 'Some would, some wouldn't. In any case the authorities could not prevent the wearing of a pendant on a watch-chain while on duty. A *decent* badge could be worn when off duty.' The badge was accepted. Three thousand were initially ordered, manufactured by Thomas Fattorini of Bradford for sale at 9 pence each. They were made in the form of lapel badges and watch chain fobs for men and brooches for women. Wearing of the badge was optional, but 'Nevertheless annual conference and other official delegates are strongly urged to procure badges without fail.' There was clearly a lingering concern about employer permission to wear

Figure 3.4   Enamel and brass badge of the National Asylum Workers Union c.1910s. It must surely hold the record for including the greatest number of allegorical allusions to trade union principle. The all-seeing eye (historically of God, in union legend, of the treasurer!) hovers above a bundle of sticks signifying strength through combination, across which are the clasped hands of unity. Above them on the scroll, is the maxim 'all for one for all' which is surmounted by the scales of justice, and for good measure, a wheat sheaf symbolising abundance appears under the clasped hands.
Joe Fleming collection, photograph by Dean Bennett.

the badge at work, as the full-page advert for the introduction of the badge in the May 1914 issue of the *National Asylum Workers Union Magazine* makes clear:

IMPORTANT NOTICE
'Members should not wear these badges on the official uniform where the institution rules forbid such adornment, but all branches should immediately request permission from their respective visiting committees to wear the badges whilst on duty'.

Evidently the concern was justified, as thirty-four other nurses walked out in sympathy with the original five sacked at Bodmin. It is not clear if the members had asked permission to wear the badge or had been refused it, and were wearing them in defiance. However, the medical superintendent, no doubt trying to show who was boss, dismissed the other thirty-four and then offered to reinstate all but the original five.[129] The reply was 'all or none', which they had inscribed on a protest banner.

Fifty women nurses were on strike for the right to wear the union badge on duty, in conjunction with other improvements. All fifty were dismissed, and it is said that 'The strikers – who were resident staff – were billeted and provisions in plenty were delivered to the picket lines. The town crier announced strike meetings and the Salvation Army preceded the strikers as they marched through the town.'[130] The following resolution was passed after a visiting committee and Shaw, the NAWU secretary, had visited Bodmin: 'that the visiting committee recognises the NAWU and that the Asylum employees, being members of the union, be allowed to wear the official union badge in such a position as not to cause an injury to patients.'[131] All strikers were reinstated, and the badge had triumphed. The real objections to the badge would no doubt have been the same as the PMG's, being seen as symptomatic of a loyalty over that of the profession, which is still the government card played against nurses today when they complain of poor pay and conditions. In this instance, it seems that the employers argued that the badge may be harmful to patients if it got caught in their clothing, or scratched them. This concern was still present in nursing amongst members of the National Union of Public Employees (NUPE) at least, in modern times. As a Brother McDougall (Doncaster Hospitals) pointed out at NUPE's 1982 conference:

I think it is time the union looked at the shape of the badge it produces because the members employed in the health service are not allowed to wear the one that is made now [a three-pointed triangular badge]. We want a round badge we can wear in the vicinity of the workplace and near the patients.[132]

The same point was raised again at the 1984 conference when a Brother A. Moore (Stockport Hospitals) raised the concern that 'Nurses and members of staff with close patient contact are afraid of injuring the patient with the existing pointed badge, for example, when lifting or turning a patient.'[133] This issue therefore was no longer solely a managerial point of contention.

The NAWU became the Mental Hospital and Institutional Workers Union (MH&IWU) in 1930, and in 1931 published a book on its history since 1910, for its twenty-first birthday. On the inside back cover, there is an advert for the union's badge which reads as follows: 'The union's badge is made of solid silver and its neatness, beauty and unobtrusive appearance will commend itself to all members. There is no lettering on the front of the badge but the initials "MHIWU" are on the reverse.' A legacy of 1918 perhaps? If the NAWU badge had so much iconography of solidarity on it as to attract the unwelcome attention of the medical superintendent and cause the subsequent strike, then presumably the MH&IWU were trying to be a little less overt in their choice of design, but to eradicate all symbols and lettering from the front of the badge, is perhaps going a little too far. It none the less shows the seriousness with which the badge was taken.[134] Certainly given the nature of the economic climate of the time, caution would have been advisable. The radical differences between the NAWU and the MH&IWU badges are outward signs of the change in union policy after the name change. An appeal published in the *Mental Hospital Workers Journal*, in July 1932 places emphasis on the 'professionalising' and status raising of nurses. It is noted that 'The "objects" of the new union were achieving "reasonable hours of duty and a fair rate of wages". The problems and grievances now received less attention in the union journal than they had previously.'[135]

Police Unions

In Britain, attempts to organise police never met with much success. The most notable attempt was the formation of the National Union of Police and Prison Officers (NUPPO) during the 1919 police strike in Liverpool and London.[136] The failure of the strike led to the formation of the present Police Federation, a representative body without the rights of action of a trade union. The NUPPO however, continued to function until the Second World War and issued its own badge, which was round in blue and green, with an ivy leaf design in the centre and the union's initials. In Australia, state police organisations have had permission to affiliate to the Australian Council of Trade Unions (ACTU) and state trades councils. However, even there they had to be careful. The Victorian Police Association, one of the oldest police unions, was established in 1917:

> In 1920 it was decided to issue an Association badge, and permission was sought from the Victorian premier for a badge incorporating a crown attachment. Permission to wear a badge was granted on 14th February 1921. A final design was approved in June 1921, and an amount of 2/6d was charged to each member to cover the cost of manufacture. The badge always remained the property of the Association. In October 1930, the Association was declared an illegally constituted body, and a new Association was formed known as Police Association Victoria.[137]

In 1923, on 31 October, a police strike took place in Melbourne

> ... when a group of constables at Russell Street Police Station refused beat duty in protest over the use of four special supervisors in plain clothes, who were appointed to watch the men on duty. The strike spread rapidly, with over six hundred police refusing duties on 1st November. The government broke the strike by discharging these men and enrolling Special Constables, and recruiting replacements.[138]

This is uncannily like the events in Britain in 1919. Like the NUPPO in Britain, the victimised strikers formed their own organisation, 'The Police Strikers Association', who also issued their own medallion or fob to commemorate their stand. Even in recent years, police organisation and outward expression of belonging to it has been a contentious issue. The Police Association of Tasmania, established in 1923, registered as a union in 1956. The placement of their badge was precisely defined: 'worn on the centre of the left tunic pocket, below the button, until the wearing of the badge while in uniform was disallowed in 1977'.[139] Thus the lapel badge acts as an interpretative tool and an attractive way to engage with labour history. In relation to badges of uniformed workers in general, it is worth remembering the nursing badges cited in the preface, that the badge asserts 'this is what I am.' The NAWU badge, or any union badge for that matter, in many instances holds these kind of connotations for its wearer, and in some instances as discussed above, is the outward expression of principles and standards which must be defended.

Other Developments

Other trade unions began to issue badges and fobs to commemorate strikes and events in the same period. The NUR and ASLEF issued such items to commemorate the strikes of 1911, 1919 and 1924, the first two commemorating the joint action by the two unions. In Australia, a silver medal was awarded to participants who made an outstanding contribution to the sugar workers' strike of 1911, which led to the winning of the eight-hour day and a minimum wage of seven shillings.[140] The obverse of the medal reads: 'Firm, Solid and Together We Stand', whilst the reverse pictures sugar cane and tools. The successful 1913 strike of the Australian Ferry and Tugboat Employees Union, for the eight-hour day, was also commemorated by a silver medal.[141] The minutes of the union's Sydney branch record that on 9 April 1913: 'each and every member subscribe two shillings and sixpence to allow a medal to be struck to commemorate the victory of employees in obtaining a valuable reduction of hours enabling members to be placed on the basis of a forty-eight hour week.'[142]

The British general strike in 1926 saw the issue of a silver merit badge by the National Union of Printing, Bookbinding and Paper Workers and a small enamel fob by the TGWU, which reads 'Comradeship 1926'.[143] The Miners Federation of Great Britain issued miniature davey lamps in brass, silver and gold with long needle pins for fixing to the lapel. These were sold to raise funds for the miner's families and were also used as awards to supporters (see Figure 3.5).

There would seem to be far fewer badges issued to commemorate or lend support to campaigns in the early years than in recent years (as is explored in the following chapter). Such strike badges that are known from earlier periods are also expressions of victory, in strikes that were won, whereas the biggest defeat of all, 1926, seems to have sported very few commemoratives in the way of the badge. Again, there may well prove to be strike badges from the early years that would disprove this theory, but as yet they have not come to light.

Figure 3.5   Watch chain fob of the Transport and General Workers Union commemorating its members' participation in the 1926 General Strike and brass Davey lamp pin issued by the Miners Federation of Great Britain (also in silver and gold) in 1926 to raise funds for striking miners. For such a momentous event, it is surprising that so little was made to commemorate it by the unions concerned.
Joe Fleming collection, photograph by Dean Bennett.

The badge, more than any other form of iconography, permeated the working lives of those who wore it, at some considerable risk. The omnipresence of the straightforward membership badge, quite apart from the quarter badge, had a dramatic impact on labour relations and the fight for recognition. Even the infamous W.V. Osborne of the 'Osborne judgement' was advocating the use of a badge by pickets as a means of identification, though for more suspect reasons perhaps:

> The wearing of a distinctive badge by pickets would be of distinctive advantage. It would invest the pickets with some authority and avoid interference from the police; on the other hand police could prevent unauthorised persons from loitering in the vicinity of

a dispute under the pretext of being pickets and further the badge would assist in the identification of pickets in the event of them committing unlawful acts.[144]

The badge aroused emotions both sympathetic and antagonistic towards it and what it represented. It is a peripatetic item, openly proclaiming the wearer's membership. It was not hidden away on the parlour wall, or stored in the lodge meeting place – to wear a badge was to wear one's principles on one's lapel. Sometimes, as has been shown with the dockers, it was worn cautiously or invertedly, but it was always there serving a purpose whether as a means of membership control, or simply to assert a self-confidence in the strength of the union. They also invited further inquiry from the curious, as one member of the National Union of Clerks noted in 1927:

I have been drawn into conversation on the topic of trade unionism, simply and solely because of the badge. Many persons have scrutinised the badge in tram-car, train and bus; and we may rest assured that in nine times out of ten, it acquaints them for the first time in their lives that there is a union for ... oh what shall we call them? er ... Clerks.[145]

Similar points were being raised in the 1980s when motions to provide free badges to new members as an aid to recruitment were debated at the annual conferences of the National Union of Public Employees (NUPE) between 1980 and 1988.[146]

However, badge wearing can also lead to confusion in some cases. One member of the Civil and Public Services Association (CPSA) relates how in 1979, he questioned a fellow shopper in a supermarket, on noticing he was wearing a 'CPSA' badge that he had not seen before:

... [I asked] which branch are you in? to which he replied 'Bradford'. So I tried again: which department?, and he replied rather confused 'Bradford'. I tried one further time: I was in DNS, which branch or department are you in? To which he turned to me rather sharply and said: 'Look mate, I can't say this any more plainly, but I am a member of the Bradford Clay Pigeon Shooting Association'!.[147]

This then begs the question of whether the union badge is designed solely for mutual recognition in the workplace, or as an advertising device to a wider public. If the latter is the case, then clearly initials on their own are not adequate for the task. This is especially so today, when the trend seems to be towards stylised logos which are incomprehensible even to members, let alone the public.

A 1980s example of a badge system of the American Hotel Employees and Restaurant Employees International Union, which we first encountered in Chapter 2, has echoes of the NUDL's quarter-badge system:

The union button proudly worn by waiter, bartender, cook waitress or other service says you are in a union house. Look for the button on the worker who serves your meal or drink. Look for it when you register at a hotel. These work buttons of the Hotel

Employees and Restaurant Employees International Union are marks of high craftsman-
ship. They are signs of fair wages and decent working conditions achieved the union
way. They are symbols of organization of collective bargaining in the American way.
The colours on the buttons, blue, green, white, gold and red represent our various crafts:
bartenders, waiters, and waitresses, cooks, service employees and miscellaneous.[148]

KOKURO

Even in the 1990s, the 'right' to declare individual membership of a union through
the wearing of its badge at work was still a principle which had to be fought for.
The Japanese National Railway Workers Union, known as KOKURO is one such
case:

> Not long after its formation in 1946, KOKURO drew up its official union badge as a
> symbol of solidarity, and its members [have] wor[n] the badge ever since. Before the
> privatisation of the National Railways (JNR), the railway authorities had not called the
> worker's practice of wearing their union badges into question. However, the succeeding
> railway (JR) companies following the privatisation totally banned this practice ... 'viola-
> tors' have been persistently asked to take their badges off with the threats of cutbacks in
> the bonus payments, regular salary increments and even their qualification for promotion
> tests. Th[ese] rigid restrictive measures against the wearing of trade union badges led to
> labour – management disputes, resulting in battles before the law court as well as the
> labour commission.[149]

One way in which the union sought to gather evidence for their case was by
enlisting the aid of the International Transport Workers Federation (ITF) to which
they are affiliated, to canvass other international affiliates on their customs or
agreements over the wearing of the union badge at work. Some twenty-five unions
replied (see Appendix 3). In the main, other unions from countries as diverse as Fiji
and Sweden, even Turkey, replied that although they had no specific agreement
over the wearing of badges, their members generally did wear them, and had no
problem from management for doing so. Those unions who did cite instances of
either historical or recent problems on this issue were Australia, Britain, Canada
and France. The Australian cases were the historical ones cited earlier in this
chapter, whilst the British instance arose from the former British Railways, whose
staff guidelines noted: 'With the exception of staff employed within the InterCity
business one small standard badge identifying trade union membership may be
worn by employees on the left lapel of the uniform jacket, or similar.'[150] It was the
exception of the 'InterCity business' that ASLEF had objected to. The Canadian
instance was a case in which Air Canada challenged the right of its employees to
wear the union badge, but the union won the case. In France, the 1968 Labour Act
enshrines in law what is permitted and provided for in terms of union activity,
anything not stipulated in this act, is deemed illegal. As wearing union badges is

not stipulated, it is technically illegal, though there does not seem to have been a precedent set by employers or unions over it. Unions were asked to supply examples of the badges worn at work by members, and these were photographed, each in comparison in size to the NRWU/KOKURO badge, and appeared in the report. Overall, the NRWU/KOKURO found that:

> The survey has made clear that almost all of the transport workers throughout the world are allowed to wear their trade union badges without any restrictions. It is our conclusion that to wear trade union badges while on duty is approved as a matter of course in most of the countries, which fact is very suggestive in judging the propriety of disciplinary measures taken by the Japanese railway authorities against KOKURO members.[151]

In November 1999, the Tokyo Supreme Court rejected the final appeal of the East Japan Railway Company against the wearing of the union badge at work by their employees, resulting in a victory for Kokuro.[152]

The above suggests that the badge is still seen as a threat by employers today, every bit as much as in the earlier examples, when recognition struggles were rife. The badge permeated the labour movement and was utilised for many purposes. It was used by the American Knights Of Labor, as an incentive to encourage members to pay their contributions in large advances: 'By 1890, any member who sent in a yearly, or two half-yearly subscriptions could choose a premium of a watch charm or enamelled badge.'[153] It should also be noted that the badge has always been one of the first items produced by breakaway unions to proclaim their presence and assert their legitimacy. The Union of Railway Signalmen and the National Passenger Workers Union are two British pre-Second World War examples of unions whose badges found more recognition amongst collectors than the issuing organisations ever did by employers or fellow trade unions. The Federation of Professional Railway Staff, a split from the train drivers union, ASLEF after the 1982 strike, issued three badges for its membership, which was only measured in the hundreds. Perhaps the most recent breakaway union, the 150-member Irish Locomotive Drivers Association (ILDA), is the most interesting. It sought in 2000 to gain recognition from Irish Rail, who refused it, as did the Irish Council of Trade Unions. Irish Rail sued the union for loss of revenue caused by a union-inspired strike. The ILDA called on members to contribute £500 each to a fighting fund, which apparently was met, members raising the money by borrowing from credit unions. Interestingly, however, in the midst of such perilous financial conditions, the union produced a large, colourful enamel membership badge![154] The badge was most often used however, as a reward for those who excelled in recruitment. For example, Aslef, in 1905, had a silver medal especially inscribed as a present for those who secured twenty-five or more members.[155] Between 1910 and 1913, 'silver medals for procuring twenty five members went out constantly, hundreds of them.'[156] The Workers Union even issued a silver signet ring picturing two clasped hands to honour 'outstanding recruitment efforts of at least one hundred members in any one quarter'.[157] The Heating and Domestic Engineering

Union on introducing long-service badges in the 1950s found a surprisingly large number of eligible members, including a family in the Downham branch who had a total of 166 years service between them over four generations, the great grandfather having joined in 1858![158]

Does Size Matter?

The small size of most white-collar union badges are surely indicative of the discretion used when wearing them. The National and Local Government Officers Association (NALGO, now part of UNISON) badge until the 1980s had always retained its same small dimensions. The increase in its boldness and size in the 1980s, was perhaps indicative of the union's growth and rise in prominence, an opinion concurred with by others.[159] In the UNISON collection[160] there is a tiny badge of the Bank Officers Guild (BOG, 1917–47, later the Banking, Insurance and Finance Union) and which UNISON believe to be the smallest badge ever made. One white-collar union, the National Union of Clerks (NUC), issued badges before the First World War and even called for design suggestions which were reproduced in its journal *The Clerk* (March and April 1912) and which were taken up by the membership with zeal. By 1927, however, a member wrote to complain about the lack of the badge's visibility on the jackets of members:

> Now we know that doctors, lawyers, judges etc., do not wear badges. But they wear the other 'rigging' of their callings; or in other ways announce their profession, by door plates, titles etc ... 'What does the union lose because badges are so scarce? How are we to know of fellow members of trade unionism? Shall we adopt a special dress like clergymen, Quakers, barristers when practising; judges when sitting down?[161]

The size of a badge is probably not an arbitrary arrangement, as one trade union badge collector illustrates:

> The smallest badge in my collection belongs to the massive Spanish union, UGT. When I expressed surprise to the donor of this 0.5 cm red dot, she explained that under Franco, unions had grown used to operating clandestinely and it was clearly taking some time for them to come to terms with flamboyant self-publicity. Perhaps she was just winding me up. For just a few weeks later I received from the same source the biggest item in my collection, a delegate's badge to that year's UGT conference. It's an impressive baked terracotta medallion on a leather thong.[162]

Leisure and Recreation

The union badge also permeates the social life of its members. Trade unions in nineteenth-century Britain were often highly patriotic. It is often wrongly assumed that because unions were sometimes militant industrially, they were also militant politically, which is far from the truth. Examples include button badges issued by the Enginemen, Firemen and Cleaners Association of Australia in 1917 and 1918, celebrating Australia Day and their South Australian branch badge issued to 'help our defenders' in the First World War.[163] The South Australian Commercial Travellers and Warehousemen's Association' 'carnival' medallion of 1914 states 'For King And Empire' whilst they issued an attractive badge to raise funds for the 1917 'Nurses Day'.[164]

In terms of dedication, an employee of the former National Union of Agricultural Workers related how the union supposedly deposited one of their old National Agricultural and Rural Workers Union enamel lapel badges in the centre of the foundations of their head office in Gray's Inn Road, London, when under construction.[165] This has strong overtones of religious customs such as the use of grave goods (belongings of the deceased, buried with them) and in terms of consecration or purification of the ground, whilst such modern trends such as time capsules also come to mind.

The TGWU, ASLEF, and the AEU all issue retired members badges of some kind. The former AEU issued badges for its annual retired members' outings, the first of which took place in Birmingham in 1908.[166] The former ASE also issued badges for its cycling clubs (see Figure 3.6).

In the inter-war period, working-class recreational organisations became popular, such as the Workers Travel Association[167] and the British and National Workers Sports Associations.[168] The union badge as a source of recreational representation is mentioned by Alex Spoor in his history of NALGO (now part of UNISON), which in the 1920s was still more of a professional association than a trade union:

> In 1925, the Council asked Hill to produce a Nalgo sports badge and a few weeks later he patented his design: 'The discobolus on a blue shield imposed on a larger brick-red shield, with at the top, a helmet and floral device and a black chevron on each side, the whole surmounting a scroll bearing the name of the appropriate branch'. It was an imposing object for a blazer pocket (sew-on variety) and was widely used until a facetious mayor suggested that the discobolus represented 'Nalgo members throwing away rate payers money'. At once, a sensitive NEC dropped the badge, replacing it with the 'crest' Hill had designed for Nalgo's official seal a few years earlier ... .[169]

In Australia, the Amalgamated Workers Union had its own uniformed brass band. It is commemorated in the 30 mm button badge issued in 1904 when the band won the Commonwealth Championships in Ballarat, and pictures a posed sepia photograph of the band in full uniform.[170] In Britain, the National Communications Union during the 1980s, sponsored a brass band for which they issued an attractive embroidered uniform badge in yellow and black, picturing an old-fashioned telephone. These social aspects of trade union organisation are sadly those which receive the least attention by both the media and academics, and are deserving of a greater study in their own right.

**Figure 3.6   Membership badge of the Battersea Cycling Club run by the
                Amalgamated Society of Engineers c. 1900s. The recreational and
                social events and organisations run by trade unions in the first
                half of the twentieth century are too often overlooked in defer-
                ence to concentration on industrial confrontation in labour
                history. A detailed study of such auxiliary organisations would
                certainly help to contextualise the economic and industrial
                aspects of trade unions and place them as far more organic and
                embedded in wider community culture than is usually acknowl-
                edged historically, and which Thatcherism did its best to deny in
                more recent times.**
Mark Organ collection.

The TUC in 1933 issued a booklet setting out the proposals for the celebrations
of the Dorsetshire labourer's centenary. There were proposals for football matches
between international trade unionists and 'the best team we can pick from the
National Workers Sports Association'.[171] The NWSA issued a special triangular
badge with its own logo on it, and the commemoration of the Dorsetshire labourers.
They also issued prize medallions for winners of the various sporting events again
with the TUC/Tolpuddle inscription.[172] Artistic medallions were issued by the TUC

itself and sold to people taking part in the celebrations which was the subject of a design competition.[173] Other organisations such as the London Labour Party Sports Association also catered for working-class recreation and issued medals and badges.

Honour and Pride

Badge awards for recruitment, voluntary service to, and long membership of trade unions have been common over the years. Badges were originally awarded to activists who had recruited various numbers of new members. By the 1950s however, the TUC began to feel that awards for voluntary service to the union were more useful and appropriate than recruitment awards.[174] This perhaps reflected the relatively secure position of trade unions at the time, the achievement of the closed shop in many industries, etc. which ensured union membership, whilst conversely, the rise of youth culture served to lure new blood away from active service in the union, which in the 1950s and 1960s was seen as old fashioned.

When the National Union of Sheet Metal Workers introduced long-service badges in 1952, the meter makers' section from the firm of T. Glovers had more than one thousand years' membership between the twenty-two members.[175] The use of the badge as a symbol of reward, merit or office in the labour movement, is as important as its use as a means of membership control or solidarity. In 1935, F.P. Harries, secretary of the TUC's organising department, extolled the virtues of trade union banners, and called for more of them to be seen on demonstrations. He went on to ask:

> And what about Trade Union badges? Can they not be regarded as the medal ribbon of the industrial fighter? It is very gratifying to notice at conferences and meetings that a number of members present carry in their buttonholes the Congress Award badge for recruiting new members. Many of these badges are worn at the risk of losing employment, and are a much more valuable symbol of citizenship than any old school tie.[176]

In July 1957, it was reported in *TUC Labour* that:

> New dignity has been added to the proceedings of Brierley Hill Trades Council. The president W.E. Nutting, holder of the British Empire Medal, now wears a silver gilt badge of office when he takes the chair at the Council's meetings. Suspended from a blue silk ribbon, the badge has as its centre piece a factory building and flames to represent engineering, fire fighting, iron and steel, blastfurnaces and other such manufacturing industries. Bricks and crossed paint brushes are symbols of the building, civil engineering, clay and brick making industries. Transport is represented by a wheel, baking by a wheatsheaf and glass making by an hour glass.

The National Union of Printing, Bookbinding and Paper Workers in 1952, gave due consideration to their merit awards:

Our gold medal has been referred to as the Victoria Cross of the union and obviously, it is undesirable that it should be granted in any indiscriminate manner. On the other hand we have frequently had cases where the award of the Diploma of Merit was hardly sufficient recognition of services rendered.[177]

It was decided to award the gold medal for outstanding services rendered and not simply for long service.[178] There have always been specific rules governing the award of special badges to union members. As long ago as 1913, the Railway Workers and General Labourers Association of New South Wales, established in 1908, stated the following in Rule 40:

Life membership: any member of the union having attained the age of sixty and having been a financial member of the union from its conception, shall be admitted as a life member of the union. A membership ticket shall be issued free of charge and shall carry with it all the benefits and privileges of this union. The executive shall issue to such life member a silver badge.[179]

The Australian Meat Industries Union for instance, award their nine-carat gold badge to union officials for *services*, whilst a silver version is awarded for *assistance* to the union. The New South Wales Teachers Federation issues gold badges at its annual conference to members nominated by constituent teachers associations. The member must have at least fifteen years' membership to be eligible.[180] To obtain the life membership badge for outstanding service of the Secretaries and Managers Association of Australia:

The nominee must have been a member for at least ten years, and the nomination must be approved by two thirds majority of the council. Only one can be awarded per year. To 1989, ten had been awarded including four to the founding executives. The badge is also issued with the legend '21 Club' on the bottom bar. Awarded for twenty-one years membership of the Association.[181]

Obvious pride in being awarded a distinguished badge is demonstrated by one correspondent from Australia. He noted that throughout the ninety-year history of the Australian Journalists Association, his father and himself, were the only father and son to be awarded the union's gold honour badge in 1959 and 1989 respectively.[182]

Trade union journals often carry reports of awards to long-serving members of the union such as the Transport Salaried Staffs Association gold medallion (see Appendix 2), or the gold medallion of the National Union of Railwaymen's Orphan Service, awarded to one Harry Tarr by the London Orphan Fund Committee.[183] Similar was the 'Order of Industrial Heroism', awarded by the *Daily Herald* (owned by the TUC and Labour Party until 1929) between 1923 and the 1950s. This was set up to 'recognise acts of courage by working men and women both at work and outside of work'.[184] Such awards were the labour movement's equivalent of the

OBE or Legion of Honour. Perhaps the most novel of all award or commemorative badges issued by a trade union was that issued by the Amalgamated Society of Railway Servants (ASRS) around 1890 for 'Help', the railway dog. He was introduced at the 1881 ASRS Conference by a delegate Climpson who had bought a dog, Fred to act as a travelling collector for the ASRS Orphans Fund. Fred and a further dog had both died during the year, Help however worked for the Orphan Fund until 1889. Help was a collie and collected over £1000 during his working career for the ASRS. After he died, he was stuffed and placed on Brighton station to continue to collect for the fund. He continued to raise 12–15 shillings a week.[185] Peter Carter remembers him still on the platform in the early 1950s: 'He had a collecting box strapped to his back, and he may have been a bit moth-eaten by then, but remained an invaluable fund raiser for the Orphan Fund':[186]

> The ASRS issued a badge, 'Help, Our Noble Railway Dog', although it is uncertain whether the badges was first issued during his lifetime or on his death. The fob is enamelled on both sides dark blue, light blue on one side with a brass locomotive and the union title in full around the outer ring. The reverse is a portrait of Help on a grassy background with the caption 'Help Our Noble Railway Dog' in brass on a dark blue outer ring.[187]

One member of ASLEF tells the story of a special commemorative teaspoon which had as its finial an enamel badge of the ASLEF Woman's Society:

> This spoon was presented to me being the first baby born to commemorate the forming of the women's branch of Eastleigh in 1927. I'm now in my 70th year having done 47 years on the footplate. I followed my father and two brothers on the footplate, all strong trade unionists. My mother helped keep the Eastleigh pickets supplied with refreshments in the 1955 strike.[188]

Membership badges were often supplied to members on joining the union as a means of establishing an outward affinity with union principles, as well as a useful way of identifying and advertising the union.[189] The 1918 constitution of the National Warehouse and General Workers Union stated that 'a book of rules, a badge and a membership card shall be supplied to all members on entry.'[190] Rule 31 of the New South Wales branch of the Australian Foremen Stevedores Society, formed in 1939, similarly states that 'A uniform badge of an approved design shall be issued to each member of the branch upon completion of his probation period at a cost to be born by the said member.'[191] Likewise, Terry Thomas, an elite toolmaker member of the British AEU in the 1950s, recalls that receiving the badge was part of an engineer's rite of passage, which he believes to have ended around 1970. After having been sworn in as a member of the AEU, a rule book and badge was given to the new member. The badge, he recalls, was seldom worn in the general course of things, but was kept in the (mainly older) member's tool box, but when a dispute arose in the factory, the badge would be immediately brought out, and pinned on as a sign of defiance and an assertion of strength. Even in 1974, the rule book of the Laminated and Coil Spring Workers Union, Rule 23 stated: 'Every member is expected to be in possession of a badge.'

We have seen that the trade union badge has very strong identity traits. The quarter-badge and tally system were, functionally, a significant means by which an efficient system of organisation could be realised and maintained. Symbolically, these badges represented a value system, an assertion of the workers' human dignity which their station in life and estimation by their employers often did not. On uniformed workers, the membership badge invoked this value system as being of equal worth to employer-imposed work codes. It symbolised a will to influence control and aspired to a level of self-determination, which the uniform, by definition, sought to deny through conformity. Many uniformed workers took immense pride in their uniform; the addition to it of a union badge or fob, enhanced one's sense of self in relation to it. What then, in the contemporary labour movement is the role of the badge? And to what use is it put? This is the subject of the next chapter.

Notes

1   J. Sexton, *The Life of a Docker's M.P.* , London, Faber & Faber 1936, p. 102. John Smethurst notes, however, that 'Edward McHugh, a foundation president of the NUDL in 1889–90 is credited with the introduction of the system of control badges operated by the American Longshoremen's union on the Eastern seaboard of the United States of America, during one of his many visits during the 1890s', J. Smethurst, 'The Badge, Insignia of Membership or a means of membership control', *Trade Union Badge Collectors' Newsletter*, No. 64, Summer, 1998, p. 10.

2   'The National Union of Dock Labourers in Great Britain and Ireland' was established in Glasgow in 1889. It relocated to Liverpool shortly afterwards. Due to expansion into other areas, and the absorption of other waterfront unions it changed its name in 1912 to the N.U. Dock Labourers & Riverside Workers, and in 1919 to the N.U. Dock, Riverside & General Workers. However, it is usually simply referred to as the NUDL. See E. Taplin, *The Dockers Union: A Study of the National Union of Dock Labourers 1889–1922*, Leicester, Leicester University Press, 1985, pp. 103–104, 138.

3   Pelling, 'The Knights of Labor In Britain', pp. 320, 322. Sexton stated he belonged to the Local Assembly (branch) of the KOL in Bootle which existed between about 1883 and 1885. It was broken up as a result of a small, unsuccessful strike (Sexton, *Life of a Docker's M.P.*, p. 79).

4   Sexton, *Life of a Docker's M.P.*, p. 102.

5   M. Russell, *Men Along The Shore: The International Longshoremen's Association and its History*, New York, Brussel & Brussel, 1966, p. 28.

6   Ibid., pp. 22–23.

7   Sexton, *Life of a Docker's M.P.*, p. 102.

8   Smethurst and Devine, 'Trade Union Badges', p. 86.

9   P. Carter, 'New Badges Will Be Issued On Monday: a further look at the Liverpool

Carters Union badge', *Trade Union Badge Collectors' Newsletter*, No. 50, September, 1995, p. 8.

10 P. Carter, 'The Liverpool & District Carters & Motormen's Union', *Trade Union Badge Collectors' Newsletter*, No. 3, April, 1985, pp. 3–4.

11 Carter, 'New Badges Will Be Issued', p. 9.

12 Devine, 'Who Dares', p. 59.

13 *Liverpool Mercury*, 24 February 1890, p. 5.

14 P. Carter, 'What's In a Name!', *Trade Union Badge Collectors' Newsletter*, No. 48, May, 1995, p. 4.

15 See J. Lovell, *Stevedores and Dockers: A Study of Trade Unionism in the Port of London 1870–1914*, London, MacMillan 1969, p. 148; p. 249, n.44–45.

16 There is a photograph of Tom Mann, the first president of the Federation wearing the badge in the International Transport Workers Federation archive, London.

17 P. Carter, 'Federation Buttons Shall Be Worn!', *Trade Union Badge Collectors' Newsletter*, No. 51, November, 1995, p. 6.

18 S. Erixon, *Stockholm's Hamnarbetare*, Stockholm, Nordisk Rotogravyr, 1949.

19 Lovell, *Stevedores and Dockers*, p. 80.

20 Ibid., pp. 124, 130 also makes further references to the DWR&GWU card inspection system.

21 Pelling, 'The Knights Of Labor In Britain', p. 322.

22 Taplin, *The Dockers Union*, p. 34.

23 *Liverpool Mercury*, 21 July 1890, p. 5.

24 Taplin, *The Dockers Union*, p. 40.

25 Smethurst and Devine, 'Trade Union Badges', p. 85.

26 Ibid., p. 86.

27 Carter, 'New Badges Will Be Issued', p. 7.

28 Ibid., p. 5.

29 Ibid., p. 10.

30 Ibid., p. 9. Similarly, the Longshoreman's United Protection Association in New York, in the mid-1880s, had 'beach walkers', officials who patrolled the docks checking badges were correct. This adds to the suggestion that the quarter-badge system originated from them: Russell, *Men Along The Shore*, p. 28.

31 Sexton, *Life of a Docker's M.P.*, p. 102.

32 Ibid., pp. 102–103.

33 G. Milligan, 'Mersey Dockers 30 Years Struggle', *TGWU Record*, 1923, June, cited in Taplin, *The Dockers Union*, pp. 43–44.

34 Sexton, *Life of a Docker's M.P.*, pp. 102.

35 P. Roach, personal communication to P. Carter, 20 May 1975. My thanks to Peter Carter for making this available. See also A.J. Corfield, 'Dockers Trade Unionism In Liverpool', *TGWU Record*, 1964, December, pp. 35–37 for further reference to the NUDL quarter-badge.

36 A historian and former branch secretary of the Willesden branch of ASLEF, the train drivers' union, notes that in the 1890s 'trade union badges were worn beneath the coat lapels.' Thus dockers were not alone in this practice (Mr A. Moynahan, personal communication 1998).

37 Carter, 'The Liverpool & District Carters & Motormen's Union', p. 4.

38 J. Sexton (writing as 'Citizen'), *Liverpool Labour Chronicle*, 1 July 1895, p. 1.

39   Sexton, as 'Citizen', p. 1.
40   Devine, 'Who Dares', p. 59.
41   Smethurst and Devine, 'Trade Union Badges', pp. 88, 86–88 See also, pp. 54–55 for an illustration and example of such a studded belt belonging to Myles Kinsella, a Dublin docker; Erixson, *Stockholm's Hamnarbetare* for an example of a Swedish docker's belt, similarly studded with quarter badges of the International Federation of Ship, Dock and River Workers, later to become the International Transport Workers Federation. Carter, 'What's In a Name!', p. 5 reproduces the illustration.
42   Smethurst and Devine, 'Trade Union Badges', p. 85.
43   Devine, 'Who Dares', p. 60.
44   Taplin, *The Dockers Union*, p. 94.
45   *Liverpool Daily Post and Mercury,* 21 June 1911, p. 7.
46   L&DC&MU circular, 25 March 1939; Muller, pp. 143–144.
47   T. Topham, 'The Unofficial National Docks Strike of 1923: the Transport and General Workers Union's first crisis', *Historical Studies In Industrial Relations*, No. 2, Keele, Keele University Centre For Industrial Relations, 1996, p. 35.
48   TUC annual report,1923 The 'PC5 methods' referred to was a scheme set up by Havelock Wilson, secretary of the National Sailors and Firemen's Union, which with the complicity of the ship owners, excluded members of unions other than the NS&FU from working on merchant ships. See K. Coates and T. Topham, *The History of The Transport And General Workers Union Volume One: the making of the Transport and General Workers Union, the emergence of the labour movement 1870–1922*, Oxford, Blackwell, 1991, pp. 790–795.
49   W. Milne Bailey (ed.), *Trade Union Documents*, London, G. Bell & Sons, 1929, pp. 475–476.
50   Milne-Bailey, *Trade Union Documents*, pp. 474–476 describes the use of tallies in the Bristol Docks in 1919; see Taplin, *The Dockers Union*, for the Liverpool system; P. Carter 'Engage The Badgemen', *Trade Union Badge Collectors' Newsletter*, No. 59, 1997, May, pp. 3–9 for the Belfast and Glasgow systems. It should also be noted that badges and tallies were extensively used in industry both as employment registration (especially during the Second World War) and safety devices (particularly within the mining industry). See for example I. Johnson and L. Johnman, 'Lost Horizon', *Guardian (Weekend)*, 28th March 1998, p. 30 for the example of the shipyard timekeeper.
51   Carter, 'Engage the Badgemen', p. 4.
52   Ibid., p. 5.
53   Ibid., p. 7.
54   Ibid., p. 8.
55   Carter, 'Liverpool & District Carters and Motormens Union', p. 3.
56   *Liverpool Mercury,*18 April 1890, p. 5.
57   F. Whitelaw, 'The National Warehouse and General Workers Union', *Trade Union Badge Collectors' Newsletter*, No. 34, 1992, August, p. 9.
58   Devine, 'Who Dares', p. 60.
59   J. Dash, *Good Morning Brothers*, London, Lawence & Wishart, 1969, p. 68.
60   Although quarter badges are known in Australia, such as the early example of 'The Stevedores Union' which is known to have been issued with '1, 2, 3, and 4' in the centre. Other Australian dock and riverside union badges bear the same traits as British ones, such as registration and membership numbers stamped on obverse and

reverse, etc. At least one example is known of a half-yearly badge, issued by the Railway Workers and General Labourers Association of New South Wales: Smith, *Emblems Of Unity*, pp. 232, 267–277, 217.

61 Ibid., pp. 115.

62 'Report Re Shipping Meeting 23rd January 1943: Mr. MacLaren submitted design of proposed badge to be struck. Initial cost would be £70. Meeting had agreed that 2/- deposit be made on all medals, which would remain the union's property' (Central Executive minutes, 24 November 1943, p. 2). There was some problem with the running of the system, regarding the hours in which 'medals' were issued to new members. The Sydney Shipping Section organiser, a Mr MacLaren was not always able to be attendant to issue them. This was resolved by authorising other union officers to issue them (Central Executive Minutes, 8 December 1943, p. 3; 16 February 1944, p. 3). It was agreed that there should be 'Refusal to work with non-medal men after 31st March each year, except in cases where snipers are used because of shortage of Waterside Workers' (Central Executive minutes, 16 February1944, p. 4). The secretary of the Australian Services Union, NSW clerical and administrative branch, states that 'The system worked successfully and was the beginning of a system which gave rise to the registration of casual shipping clerks in the Port of Sydney. The Commonwealth Employment Service instituted a "Pick-Up Centre" at which casual shipping clerks were registered and available for work by rotation of registered number so that all work was allocated on an equitable basis', Michael Want, personal communication, 11 June 1998.

63 Smith, *Emblems of Unity*, pp. 143–151.

64 Ibid., pp. 182–186.

65 Ibid., pp. 276–277.

66 Ibid., p. 84.

67 Ibid., p. 225.

68 Ibid., pp. 241–245.

69 Personal communication from Mr H. Pridmore in 1987, a retired USDAW member who worked in the stores department of NUDAW's head office from 1929.

70 Personal communication, 18 February 1987. Mr Murt has since died and his collection was donated to the GMB college in Manchester. His letter confirms that the system was used in the same way as the Liverpool dockers:
'I cannot determine the period in time in which the quarterly badges were issued, but they were still being issued in the early part of 1950 and the earliest dated one I have in my collection is 1923. The badges were stamped with an identifying number on the back and the number was kept in the register against the name of the recipient. Cases of false pretence were dealt with very severely, often by the removal of the member's trade union card. The members were selected for work from a stand and the badge signified that they were in benefit and eligible for selection, no badge, no job, it was as simple as that. I understand that the custom arose because of a membership dispute between the Ship Constructors and Shipwrights Association and the Liverpool Shipwrights Association'.
Private British collections known to me also contain examples of quarter badges from the following: Scottish National Horsemen's Association; Amalgamated Carters Society of Glasgow; Liverpool Tinplate Workers Society; and the Boilermakers Society, which suggests the use of the system was widespread.

71 Hammond, *Trade Union Badges*, p. 57.
72 C. Williams, *One Hundred Years of Progress 1880–1980*, Derby, National Union of Mineworkers, 1980, p. 2, illustration 3.
73 A.R. Griffin, *The Notts Coal Field 1881–1981*, Nottingham, Moorland Publishing, 1981, p. 108.
74 Williams, *One Hundred Years of Progress*, p. 2.
75 Smethurst and Devine, 'Trade Union Badges', p. 95, n.39.
76 Derbyshire Miners Association, minutes, 5 April 1891.
77 Ibid.
78 Smethurst and Devine, 'Trade Union Badges', p. 86.
79 Ibid.
80 Hammond, *Trade Union Badges*, p. 161; P. Dunn, National Museum of Labour History, personal communication, 1998.
81 Smethurst, 'The Badge: Insignia of Membership', pp. 10–18.
82 A. Tuckett, *The Scottish Carter*, London, George Allen & Unwin, 1967, p. 96.
83 Ibid., pp. 108.
84 S. Cherry, Curator, Cork Public Museum, personal communication, 19 January 1998.
85 Smethust and Devine, 'Trade Union Badges', pp. 54–55.
86 C. Desmond Greaves, *The Irish Transport and General Workers Union: The Formative Years*, Dublin, Gill & MacMillan, 1982, p. 21. See also pp. 21, 28–30, 43, 100, 266, 290, 329 for further references to the badges of the NUDL and ITGWU. See also the following: *Fifty Years of Liberty Hall* (1959), Dublin, ITGWU, for further illustrations of ITGWU badges; P. Doyle and J. O'Down (eds), *The Parliament of Labour: 100 Years of the Dublin Council of Trade Unions*, Catalogue prepared for an exhibition in the Dublin Civic Museum 7 October–31 December 1986, Dublin, Irish Labour History Society. This illustrates (amongst others) badges of the Irish Regular Chimney Cleaners Trades Union and The Irish News Vendors Trade Union; Swift, *History of the Dublin Bakers*, which illustrates a large number of guild emblems and describes the trades processions there in the nineteenth century.
87 Smethurst and Devine, 'Trade Union Badges', pp. 89–90.
88 Smith, *Emblems Of Unity*, p. 31.
89 J. Knapp, General Secretary National Union of Railwaymen, personal communication, 3 August 1987.
90 J. Hammond, 'Wear The Union Badge', *Trade Union Badge Collectors' Newsletter*, No. 65, August, 1996, pp. 3–7.
91 Smith, *Emblems Of Unity*, pp. 191, 118.
92 K. Sinclair, 'Trade Union Badges; A Neglected Part of Trade Union History?', *Trade Union Badge Collectors' Newsletter*, No. 35, October 1992.
93 Smith, *Emblems of Unity*, op. cit., p. 86. See also 'Badge Show Rules', *Barrier Daily Truth*, reprinted in *Trade Union Badge Collectors' Newsletter* No. 36, January, 1991.
94 Smith, *Emblems Of Unity*, pp. 86–87.
95 Smethurst and Devine, 'Trade Union Badges', p. 88.
96 Ibid. At the 1982 conference of the National Union of Public Employees, an opponent to the issuing of badges free to new members protested in as much ignorance of the union badge's history as everyone else: '... and what you will also find – and I have seen this – is youngsters in the streets wearing the badges presented to their fathers because they have afterwards left the union. The badges are never returned. If you

supply them with a badge, are you going to say, "We'll give you a free badge but if you leave the Union, you'll have to return it?"', (NUPE annual conference report, 1982, p. 381).

97   Smith, *Emblems of Unity*, p. 234.
98   Ibid., p. 252.
99   Ibid., pp. 253–254.
100 K. Fuller, *Radical Aristocrats*, London, Lawrence & Wishart, 1985, p. 33.
101 Gorman, *Images of Labour*, p. 33.
102 Fuller, *Radical Aristocrats*, pp. 33–34.
103 The LPULVW was established in 1913 as a result of a name change to incorporate a wider area of recruitment. It was formally the London Cab Drivers Trade Union (LCTU) which was established in 1894 (A. Marsh and V. Ryan, *The Historical Directory of Trade Unions, Volume 3*, Gower, Aldershot, 1987, p. 238). In January 1913, the LCTU went on strike to secure cheaper petrol, as the cab companies were trying to institute a rise in cost from 8d to 1/- a gallon (Gorman, *Images of Labour*, p. 182); Marsh and Ryan say the dispute was over free petrol, Gorman that it was a cost increase). After the dispute was over (which the union won), they changed their name to the LPULVW (Marsh & Ryan, *Historical Directory ... Vol. 3*, p. 238). The LCTU strike was in January 1913 and the Tillings dispute in September of the same year. It would be pleasant to think that the LPULVW 'Victory 1913' badge was issued as a rebuff to Tillings, but it may have been issued for the petrol strike, if the name had been changed from the LCTU to the LPULVW before the badge was ordered.
104 Fuller, *Radical Aristocrats*, p. 32.
105 Ibid., p. 33.
106 Ibid., p. 55.
107 See *The Story of The TGWU*, TGWU, London, 1977, p. 29 for colour illustration.
108 Smith, *Emblems of Unity*, p. 16.
109 For the full details of the arguments for and against the right to wear the badge on uniform, see *Proceedings Of The High Court Of Australia (1913) 'The Australian Tramway Employees Association and The Prahran And Malvern Tramway Trust And Others'*, pp. 680–719. The union's case rested on the argument that the matter was an industrial dispute, whilst the employers argued it was a contravention of company bylaws and therefore rendered the union open to prosecution. The union badge is repeatedly referred to as being 'worn on the watch chain', that is, a fob; perhaps a distinction could have been made between wearing it 'with' rather than 'on' the uniform therefore.
110 Smith, *Emblems of Unity*, p. 191.
111 Ibid., p. 80.
112 Ibid., p. 54.
113 Ibid., p. 170.
114 G. Smith, 'Badges of the New South Wales General Strike 1917', *Journal of the Numismatic Association of Australia*, Vol. 5, 1991, p. 54; G. Smith, 'Badges Trace The History of New South Wales Railways', *Australian Coin Review*, 1985, June, p. 26.
115 Smith, 'Badges of the New South Wales General Strike 1917'.
116 *Postmen's Gazette*, 15 November 1913. See also *Daily Herald*, 4 November 1913.
117 Ibid., 2 February 1913, p. 82.

118   Ibid., 21 February 1913, p. 83.
119   Ibid., p. 83.
120   Ibid., p. 83.
121   Ibid., 21 February 1914, p. 83.
122   GPO rule 45, paragraph: 'Badges', sub-paragraph 5 'private badges'.
123   'Union Badges Ban Beaten', *Public Service*, 1985, reproduced in *Trade Union Badge Collectors' Newsletter*, No. 7, February, 1986.
124   I. Monkton, 'Worn With Pride: The Badge of Nobility', *Landworker*, 1991, February, p. 5.
125   Railway Service Joint Committee Clothing Subcommittee Minute, 23 March 1990, pp. 4–5.
126   British Railways Board, personal communication to ASLEF, NUR, TSSA, 4 June 1990.
127   L.W. Adams, ASLEF, personal communication, 6 April 1998.
128   *Mental Hospital and Institutional Workers Union, Twenty-First Anniversary History*, Manchester, 1931, p. 24.
129   M. Carpenter, *All For One*, Surrey, Confederation of Health Service Employees, 1980, p. 23.
130   Ibid.
131   *MHIWU Twenty-First Anniversary History*, p. 24.
132   An example of the MHIWU badge exists in both the TUC and UNISON collections in London. The badge is small, and in the shape of a blue cross with no lettering or other iconography. The initials are on the reverse. Even in 1970, a similar situation to that of Bodmin could still arise. Six hundred nurses, members of the Confederation of Health Service Employees (the successor to the MHIWU) in thirteen Manchester hospitals were banned from wearing their membership badge 'the size of a shilling' under the administrator's 'no badge rule' (*Manchester Evening News*, 20 November 1970). The nurses threatened to strike, but the dispute was resolved amicably.
133   M. Carpenter, *Working For Health: A History of COHSE*, London, Lawrence & Wishart, 1988, p. 109.
134   NUPE 1982 conference report, p. 381.
135   NUPE 1984 conference report, p. 366.
136   V.L. Allen, 'The National Union of Police and Prison Officers', *Economic History Review*, Vol. XI, No. 1, 1958, pp. 174–182; G.W. Reynolds and A. Judge, *The Night The Police Went On Strike*, London, Weidenfeld & Nicholson, 1968; A. Marsh and V. Ryan, *Historical Directory of Trade Unions Volume 1*, pp. 164–165; Gorman, *Images of Labour*, p. 98; *Trade Union Badge Collectors' Newsletter*, 1996, January, April.
137   Smith, *Emblems Of Unity*, p. 260.
138   Ibid., pp. 204–205.
139   Ibid., p. 203.
140   Ibid., p. 35.
141   G. Smith, 'Union Badges of the 1913 Ferry Strike', *Australian Coin Review*, 1992b, October, pp. 34–35.
142   Smith, *Emblems Of Unity*, pp. 154–155.
143   One contemporary activist in the TGWU still wears the 1926 TGWU strike fob, on the watch chain attached to a pocket watch commemorating the campaign for the

eight-hour day. He wears these to 'keep me going during union negotiations' (J. Fleming, personal communication, 1998).

144   W.V. Osborne, *Sane Trades Unionism*, London, Collins, 1912, p. 200. The Osborne Judgement was a legal ruling which required trade union members to contract into rather than out of the political levy, thus putting the onus on the union to convince members of the importance of contracting in. Previously it had been automatic, with the levy going to the Labour Party. A legal challenge by Osborne, a branch officer of the Amalgamated Society of Railway Servants, and a staunch Liberal Party activist, reversed this procedure in 1908, but it was later reinstated by Labour. The Conservative government's attempt to reverse the procedure again in the 1990s by requiring a ballot of the membership to decide on the political levy backfired when members voted overwhelmingly to retain the system as it was.

145   S.H. Rudd, 'About Badges', *The Clerk*, 1927, August, p. 126.

146   Those for the motion argued that the badge was a good aid to recruitment; those against, opposed it on cost grounds.

147   A. MacAllister, personal communication, 1998.

148   Reproduced in *Trade Union Badge Collectors' Newsletter*, No. 20, July, 1988.

149   National Railway Workers Union (NRWU) – Kokuro, supplement 1994, p. 1.

150   NRWU supplement, p. 57.

151   Ibid., p. 6.

152   Weir, *Beyond Labor's Veil*, p. 247.

153   See also Raynes, *Engines And Men* 1921, p. 142 for the description and account of a special conference medal issued by ASLEF for visiting US conference delegates in 1909.

154   A. Redpath, personal communication, 24 April 2000. For the story of the Union of Railway Signalmen, see A.J. Redpath, 'Safe Passage For The Railway Traveller – The Union of Railway Signalmen', *Trade Union Badge Collectors' Newsletter*, No. 54, June 1996.

155   Information supplied by International Transport Workers Federation, Tokyo office, 4/2/2000.

156   Raynes, *Engines And Men*, p. 170.

157   *FTAT Record,* March 1981. See Unison collection, London for an example.

158. Brake, *Men of Good Character*, p. 345.

159   S. Cusack, 'Is Size Important?', *Trade Union Badge Collectors' Newsletter* 1994, June, p. 9.

160   See also the following: Blaenau Ffestiniog (slate) Miner's Support Group, p. 55 for the example of a strike badge made from slate; National Union of Railwaymen, *Unity House Souvenir*, London, 1980, p. 9 for a photograph of a delegation outside Unity House (the NUR's head office) when it was opened in 1910 wearing distinctive commemorative medals; 'Trade Union Badges', *Men and Metal* (journal of the Iron and Steel Trades Confederation), 1965, November, pp. 326–327 on international trade union badges and their uses; Gorman, *Images Of Labour*, pp. 38–39 for further comment on the badge as a marketing tool and p. 36 for illustrations of button badges used as publicity items in British election campaigns in the early 1900s, see T. Hake, *Political Buttons Book III 1789–1916*, Pennsylvania, Hakes American and Collectables Press, 1987 for American equivalents.

161   Rudd, 'About Badges', p. 126.

162   Cusack, 'Is Size Important?', p. 9.
163   Smith, *Emblems Of Unity*, pp. 108–109, 230.
164   Ibid., pp. 228–229.
165   Headland House in Grays Inn Road, London, recollection of conversation in early
       1980s.
166   A. Harlow, personal communication, 1987; P. Carter, 'A Prize If You Are Spotted',
       Trade Union Badge Collectors' Newsletter, No. 67, 1999, Spring, pp. 12–14.
167   See H. Walker, 'The Workers Travel Association 1921–1939', *Bulletin of The Society
       for the Study of Labour History*, No. 50, 1985, Spring.
168   See S. Bird 'The British Workers Sports Association 1930–1960', *Bulletin of The
       Society for the Study of Labour History*, No. 5, 1985, Spring, pp. 7–9; S.G. Jones,
       *Sport, Politics and the Working Class: Organised Labour and Sport in inter-war
       Britain*, Manchester, Manchester University Press/St. Martins Press, 1988.
169   A. Spoor, *White Collar Union* (NALGO), London, Heinemann, 1967, pp. 101–102.
170   Smith, *Emblems Of Unity*, p. 34.
171   W. Citrine, *How We Will Commemorate The Dorsetshire Labourers Centenary*, Trades
       Union Congress, London, 1933, p. 7.
172   National Museum of Labour History collection, Manchester.
173   Citrine, *How We Will Celebrate*, pp. 7–8.
174   P. Carter, 'Meritorious Service – Badges For Recruitment', *Trade Union Badge Col-
       lectors' Newsletter*, No. 67, 1999a Spring, p. 8.
175   Brake, *Men of Good Character*, p. 412.
176   F.P. Harries, 'Forth The Banners Go!', c.1935, reproduced in *Trade Union Badge
       Collectors' Newsletter* No. 42, 1994, February, pp. 67–68.
177   C.J. Bundock, *The Story of the National Union of Printing, Bookbinding and Paper
       Workers*, Oxford, Oxford University Press, 1959, pp. 560–561.
178   Ibid., p. 561.
179   Smith, *Emblems Of Unity*, p. 217.
180   Ibid., pp. 41, 195.
181   Ibid., pp. 221–222.
182   Mr A. Wild, personal communication, 9 July 1998.
183   *Transport Review*, 06 April 1984.
184   P. Carter, 'Daily Herald Order of Industrial Heroism', *Trade Union Badge Collectors'
       Newsletter*, No. 49, 1995, July, pp. 5–7; 440 such awards were made in total. See
       W.H. Fevyer, J.W. Wilson and J. Cribb, *The Order of Industrial Heroism*, Guildford,
       Surrey, Orders and Medals Research Society, 2000.
185   P.S. Bagwell, *The Railwaymen: The History of the National Union of Railwaymen*,
       London, George Allen & Unwin, 1963, pp. 124–125.
186   P. Carter, 'Help And The Cromford Strikers', *Trade Union Badge Collectors' News-
       letter*, No. 60, 1997b, July, p. 9.
187   Ibid.
188   'Spooning Up History With a Selhurst Veteran', *Locomotive Journal*, 1997, July, p. 3.
189   One boyish-looking seventeen-year-old wrote with a tale involving his new CPSA
       badge, when he joined the civil service straight from school. He was in the habit of
       paying half-fare on buses and for attendance at football matches because he looked so
       much younger than his years. On joining the CPSA, he was pulled out of a crowd of
       football supporters at the 'boys' entrance to the ground. Protesting, he suddenly

realised that his 'shiny new' CPSA membership badge had given him away: 'I dare say there could not have been many 15 year-old CPSA members, so therefore the stewards guessed I was older than I was pretending to be' (personal communication, 1998).

190   Whitlaw, 'National Warehouse and General Workers Union', p. 9.
191   Smith, *Emblems Of Unity*, pp. 59–60.

Chapter 4

An Epoch of Minority Symbolism?
The Pervasion of the Badge and the
Contraction of the Union

Wearing badges is not enough.[1]

In this chapter, we will explore the resurgence in the use of badges over the last two decades in the labour movement, and question if they might articulate a deeper meaning than might at first seem to be the case. Questions of gender, race and particularism are addressed to site the badge in a wider context. The badge has become a familiar appendage of the trade union movement, entrenching itself in many areas. Yet its use as a propaganda tool in the labour movement in Britain, was late in coming. This use, although perceivable in earlier decades, has only become predominant since the 1970s.

It is useful to note the spread of the badge, and especially the tin or button badge into wider spheres of popular culture and society, in order to place trade union adaptation of it into context.[2] Primrose Peacock in her book *Buttons For The Collector*, gives some indication of the tin badge's early permeation. Buttons in the sense used by Peacock are those normally used for the fastening of garments as opposed to the lapel badge variety, although she does talk briefly about 'pin-backs':

> To a button collector, the term lithograph includes photographs and other methods of printing, and is used to describe a variety of buttons which were first made during the 1880s, but which did not become very fashionable until the early years of George V (1911). During that time there was a fashion craze, first for buttons which portrayed actresses and other personalities and later, when waistcoats became popular with men's sportswear, sets of buttons depicting any pretty girl or sporting activity were worn. Such buttons were popularised by the development of celluloid, but in Britain were considered common by the upper classes. Ladies of breeding would not "know" a man who wore theatrical buttons, in the same way that my grandmother did not "know" any woman that dyed her hair.[3]

After the first mass-production of the button badge in 1896 it would have been a simple matter of modification to transform the celluloid waistcoat buttons into lapel badges by altering the fixing on the back, and the 'craze' for such items would seem to have become an established custom: 'The majority of modern 'pin-backs' are celluloid or plastic and they range from quaint to vulgar. British people will remember the "I like Ike" campaign after WWII. More recent slogans are not so complimentary.'[4]

In America, the button badge has, since 1896, been used for every conceivable purpose, including protest. In the 1960s it was used in large numbers there, reflecting the disillusionment with the establishment of the time. It was used by the civil rights movement, anti-Vietnam war lobby, nuclear disarmament groups, and as an expression of alternative culture in musical, social and political culture generally. In Britain, the establishment political parties had used the button badge from the later 1900s to a small extent as a publicity tool, by issuing buttons with portraits of the candidates on them. The Communist Party had also used button badges for hunger marches in the inter-war period, as well as for the commemoration of May Day before the Second World War. Although they were issued in Britain in the 1950s and 1960s, it was never on the same scale as in the US, and it was not until the 1970s that the button badge made a real impact on labour culture in Britain.

The material conditions of the 1970s must be sketched out to some extent in order to trace the pattern of the current distribution of the badge. These conditions broadly follow political agendas of the period: first the Heath government of 1970–74, second the Wilson/Callaghan government of 1974–79, and finally the various Conservative administrations beginning in 1979. The badge in these periods becomes a symbolic iconographical expression of the ebb and flow of industrial relations and sociocultural practice, marking beginnings and ends of certain trends, and perhaps in recent years, of an epoch.

The first significant phase, from which the rise of the badge as a conveyer of cause or as an explicit protest weapon in the modern period in Britain, is traceable is that of the Heath government, and especially the 1971 Industrial Relations Act. From the end of the Second World War until this time, union disputes had been largely internalised and concerned observation of demarcation, and spheres of influence, which were largely resolved through the TUC and union amalgamation. Two major national issues, however, were the implementation in the early 1960s of the Beeching cuts in rail services and the widespread pit closures of the late 1960s under Lord Robens. The Beeching cuts were to be commemorated posthumously by the train drivers' union, ASLEF, in the form of the badge as will be seen later. The pit closures of the 1960s were hardly contested, the focus of attention being the level of severance pay, and so does not relate to the union badge in its role as a means of protest.

The 1971 Industrial Relations Act marks a major discontinuity in post-war labour history. For the first time since 1945 overtly anti-union legislation had been enacted (*In Place Of Strife*, drawn up by Harold Wilson and Barbara Castle in the 1960s was never implemented and so cannot be said to mark a discontinuity). The effect of the 1971 Industrial Relations Act however was to cause a major rupture within the TUC over registration and compliance with it, and caused several large unions (albeit temporarily) to disaffiliate from the TUC. The use of legislation from that time on was to become the norm in industrial relations. The dockers known as 'The Pentonville Five' gave British labour its first post-war martyrs. The notorious builders' strike of 1972, and the Shrewsbury trials reiterated this trend. Balanced against this were the victories of the workers in the Upper Clyde Shipyards (UCS) and the two miners' strikes of 1972 and 1974. These victories, which were contributory towards bringing down the Heath government, were set against a background of continuing amalgamations, the two most notable ones being the engineers (AUEW) in 1970 and the building workers (UCATT) in 1971. The tradition of unity being strength via amalgamation, and the ultimate victories of the two miners' strikes represented to the unions the justness of their cause and the victory of labour over repressive anti-trade union legislation. The UCS dispute in particular highlighted the influence of the shop stewards' movement. This had been growing and consolidating itself since the 1950s and was partly responsible for the resurgence of the badge in the labour movement in the later 1970s, as will be examined later.

The introduction in this period of anti-union legislation and the resistance of the shop stewards *ipso facto* marked both the beginning of iconographical resurgence and discontinuity of design. The demonstration against the Industrial Relations Bill in 1971 saw the biggest procession of trade unionists since the 1926 May Day celebrations, many of the old banners being given their first public airing for years and probably in many cases, their last. It is noted that several of the then more recently established unions had prepared new banners especially for the demonstration, far more simplistic in design than their opulent predecessors,[5] and this implicitly was to become the norm in banner-making in subsequent years. Poplin and silk-screened designs replaced the expensive banner silk and embroidery of the past. Meanwhile, the legislation of the time and the solid shop steward-organised resistance to it, saw the first sparse use of the badge as a propaganda weapon in the labour movement.

Button badges such as 'Kill The Bill' and 'Free The Shrewsbury Pickets' were issued in this period, whilst 'Solidarity With The Miners' button badges were issued during both the 1972 and 1974 miners' strikes (and reappeared in 1984). Sparse as the use of the badge was in this period, it was used when the struggles were in progress. Only two commemorative (enamel badges) were issued after the events were successfully concluded. These were the Kent and South Wales area NUM badges for the 1972 miners' strike. None at all were issued for the 1974 miners' strike, compared with the many hundreds that were issued for the 1984/85 miners' strike. This seems to indicate that the burgeoning of the badge in the postwar labour movement occurs only when it is losing or after it has lost, rather than when it is winning a battle. In 1989, only one commemorative enamel badge was made to mark the fifth anniversary of the 1984 miners' strike; in 1994, there were at least six to commemorate the tenth anniversary. That more pits had been closed as a result of the 1992 Heseltine cuts no doubt increased the imperative of commemoration – a faint echo and personal token of a community's existence. Designs from

1985–86 were revamped and struck in different colours to commemorate the repetition of the same process of protest, as with for example, the Lancashire Women Against Pit Closures, who camped outside colliery gates on anti-closure vigils during 1992.[6]

The election of a Labour government in 1974 was seen as the ultimate victory over the 1971 Act. The legislation passed under it was favourable to organised labour, and for the first half of its administration, there was general industrial contentment and an absence of the badge in a campaigning role is noticeable in this period. By 1977, inflation was increasing, unemployment was rising and public sector wages were being eroded, along with cuts in public expenditure, leading ultimately to the 'winter of discontent'. An increasingly directionless and moribund Labour government seemed incapable of solving the problems. It is at this point that the button badge as a campaign weapon and a conveyor of protest came into its own. An early example was the 'Stuff The Jubilee – Fight The Cuts' badge issued by the Socialist Workers Party (SWP) in 1977 on the occasion of the Queen's silver jubilee.

The tin badge enjoyed a renaissance in 1970s Britain, but not only in the political or labour field. It was seized upon by advertising agencies, and used as an effective promotional medium for the sale of everyday items. It was also used by newspapers and magazines in a similar way, and by record companies to promote rock bands and the culture that surrounded them. The button badge was also being used as an introspective proclaimor of esoteric statement. Slogans such as 'keep on trucking', 'just passing through' and tantric designs were commonly reproduced on button badges at this time.

There were also the 'fun' button badges. Statements such as 'I'm Bored', 'Tomorrow We Must Get Organised', etc. were quite prevalent. These were reflective of a kind of office humour, but also proved highly popular with school children usually to the alarm of parents who viewed them with distaste.[7] Enamel and button badges however, had been utilised for children's clubs by cinemas, newspapers, comics, magazines, etc. since the 1920s, many of which are now highly sought after by collectors with a taste for nostalgia.

It was not directly from the labour movement that the phenomenal outbreak of badge wearing occurred at first, but from two outside sources. The increase in racist attacks, the rise of the National Front, and the alienation and disaffection felt by much of youth at this time expressed itself in opposition to a seemingly ineffective Labour government.[8] It was ethnic minorities and working-class youth who were *losing*, and it was they who acted as a catalyst for the explosion in the use of the badge. The Socialist Workers Party (SWP) had organised 'Rock Against Racism' (RAR) and 'The Anti-Nazi League' (ANL) movements in 1976 and they took off in a big way, especially with youth who were the specific target. Anti-racist button badges were issued for all sorts of social groups. Many rank-and-file trade unionists wore the badges of Engineers, Miners, Nurses, even TUC 'against the Nazis' (Figure 4.1).

Figure 4.1   Anti-Nazi League Badges. The Anti-Nazi League in the 1970s, was a popular movement which served as a platform to bring together political activists, disaffected youth and different ethnic and cultural groups in a way which was a precursor both of the trade union-sponsored 'event' festivals of the 1980s and 1990s and of ecological and other pressure and activist groups of the 1990s. These badges were endemic in 1977–78.
Author's collection.

Coinciding with this was the emergence of the youth cult of 'punk rock' in 1977. Culturally this incorporated largely anti-racist, nihilistic and socialist tendencies and was naively political in its music. It offered a mass youth market for the SWP/ANL/RAR. Racists sought to infiltrate the punk scene early on, encouraged by the naive fashion amongst punks at first, for wearing Swastika armbands as a form of shock tactic to an older generation rather than an assertion of political conviction. Punk's mass expression was overwhelmingly anti-racist. The two big Carnivals Against The Nazis in 1978 and 1979 were RAR/ANL's high point.[9]

In conjunction with the musical badges, which expressed in the main either nihilistic or socialistic slogans and which were produced largely by record companies and petit-entrepreneurs out to exploit the phenomenon, the ANL/RAR badges were sold and worn in vast quantities. The button badge was a popular part of the livery of any punk. The SWP's 'Bookmarx' outlet, did a roaring trade in anti-establishment slogan badges. Initially badges were issued in three-inch (75 mm) diameters but these proved unpopular, and were soon reduced to minuscule size, down to a half-inch (12.5mm), but more usually between one and one-and-one-quarter inches (25–31 mm), in order that the maximum number of them could be worn on one lapel, which was the fashion at the time. The Better Badges firm in London's Portobello Road for instance, issued enormous quantities of such badges.

The implicit informal alliance between left-wing politics and youth culture was symptomatic of Labour's failure to act as a campaigning body. This gave the impression of cutting the ground from under the unions' feet, temporarily usurped by external bodies. The movement represented vigour to youth, an outlet for frustration. They had as little respect for the unions as they did for the government – they were all regarded as part of the establishment. It is from this point that trade unions began to try and recruit more young workers into the movement as a whole. Similar campaigns had been tried in the early 1960s, when youth culture had offered an alternative identity to that of the work place. Notably, campaigns were initiated by the National Union of Boot and Shoe Operatives (NUBSO) and the National Union of Tailors and Garment Workers (NUTGW) at that time. 'Anarchy In The UK' as a youth anthem was not one which trade unions saw as conducive to the next generation of their officials and activists.

With the election of a Tory government under Thatcher in 1979, the SWP placed its emphasis in other areas. ANL and RAR were largely abandoned (although ANL was revived in the late 1980s). Youth culture changed again, and the populist upswing of the late 1970s ebbed away. One of its practices though, the use of the button badge, remained and was used from below to a great extent by groups of workers in dispute, in a way it had not been (prior to 1977) used before in Britain. The innovative idea of making badges for various groups 'against the Nazis' and so making the cause that more close to those who wore them, was perhaps the idea for the issuing of localised dispute badges. To commemorate Thatcher's election in 1979, the *Morning Star* newspaper hurriedly issued a copious number of 'I Didn't Vote Tory' button badges. In origin a bitter political statement, the slogan was quickly appropriated by commercial interests, and was printed on posters, t shirts, mugs, postcards, even teatowels. Whilst illustrating the power and wide distribution of the badge, this example also shows how 'serious' rhetoric is often converted into music-hall satire or self-mockery. The unions, seeing the popularity of the button badge, probably adopted it as a propaganda tool, as a means of regaining their established position as the vocal expression of the working class. This tendency seems to have begun at the bottom and percolated upwards via shop stewards at branch level in disputes. Shop stewards, the means by which rank-and-file dissent had come to be articulated, now used the badge as a means for that articulation. Unions such as the TGWU had recognised and accommodated the stewards' movement, rather than try to distance itself from it; by such means the badge percolated upwards, to be used also as a means of expression of conviction at national as well as local level, from around the end of the 1970s. The steel strike of 1980 was probably the first instance in which the button badge was overtly issued by British trade unions on a large scale.

The button badge as a campaign tool was again invoked in the 1980s, principally through the Campaign for Nuclear Disarmament (CND), but also in other areas, though nowhere as explicitly as in the 1970s. CND's use of the badge was revived when the movement itself revived in the early 1980s. It imitated the RAR/ANL device of issuing badges for various social groups 'against the Nazis', by adopting the same and other social groups 'against the bomb'.

It is important to differentiate between the two types of badge that have become prevalent as a means of protest in the last three decades. From 1977 to 1982, it had been the button badge that had been utilised. From 1982, and especially from 1985, it has been the enamel badge. The earliest use of the enamel badge as a protest or publicity tool in the contemporary period seems to have been one issued by the South Yorkshire Regional Committee of the Iron and Steel Trades Confederation (ISTC), to commemorate the 1980 national steel strike, again a campaign that was lost. But it was 1982 which marks the real beginning of the renaissance in enamel badge manufacturing. This is not an arbitrary date. It was the year of the ASLEF strike, which coincided with the Falklands War. The dispute (over flexible rosters) was lost, and the enamel badge was used by ASLEF to commemorate the loyalty of those who had struck, branch and regional badges being issued in their hundreds, and which were still being issued for several years afterwards. The ASLEF dispute has poignancy perhaps because of its coincidence with the Falkland Islands war. A placard on an English naval dockside seen in a television news broadcast warned: 'Call Off The Rail Strike, Or We'll Call An Air Strike.' An industrial dispute at a time when so many people were wrapping themselves in the Union Jack was never likely to curry much favour with the public. The use of the enamel badge rather than the tin one was perhaps also symbolic of the ambivalence towards the union from the public. As such, the dispute needed a more permanent symbol of loyalty than a transient button badge.

The nature of industrial relations under Thatcher had deteriorated rapidly. The onslaught of the Tory government, and the reactionary atmosphere engendered and encouraged amongst employers, meant that strikes were no longer short protest affairs, but had rapidly turned into lockouts, with the replacement of strikers by non-union labour. As days turned into weeks and weeks into months, those in dispute needed a source of income to sustain their struggles. One way of providing this was by the sale of enamel badges. The more ephemeral button badge was unsuited for this purpose, as it was more like a give-away item, or could only be sold for pennies, whereas enamels could be sold for much-needed pounds. As a fund-raiser, the enamel badge has come into its own. Quite apart from the social connotations, this has been enabled by competition amongst manufacturers. Two firms in particular, Adams Badges of London and Badges Plus of Birmingham, both established in the late 1970s, issued a large portion of the enamel dispute badges of the 1980s (see Chapter 5). A reduction in the cost of production of enamel badges, by these firms at least, made the enamel badge as a fund-raiser and proclaimer of cause an even more lucrative idea.

The 1984–85 Miners' Strike

The threatened mass closures of mines on supposedly economic grounds all over Britain by the then National Coal Board in 1983, led to a national strike against pit closures in March 1984 which lasted until March 1985. During 1984,[10] enamel badges were issued by striking miners, but with the minimum of wording, usually, just the name of the pit and the date '1984'.[11] This is because they were intended as a means of identification for pickets, picketing away from their home colliery. The button badge was also used to a great extent during the strike, acting as a means of celebrating support from other areas and unions (often more in spirit than in action, as will be discussed later). Photographs of miners festooned with badges, looking like walking exhibitions,[12] brings back to mind General Gordon's suggestion that blue cockades should be worn for mutual recognition. However, the majority of the badges worn, were ordinary membership badges of other unions, as well as of county miners' unions that formed the highly federalised NUM. They are perhaps symptomatic of the need for and the belief in outside support, characterised by the extensive swapping of badges between miners and supporters on picket lines and at rallies, galas and demonstrations during the miners' strike. They were none the less badges that had already existed before the strike began of all sorts of unions including overseas ones.

   The conclusion of the miner's strike in 1985 marks the real acceleration of the production of the enamel badge, again after the strike had been lost. Such badges are regarded as war medals and battle honours, especially those issued during the strike, and shortly afterwards. Those issued later on were produced mainly to raise funds for the sacked miners, and were seen largely as precisely that. Some later issues, however, were also produced by NUM branches who did not have the means or funds during or shortly after the strike to issue their own badges at the time. All of these, though, would be bought for fundraising purposes. They were (and still are) seen as different from those issued closer to the dispute itself. Such cathartic and traumatic experiences often require counselling. As both a form of therapy and of commemoration, clubs are formed which act, at least subconsciously, as self-help groups. In 1985, the '5.3.85 Club' was formed. This denoted the date on which a national return to work was made. Only those miners who had stayed out until the end of the strike were admitted, and entitled to wear its badge. This has at least one historical precedent in the 1918 Australian organisation known as 'the Lilywhites', veterans of the 1917 New South Wales strike discussed in Chapter 3. Nothing is recorded in that instance, however, to suggest that the women – wives, mothers, etc – equally affected by such a turn of events, had any formal mutual support network, in the way that miners' wives had in the Women Against Pit Closures (WAPC) movement. More work needs to be done in this area, to allow such history to be uncovered, particularly in the field of experience outside the formal organised trade union movement, and with special reference to oral history and testimony.

The 1984–85 miners' strike resulted in a return to work without a negotiated agreement and allowed the wording on the commemorative badges to assert honour and dignity in the struggle without admitting defeat (see Figure 4.2). 'Loyal And Undefeated' and 'Loyal To The Last' were common statements on these badges, as was 'One Year's Unbroken Allegiance To The NUM'. In areas where scabbing was notable. 'Loyalist' and 'Loyal Members' are appended to the badge to distinguish them. The recurring use of the word 'loyal' though is the ultimate testimony of conviction and lack of regret in taking part in the strike.

In the contemporary sense, the invoking of principle and historical struggle, carried as much by folk memory as by documentation on the badge, again seems to be prevalent from the miners' strike onwards. Scargill's (and many others') assertion that the strike was not simply about jobs in the present, but that pit closures meant the loss of hereditary jobs which were the miners' children's by right, perhaps struck a chord with other sections of the labour movement. Certainly the miners' strike was an intensely personal one. This is demonstrated through the wording on some of the button badges issued during the strike. The Wearmouth lodge in Durham, referred to itself both as 'Harry's "F" Troop' and 'The Zulus'. The Whittle lodge in Northumberland named themselves 'The Warriors' and an enamel badge of the Northumbrian pickets refers to 'Murphy's Marauders' thus suggesting the prosecution of the strike (in a union historically, highly federal in nature anyway) on the basis of guerrilla warfare, perhaps in answer to the police armies of occupation of the colliery villages. The enamel commemorative badge of the Hickleton Main branch of the National Union of Mineworkers (NUM) in Yorkshire, declares 'Forget Not The Lessons Of Our Past', explicitly suggesting the remembrance of historic sacrifice as a reason for continuation.

The emotional resonance evoked by the miners' strike badges runs deep. In 1986, Dick Hall, a Derbyshire miner, decided to auction off his collection of four hundred miners' strike badges, in order to raise funds for the sacked miners' fund that Christmas. *The Miner*, in October 1986 reported on the decision: 'The collection of well over four hundred badges includes some exceptionally rare first editions, which are virtually impossible to obtain.' Hall himself, states 'Of course it hurts to be parting with them, most were collected in the heat of battle – but I think my feelings have got to come second to the victimised lads.' Hall's friend, Billy Seaton continues:

It must really pain him to part with the badges; some of them are priceless – about as rare as an honest Tory. For example the collection includes South Derbyshire's 'Time

Figure 4.2 Grimethorpe and Brodsworth (Yorkshire) branch badges of the National Union of Mineworkers c. 1985–86. The sense of grievance and strength through recourse to historical precedent and altruism are all too plain in the wording on these two badges from the great miners' strike of 1984–85. The maxim 'close a pit, kill a community' was an often repeated slogan at the time. Author's collection.

106

The Avenger'; the 'Kellingly Black' Allegiance badge and much prized 'Hucknall No.2' and many others which were struck in very limited numbers from a few dozen down to a handful.

Even before the miners' strike, in 1983, a postcard published by the National Graphical Association (NGA) in connection with the Warrington print dispute, pictured a ghostly appearance of the Tolpuddle Martyrs, angrily addressing a TUC General Council sitting on a fence holding its 'bottle' (that is, courage) saying 'we all broke the law when we fought for union rights.' Such invocations though, are not a phenomenon confined to recent decades. It is itself a phenomenon, each succeeding generation invoking the sacrifices of the last as the rightness of their cause. As long ago as 1919, the gold medal awarded by the Women's Trade Union League bore the motto 'Lose Not Those Things That We Have Wrought'.[13] Perhaps this tradition had been lying dormant until the 1980s, awaiting recall. The idea of preserving jobs for the next generation acted as a spark, triggering off an attestation to values. A rebirth of adhesion to traditional trade union principle is expressed in the handbill accompanying a badge of the Shirebrook (Derbyshire) branch of ASLEF in 1985. It pictures a seagull, with the words 'avarice', 'cronyism', '£7.32' and 'principles first'. The accompanying note explains the usage of the wording: 'As a branch Shirebrook supported the stand against DOO [driver-operated-only trains] putting "principles first", but within our midst we had "seagulls" that by "cronyism" and because of "avarice" were prepared to and actually did accept "£7.32" for working DOO trains before an agreement was reached.'

The other side of the coin in badge iconography is the re-emergence of 'new realism' in the 1980s rebranded as 'new unionism' in the 1990s.[14] The evangelical reaffirmation of historical struggle on the badge has been largely (though by no means entirely) in relation to dispute badges and commemoratives, usually in the wake of defeat. The more 'moderate' badges are usually in the nature of membership badges. Given the hostility to trade unionism in Britain during the 1980s and 1990s, it is perhaps a little difficult to believe that in 1975, the Australian government established the Trade Union Training Authority 'to train and develop trade union officials and members in skills required to run a trade union', which also issues its own badge.[15]

Not all redesigning of union emblematics, though, is necessarily symbolic of any compliance with softer approaches to modern industrial conditions. R.A. Leeson tells us that the Patternmakers badgered their executive for (almost) twenty years to have an emblem made.[16] The pace at which events now occur requires more speedily available iconography, almost with a sense of urgency. The changing of such union names as the 'Amalgamated Society of Wire Drawers and Kindred Workers' to the more upbeat 'Wire Workers Union' (WWU), or of the Post Office Engineering Union' to the 'National Communications Union' (NCU) in the 1980s (in both instances of which, the clasped hands of unity were retained in the design) is symbolic of the changing nature of industry and commerce. From the 1990s, new names were adopted which did not even incorporate the nature of the industry or profession in which the union organised. In a decade personified by the emphasis of style over content, three public sector unions amalgamated to become 'UNI-SON', and the Barclays Bank Staff Association became 'UNIFI' (the 'Uni' of union and 'Fi' of finance). These at least arguably adopted a soundbite name which encapsulated a key aspect of trade union rhetoric. The Society of Telecom Executives, however, in a millenial gesture, on 1 January 2000, became simply known as 'Connect'.[17] The badges incorporating the new titles are quickly ordered by unions to help promote the identity of it with the membership, whereas branch banners often take a lot longer to change. Although it has been said that the majority of branch badges are issued by the laity of the union, the NCU and WWU examples came from head office. In the cases of the Greater London Staff Association (GLSA) and the National Association of Teachers in Further and Higher Education (NATHFE), badges were issued in direct response to requests from ordinary members.[18] It is not only the badge that is used for publicising events or commemorations, although it is the most utilised and immediate one. Plates, mugs, postcards, posters, T-shirts and all other traditional and modern means of communication are being used to publicise cause and principle, with the badge at the forefront.

ASLEF continued to issue badges to commemorate branch anniversaries amongst other things, many of which were for eightieth anniversaries. This is because many of the branches concerned did not expect to reach their centenaries before they were closed, perhaps symbolising the issue of badges in advance of defeat rather than in its wake. Many ASLEF badges were issued in the late 1980s for 'dead' stations and branch lines closed under Beeching in the 1960s, though there were none issued at the time. This could be seen as no more than a ploy to cash in on the growing collectors' market, but is perhaps also symbolic of a lament for a ravaged industry, a posthumous symbol of pride in spite of defeat. It could be recognition of where the rot started, belatedly or otherwise, or as a poignant reminder of the results of that wholesale attack on the industry, acting as an implicit warning. With the privatisation of the railways in the 1990s, this seems even more relevant.

The Wapping Dispute

If the 1984–85 miners' strike symbolised Thatcher's attitude towards the state's employees, then the Wapping dispute was the imposition of this same credo in the private sector. In 1986, Rupert Murdoch manipulated a situation whereby the print unions working for his Fleet Street titles were coerced into strike action. Having got his employees out of his premises, he then sacked them, and moved his operation to Wapping, employing non-union labour and de-recognising the print unions. The dispute lasted for twelve months. The Wapping dispute also saw a large number of badges issued once the strike had turned into a lockout, and increased in number as the dispute wore on.[19] Mines, rail and print are the three best examples of this phenomenon, but many smaller local disputes have used the enamel badge for fund-raising and proclamation of cause, while the dispute is actually on (see below).

An overt assertion of alternative principle or policy by a branch to its national leadership is expressed through the badges of the London Press Branch of the former Electrical, Electronic Telecommunication and Plumbing Union (EETPU, since amalgamated with the Amalgamated Engineering Union). This branch was loyal to the sacked workers during the Wapping dispute in 1986–87, in contradiction the national leadership's policies of sweetheart deals and scabbing. It first issued its own branch badge initially in tin, later in enamel. After the Wapping dispute it issued its own long-service badges for 20, 30, 40 and 50 years, awarded in preference to the national long-service badges covering the same periods. The branch badges all picture a clenched fist as opposed to the national ones which all use Walter Crane's Angel of Light and Liberty design, as did the former Electrical Trades Union (ETU), except for their fifty-year badge which also pictures the 'Angel of Light And Liberty'.

Since Wapping

The success of Murdoch's tactics at Wapping signified to the corporate world the legitimacy of disregard for employee rights. Following Wapping, there was an intensification of such tactics throughout British industry. Many smaller disputes, caused by the same tactics as those used by Murdoch, became the norm[20] (Plate 4.3).

By the late 1990s, nothing had changed. The Liverpool dockers,[21] Magnet Kitchens,[22] Critchley Labels[23] and Project Aerospace[24] are all examples of the employer response of sacking and locking-out workers who made moderate claims for pay increases and union recognition. As a result of this position, trade unions (officially) and sacked workers (unofficially) have adopted different tactics. In the run-up to the general election of 1997, the TUC and its larger affiliates were at pains to stress a new 'user-friendly' image to both members and employers from whom they sought recognition. In imitation of New Labour's 'New Britain' mantra, the 1997 TUC congress, adopted as its slogan 'New Unionism'. However, this was a far cry from the militant adoption of the label used by the new unions of unskilled workers in the 1890s, and was partly conditioned by the fear of New Labour's distancing itself from trade unions,[25] and partly by its traditional fear of union militancy. An intensification of its new realist approach of the mid-1980s was characterised by its adoption of the music and culture festival concept as a means of attracting new members and getting its message across to the young disaffected. In this, unions were learning the lessons of the 1970s. Emphasis is placed on the services the union provides (legal aid, cheap car insurance, health care plans, etc.) which are now seen as central to people's lives.[26] In so doing, John Monks, the TUC General

**Figure 4.3   Amalgamated Engineering & Electrical Union Timex dispute
1993; National Union of Journalists Pergamon Press dispute
1989–90. Numerous localised disputes such as these came to
characterise the nature of labour unrest in the absence of work-
able industrial relations with belligerent employers in the 1980s.
Many of those involved on the union side employed the enamel
badge as both a means of raising funds to continue defending
their rights, and as a commemorative item, which, in terms of
public history, becomes a part of the evidence.**
Joe Fleming collection, photograph Dean Bennett.

Secretary, sought to equate the militant unionism of the 1890s with the new realism
of the 1990s by linking their central focus on the unskilled and semiskilled worker.[27]

Conversely, there are those who have fought and lost under such circumstances,
not least the miners. They also learned a great deal tactically as a result. Some of
these have now grouped together in the spirit of 'worker flexibility' on their own
terms. The Magnet Kitchens dispute in Darlington, England, where three hundred
workers were sacked for legally voting for a stoppage in pursuit of a wage claim, is
a case in point. During the miners' strike, workers from the Darlington factory
donated money, goods and support to the miners in Derbyshire, where most of the
mines are now closed. The ex-miners then returned the favour:

'We brought the long dispute to trade unionism' says Terry Buckeraitis, one of the
miners. 'We can't picket lawfully any more, but we can do other things'. Since their
defeat in 1985, he and 'about 70' other former members of the National Union of

Mineworkers have reinvented themselves, first as a sacked miners support group, then as 'free-range trade unionists'. Where they used to bellow on picket lines, they now 'look for new avenues'.[28]

There is also a much closer working relationship between trade unionists in this situation, environmental activists and other direct action lobby groups. The absence of any meaningful and nationally applied industrial relations apparatus over the last two decades has perhaps sown the seeds from which we are now reaping the harvest. The lapel badge in this scenario becomes another symbol of solidarity and principle, a visual testimony both to the legitimacy of the cause being advocated and the solidarity of others in its support. The wearing of hats and caps bearing multiple examples of badges of unions who (at local level) have assisted is the evidence of this assertion.

Gender

Given the sheer numbers of badges issued over the years, it would not be possible to say to what extent women have been represented in union badges, but they would seem to have been largely hidden. This is not to say that women were more active in trade unions in the early years of the century, but that as many unions had considerable numbers of female members, it would be only logical to assume that some expression of this fact would have been manifested in the badge, but apparently did not to any great extent. The National Federation of Women Workers, Society of Women Welders,[29] National Union of Women Teachers, National Union of Women Civil Servants and the Association of Women Clerks and Secretaries are a few examples of all-women unions that issued badges, the best example of which is perhaps the beautiful medal issued by the Women's Trade Union League, previously mentioned. This was awarded to a Miss Ann Loughlin in 1919, the last of its kind before the WTUL merged with the TUC in 1920. The narrative accompanying a picture of the badge relates:

> Its winner was the daughter of an active trade unionist but she found that she started work in the Leeds clothing industry [and] that the local union branch committee of the union was not at all enthusiastic about enrolling women, although the wages of the girls were sometimes as low as 3s for a week of fifty two and a half hours or more. Joining the union the day she started work at the age of 15, Miss Anne Loughlin was shop steward and propagandist before she was 21 ... [30]

Another similar example can be found in the special medal minted for the retiring presidents of the National Union of Women Teachers (NUWT). A commemorative history of the NUWT was published in 1928, a copy of which was found by a collector, Andy Redpath. The presidential medal was introduced in 1917–918 shortly after the union was formed by ex-members of the National Union of Teachers

(NUT), angry at male teachers' attitude towards women's suffrage and equal pay. The wording in the badge's centre reads: 'Pass On The Sacred Flame' and pictured a female hand passing on a flaming torch (of enlightenment) to another, and was the work of Miss Neal, the NUWT secretary and Miss Phipps, the commemorative book's author.[31]

Other than this example, however, there seems to be little representation of women on mixed-gender union badges. It is also indicative of the indifference with which badges have been met by feminists, those working in visual culture and historians generally, that this has not been noticed sooner. Over the last two decades, books have been written on the use and importance to the women's movement of banners and emblems[32] and even postcards,[33] and yet the badge has still to be recognised as an aspect of women's history, even within the women's suffrage movement when many portrait buttons of the Pankhursts and other suffragists were issued as fund-raisers.

The Women Worker's Union of Ireland issued a badge, the union being formed because of Larkin's interpretation of the word 'person' in the ITGWU rule book, to mean 'man'. The horses entering the Cork docks had to have the ITGWU 'Cork Carriers' badge in their bridle to be allowed through the gates, and therefore the ITGWU once organised men and horses but not women![34] Both ASLEF and the NUR had women's societies which issued badges, but these were supportive auxiliaries, not unions in their own right. One ASLEF member aged 70 in 1997, proudly showed off a souvenir teaspoon, the finial of which was the enamel badge of the ASLEF Women's Society. It was given to his mother on the occasion of his birth by the then new women's society branch in Eastleigh, Hampshire, he being the first baby to be born into the branch. The member remembered his mother's role in the women's society during the 1955 train drivers' strike: 'My mother helped keep the Eastleigh pickets supplied with refreshments.' He, his father and two brothers were all train drivers, and he remembered his mother 'work[ing] hard washing our overalls with the old fashioned copper. No washing machines in those days. Four sets of overalls and always clean for us every Monday.'[35]

A number of unions once issued women's section badges, including the National Union of Lock and Metal Workers, the General, Municipal, Boilermakers and Allied Trades Union (GMB), the National Warehouse & General Workers Union and the AEU (during the Second World War). This last example did not signify it was a women's section badge, rather it was made of chrome as opposed to the usual brass to make the distinction. This last example reveals a hidden element in union badges that disguises women. Some unions incorporated women into the title of the union, and hence the badge if there was a big enough female membership (though the officers seemed always to have been men). These include the National Amalgamated Society of Male and Female Pottery Workers and the Amalgamated Society of Tailors and Tailoresses. In some cases, iconographical concessions were made in the union's imagery, for example, the design of the insignia of the Amalgamated Society of Lace Makers and Auxiliary Workers which shows two clasped hands, one of which is female.[36] The Scottish Textile Workers Union, established in 1907, also issued a badge picturing both a male and a female textile operative. However, even where recognition of women is cited in the title 'male' usually precedes 'female', perhaps indicating the ratio of male to female members, but more probably asserting a male hegemony. Moreover unions such as the Dundee and District Union of Jute and Flax Workers and the General Union of Textile Workers, which both had very large female memberships, make no concession to their female members either in wording or iconography, the only distinction being that those badges intended for female members had pin rather than buttonhole fittings on the reverse. The Felt Hatters and Trimmers Unions were two separate unions, one male, one female, but which shared the same (male) general secretary and premises.[37] They also shared a common badge of membership. Women are not recognised on this badge, other than via the pin fitting (although there is a silver version of this badge in the TUC collection which has a fitting consisting of two metal loops through which a two-pronged pin is slipped, as in a cap badge fitting). This then suggests a hidden female element, masked behind an all-embracing title and the male definition of the iconography. To be fair however, even in rare instances when a union was a predominantly female one, and run by a woman, the badge chosen neither reflected these facts, nor made much of an assertive display. Such was the case of the National Union of Domestic Workers (NUDW). It was formed in 1938, by the TUC itself, as a campaign to organise poorly paid female domestics.[38] In a circular sent to members in July 1938, the question of a badge was mooted by Beatrice Bezzant, the NUDW national organiser:

> Another question on which I would like to have your opinion is that of a badge for members. As you know, most if not all Trade Unions have a Badge for members, and I have received several letters from members of our own Union, asking if and when we are going to have a badge. Would you like a badge? And do you think it would be a good idea to have a small round badge with a dark blue background and the letters N.U.D.W in gold upon it?

Evidently, the membership were either more or less in agreement, or failed to significantly respond, as the badge eventually issued was as described, but lozenge-shaped rather than round. This perhaps reflected the conservatism of the TUC who spawned the union rather than any particular desire of the union, which by May 1953 was wound up, as domestic service had largely ceased to exist as an industry by this time.[39]

Since the 1980s, it has often been heard from women delegates that the composition of union and TUC hierarchies are overwhelmingly, white, male and middle-aged. Without discussing the number of women members of unions or their proportion on executive committees etc. it is sufficient to say that during the 1990s the recruitment of women into trade unions was one of the main objectives of the labour movement. For this purpose, women's officers were appointed and recruit-

Figure 4.4   National Federation of Women Workers c.1910s; Transport and General Workers Union Region No.1 c.1988. The assertive and progressive maxim of the former is reinvoked in the latter, some seventy or eighty years later.
Author's collection.

ment material was produced specifically aimed at women. Two kinds of badges are aimed at women made by trade unions nationally, outside of the unisex national membership badge. The first are those that are issued for recruitment campaigns which often sport the female symbol and slogans such as 'a woman's place is in her union' or which utilise assertive graphics and maxims as a form of self-belief (see Figure 4.4).

On the other hand, unions have also offered their female members since the late 1970s what are usually advertised as 'the ladies' brooch', as an enamel, more permanent form of badge. These are usually round in shape and similar in design to a scarf ring. The GMB offer their women members a brooch in the shape of a brass leaf with the union logo on it, both of which are overtly and conventionally femininely decorative (see Figure 4.5).

This seems to be a visual contradiction in emphasis that needs resolving. The assertive and positive nature of women is more clearly expressed in the badges of the 'Women Against Pit Closures' movement, such as the Coventry Colliery branch issue, picturing a woman breaking the chains of oppression, and proclaiming 'proud and defiant we stand'. Such imagery away from the heat and intensity of a single issue such as the miners' strike, is perhaps a little overbearing for everyday wear, but is more representative of women's strengths and portrays women in a more

Figure 4.5 **'Ladies' Brooches' of the Furniture, Timber and Allied Trades Union and General, Municipal, Boilermakers & Allied Trades Union (GMB) c.1980s. By contrast to Figure 4.4, 'official' badges (or rather brooches) offered to women members at national level by a number of larger unions in the 1980s took the form of a more deferential accoutrement to conventional feminine dress.** Author's collection.

positive and assertive manner. It would be desirable to either replace the 'ladies' brooch' with something more representative of the campaign button variety of badge, or to do away with separatist badges altogether. At the moment it is uncomfortably tempting to ponder that the assertive tin campaign badges might be a means of attracting women into the union, but once in they are considered converted. The implicit docility of the 'ladies' brooch' or neck chain, which is also issued, seems to imply this to be the case. Attitudes are changing in some areas however. The health service nurses union, COHSE (now part of UNISON) abandoned their 'Branch Chairman' badge in 1987, and replaced it with a 'Branch Chairperson' badge. UNISON itself, in recent years has produced a 'Lesbian and Gay Members' sectional badge whilst the Manufacturing, Science and Finance Union (MSF) have also a produced a 'Lesbians and Gays In Management' (LAGIM) badge, whilst grassroots support groups such as the 'Lesbians And Gay Men Support The Miners' produced their own enamel badge during the 1984–85 miners' strike All of this is some indication of the distance travelled and reminds us that such activity is contextualised by a wider progressive change in social and cultural attitudes in recent years.

Race

Another theme that has received attention in the trade union movement is that of race. Trade unions are now seeking to present themselves as more open towards black workers, which was not the case thirty or forty years ago. Given this emphasis, the question of race in badge iconography is a pertinent subject to examine. The most obvious way in which badge iconography could be improved in this area concerns the still common clasped handshake design. This is pointed out quite interestingly in a song recorded by Ewan Mcoll and Peggy Seager, written by Charlie Mayo, about an unpopular colour bar strike that took place at King's Cross by a minority of ASLEF and NUR members in 1957.[40] The strike had no official support and was soon crushed by local leaders and activists. The claim was that promotion of black members was affecting the overtime of white members. The first verse of the song is as follows:

> My union badge shows two joined hands with a lighted flame in common fight but troubles brewing in the sheds for both these working hands are white[41]

The reference to the hands being white is to make the point of the song, as ASLEF and NUR badges of the time show the hands as either gilt or chrome, not white or indeed black, but it is a salient point. The NUR issued a badge in 1987 for the South African Railway & Harbour Workers Union, with whom they were twinned, in order to raise funds for the latter. This does indeed picture two clasped hands – one white, one black. The old GMB badge pictured two white hands, although there was no deliberate racial connotations in their colouring. Many unions that use the clasped hands device picture it in base metal, or colours other than black and white. If serious attempts are to be made in recruiting non-white workers, then the badge's iconography needs more careful consideration in some cases. If this sounds a flippant point, one has only to look at the biennial conference medals of the American Federation of Labor/Congress of Industrial Organisations (AFL/CIO), the American equivalent of the British TUC, which always picture two clasped hands, one white, the other black. Whether this came about through pressure from union members or whether it was a conscious decision is not known, but it should be borne in mind and seemed to be taken on board by some badges of the late 1980s such as that of the Southwark Trades Council (see Figure 4.6) amongst others.

The issue by the Union of Shop Distributive and Allied Workers (USDAW) of an enamel badge to mark the victimisation of two supermarket employees, 'Gary and Ross, sacked for opposing apartheid', shortly before Nelson Mandela's release from Robben Island, evoked the internationalist aspect of racism. The issue by

Figure 4.6   Calton Weavers strike bicentennial and Southwark Trades
Council badges c.1987. The Calton Weavers badge takes the
opportunity to reinvoke a dispute from two centuries previous, as
a reminder to keep the faith in the present when Thatcherite
attacks on workers' rights were at their height. Southwark
Trades Council, with that area's high-density multicultural
population, has taken care to represent its ethnic diversity in the
colour of the handshake on its badge. The plain gilt hands on the
Calton Weavers badge by contrast are left unenamelled.
Joe Fleming Collection, photograph by Dean Bennett.

UNISON of a 'Black Members' sectional badge (although the union name is not mentioned on it) and the Public Service, Tax and Commerce Union (PTC) 1996 black members' inaugural conference badge perhaps indicates the importance with which the question of equality and anti-racism is now treated in the trade union movement.

Symbolism

What does this burgeoning of the badge symbolise? It could be argued that the badge, rather than converting people to a cause, serves only to convey recognition of a cause from one member of a minority to another and gives the impression that a cause has been all but won before it has been even fully asserted. Many contemporary badges are issued by branch lay officials and activists. Compared to the small attendances at branch meetings, the badges perhaps overstate support for a cause or campaign. Many union members would perhaps not wear union badges. The badges perhaps are worn by the same activists and give a false sense of awareness of a cause, in the same way that ostensibly 'public' meetings are usually only ever attended by the same activists; this is perhaps implicit in the statement on one badge proclaiming 'Wearing Badges Is Not Enough'. The number of badges seen adorning the lapels of the converted are often quite out of all proportion to the small numbers of workers actively involved in the causes which they espouse. Many others perhaps wear the badge as a kind of trendy fashion accoutrement. In this sense modern badges are quite different from the older union badges that were worn only by the members concerned. They would be worn for years, unlike the majority issued today, which are of a temporary nature in a lot of cases, worn only whilst the cause to which they appertain is in operation, or worn by non-members to signify recognition of principle. The wearing of the badge today though probably most often symbolises a general empathy with the cause that it espouses rather than the active support which it enjoys.

It could be argued that such a burgeoning of badges acts as a smoke screen behind which the contraction of traditional industries such as mining and the railways and therefore the membership of the unions organising within them is going on apace. The miners' badges, for instance, could be said to represent an assertion of unity that was not really there. The reality, it could be argued, was division, and therefore the badges are symbolic of a cleaving together of the strikers themselves in the absence of wider support, especially so where the badge commemorates the unity of two colliery branches. The increased use of legislation during the Thatcher years aimed at breaking the unions cannot be denied. It was the second phase of Tory attack which had begun in 1971 with Heath. It was only interrupted by an undynamic Labour government, which towards its end looked increasingly as though it would have to use modified legislation of a similar nature itself. The difference was that in the early 1970s, there was nothing like the contraction of industry that took place under Thatcher; in the earlier period, industry was kept alive by artificial injections of government cash, a policy continued by Labour. The unions emerged victorious and defeated the legislation, the stewards' movement was strong and the badge was not used to express or commemorate victory. In the 1980s, legislation was implemented with a vengeance, and contraction of industry was intense. Compared with Thatcher, Heath now appears the very image of Tory moderation and the badge has been used extensively. In this sense then, the badge perhaps symbolises the end of an (albeit interrupted) epoch of Tory attack on the position of trade unions. The pronouncements of New Labour, made to placate potentially troublesome unions, have in practice only served to codify and legalise pre-existing customs (for example, the level and applicability of the minimum wage) and seem to offer little improvement.

The burgeoning of the badge has come at a time when unions are losing the battle for jobs and services. The badge then can be seen as a means behind which an ever-contracting industrial landscape is seeking to retire with grace, maintaining dignity whilst retreating, mimicking perhaps, Britain's withdrawal from empire in earlier decades of the twentieth century. Some of the largest unions seem to be collaborating with this theory. John Edmonds, General Secretary of the GMB is on record as saying '"Unity is Strength" is very, very old fashioned.'[42] It is hard to agree with him when the full name of his union is the antiquated 'General, Municipal, Boilermakers & Allied Trades Union. The union is now known by its abbreviated initials 'GMB'; 'Unity is Strength', a slogan more pertinent now than at any other time since 1926 given the level of casualisation and temporary employment under the guise of 'worker flexibility', has been replaced by 'Working Together'. Gone are the clasped hands of unity, and in come two matchstick people symbolic of harmonious working (between union and management?). This is the trade union equivalent of New Labour's abandoning of the crossed quill and spade for the softer red rose. So does this new (or rather, idealised) realism mark a departure from trade union traditions? The historical precedent of the Mond-Turner talks of 1927[43] would suggest not, but if the labour movement is to turn its back on its past heraldics and traditional symbolism, it does then mark the end of resistance and the admission of defeat and the beginning of acquiescence with policies from above.

But is this the true picture of the contemporary labour movement? There is another side to the question which is equally valid. The labour movement has since the 1980s in branch structure been busy invoking all the imagery and martyrdom of its past, not least of all through the medium of the badge. The bicentenary of the Calton Weavers strike of 1787 was commemorated on the badge of the Glasgow May Day in 1987 (see Figure 4.6). The Wapping dispute saw the commemoration of the fiftieth anniversary of the battle of Cable Street linked with the Wapping dispute in 1986, proclaiming 'Fifty Years Against Fascism'. This is symbolic of the bolstering of morale in the movement, to commemorate past glories in the absence of them today. Many unions have taken to issuing branch badges, perhaps rediscovering their own regional history and this highlights the nature of 'national' unions as actual 'federations' of branches.

Regionalism

Regionalistic representations of national union badges are not uncommon. Even in earlier years unions such as the ASW and NUR issued special badges for their Irish memberships. The Railway Clerks Association issued a special badge in 1932 for their conference in Dublin, whilst the ASE made a special badge for its delegates to the 1893 TUC conference in Belfast. The British TGWU have also made a number of special badges for their Northern Irish membership, prefixing the name with 'A' for 'Amalgamated', to distinguish it from the Irish TGWU, with whom it sometimes competes, prior to it becoming the Services, Industrial and Professional Trade Union, (SIPTU).[44] Unions such as the ASW, ASRS and ASE are known to have issued medals and badges for their branches set up in South Africa, Canada,

**Figure 4.7   Undeb Gweithwyr Môn – Anglesey Workers Union c.1918. A
stronger sense of local identity or belonging would be hard to
find in a trade union badge.**
David A. Pretty collection.

Australia and America. An even stronger sense of regional identity can be found in
the badge of the Anglesey Workers Union (an organisation comprised predominantly of agricultural workers), first issued in 1918 for the increased number of
members that year (see Figure 4.7).[45] The name appears only in Welsh (Undeb
Gweithwyr Môn) and the establishment date of 1911. The central design is the
Anglesey coat of arms and the motto 'Môn Mam Cymru' – 'Anglesey, Mother Of
Wales'.[46]

An example of modern regional badges are those issued by UCATT in the 1980s.
All bear the 'chain links' of the national design (symbolising strength through
unity), but many have regionalistic representations, such as the white rose on the
Yorkshire badge, the red dragon on the South Wales badge, the thistle on the
Scottish badge and London Bridge on the London badge. Even a scarce badge of
the Isle of Man branch of the TGWU (produced originally in the early 1930s) was
issued to commemorate the opening of their new offices on the island in 1982,
which bears the three legs of Man design. The technical and scientific union
ASTMS, not known for its proliferation of badges, did in the late 1980s issue

several badges, two of which are for health service branches. This perhaps implies a desire to commemorate the union's separate identity in these areas after the merger with the Technical Administrative and Supervisory Staffs Association (TASS) in January 1988 (now the Manufacturing, Science and Finance Union, MSF). All of this is a far cry from the days when a union would simply issue one national badge. The National Asylum Workers Union for instance, noted in its proposal for a national badge in *The National Asylum Workers Union Magazine* in March, 1914 that

> ... it has been suggested to us that if the union does not soon adopt an official badge, the London County Council section of the union will obtain one of their own! This of course would be an undesirable (and we might add unauthorised) proceeding, and it would be a ridiculous state of affairs for different 'circles' of the union to have different kinds of badges. We must have unity on the badges question as on any other.[47]

One can only wonder at what they would make of the iconographic and symbolic representations that now exist! Even the smallest outposts of empire are not without their unions and badges to represent them. The Gibraltar Taxi Drivers Union and the Falkland Islands General Employees Union (which had 450 members out of a total population of 1,759 in 1975) are two examples.

Important anniversaries have been commemorated in the 1980s and 1990s of the establishment of general unions and trades councils, which have been used as tools through which to reinvoke the traditions and principles on which the movement was traditionally based. Another perspective is offered, at least in the health service, by Andrew Redpath, a UNISON activist and trade union badge collector. During 1997, over twenty health-care branches of UNISON, issued their own badges. Redpath suspects that

> ... the reason for this is either the need to establish a strong separate identity for the union as a health care union or the fact that since the formation of NHS Trusts and local bargaining, branches have taken on more of the roles that were carried out nationally, and the local branch is now much more important within the union and branches are affirming their strong local identity.
>
> It seems that branches are much more likely to produce their own badges now than in the past, when you had to try to get the union to produce badges nationally. The nurses, midwives and health visitors badge produced by North Tyneside has spread to many other Unison branches and is getting national distribution without it being a national badge.[48]

A distinct lack of leadership from the TUC has possibly also caused unions to assert their own points of view at local level. Thatcher sought to alienate the labour movement from the very people who needed it most, portraying it as something detrimental to their interests. Events such as the Manchester Trade Union Week have been efforts at combating this, the badge playing an important role. Handbills and leaflets to the public are seldom read, but the badge invites the curious to question it further.

The localised badges are not then smoke-screens to hide behind, but are weapons to be brandished as a means of drawing strength through tradition, as reasons for continuing the collective organisation, invoking sacrifices of previous generations as moral obligations and incumbencies to resist attack, rather than a retreat, dignified or otherwise. Such badges are perhaps symptomatic of the resurgence of principle and organised discipline. If this is the case, then far from being the end of an epoch, they mark the beginning of a new one, with evangelical fervour. The badge becomes the material representation of the will to fight back, the re-inculcation of past events on the badge is perhaps to underline the thin dividing line between legality and illegality.

In Australia, which is highly federalised, state-issued badges of national federal unions have always been and still are common, many often making local distinction in both wording and imagery. These may be as simple as the fobs issued by unions such as the Grocers Employees Union, Australian Plumbers and Gasfitters Employees Union or Federated Mining Employees Union of Australia, which have stamped on the reverse: 'Property of union' and the initial of the state.[49] The next step up from this is expressed by the Federated Railway Loco Enginemen's Association of Australasia. Between 1904 and 1920, they issued a generic watch chain fob featuring a map of Australia in the centre picturing a train. On the reverse the state emblem was embossed, as opposed to a simple key letter. Until 1920, each state organisation remained autonomous within the association until registration was granted.[50] The Australian Telegraph & Telephone Construction and Maintenance Union on the other hand, went one step further by making the initials of the issuing state the central design of the badge.[51] Other unions such as Australian Timber Workers Union issued badges of their own design, incorporating the state name into the design.[52] The ultimate expression of this distinction, is the different coloured badges of a generic design, each colour representing a separate state. The Australian Tramway and Motor Omnibus Employees Association, in the 1930s and 1940s at least, had each state branch issuing 'a badge with its own initials and different coloured enamels: NSW light blue; Victoria red; Tasmania green'.[53] The Transport Workers Union of Australia in the 1940s and 1950s, issued a generic badge, to which were attached a specific coloured enamel rectangle, denoting the state. Tasmania had an: 'attachment in the shape of Tasmania'.[54] In the 1980s, the Australian Bank Employees Union issued similar badges: light blue South Australia; dark blue Tasmania; green Queensland and Victoria; red New South Wales; white Western Australia. They also issued key rings in these colours.[55] We can see therefore the progression of an assertion of autonomy or at least a strong local identity within the context of the need for a localised control system of membership.

The immediate aftermath of the 1984–85 miners' strike is probably the point at which the phenomenal resurgence of the badge took place in Britain. The miners for years had been the industrial trade unions' front-line troops. In 1972 and 1974 they had emerged victorious, recompense for 1926. In 1984–85 they were defeated, which to the Tories was recompense for 1972–74. The front-line troops had been beaten in the largest industrial dispute since 1926. The rest of the labour movement held its breath, unable to decide what position to adopt. Ideological and strategical concerns were an all-pervading concern in 1980s British trade unionism. The TUC and GMB as examples on one hand (not to mention the extreme example of the former EETPU) determined that the future laid in a sort of 'business unionism', making the union feel 'comfortable', like executive-class suites on airplanes, turning away from rank-and-file resistance, as occurred after 1926. This was reiterated in the 'new unionism' theme of the TUC's 1997 conference, the first under 'New' Labour. On the other hand, a grassroots determination to win through regardless, seeking aesthetic inspiration in the face of so many defeats has also grown since the 1980s. The revival of the theme of historic sacrifice, via the medium of the badge, helps facilitate this. Here, the badge has its role turned full circle, acting to help inaugurate a new generation into the struggle for justice that it was originally produced to uphold (as in the case of the sacked Liverpool dockers, who contrasted strongly with the suits and mobile phones of many delegates at the 1997 TUC conference), and acting 'as a useful conversation piece in recruitment work'[566] as it originally did.

The trade union badge of the 1980s seemed to symbolise either a desperate attempt to instil meaning into a flagging union movement, increasingly at odds over its aims and objectives, or an almost evangelical revival of self-confidence and self-assurance, and in so doing seemed to mark either the end of one epoch or the beginning of another, depending on the standpoint adopted. The 1990s witnessed the further decline of traditional industries, most vividly symbolised by Heseltine's pit closure programme of 1992 and its aftermath (evocatively dramatised in the film *Brassed Off*), and the election of a business-friendly 'New' Labour government. Indeed, by 1999, Trade Union Printing Services (TUPS) had been formed: 'TUPS Books was founded by redundant miners and shipyard workers who, by producing books which chronicle the social history of the North of England, have provided themselves and others with jobs.'[57] Here, what was so recently the daily working lives of so many has now been remarketed as glossy illustrated books, the covers of which picture shipyards and coal mines at sunset, in the same style as the National Trust or natural history photography, or which could also be seen allegorically as the sun setting on their particular industries. As a means of survival, and an attempt to ensure employment we all become tourists even of our own lives. The examples of spin doctoring and the heritage industry have been learned well here. In the spring of 1999, TUPS published the first issue of a magazine on the life, history and culture of North-East miners and mining, *Bands And Banners*, titled after the most commonly associated image of North-East mining. Thus, the Durham 'big meeting' which by its 110th anniversary in 1993 was virtually dead as a celebration of a living industry, found regeneration as a re-enactment ceremony, and was vigorously remarketed as a tourist attraction instead.

Many veterans from the labour disputes of the 1980s have found as much to protest about under 'New' Labour as they had under the Conservatives. At present, the TUC's new realism/new unionism of the 1980s and 1990s seems to be dominant overall, but in a still changing and ever shifting labour environment, there is everything to play for. As knowledge becomes the new currency, and as the notion of 'the citizen' is increasingly narrowly defined by technological knowledge, material ownership and the will to personal financial investment, the marginalised increase in number. The fallout from this is still to be tested, but if recent critiques are anything to go by[58] the campaigning zeal of the 1980s may have been just a foretaste of bigger things to come. As globalisation and Standardisation[59] move on apace with ever expanding international corporate amalgamations (for example, in retailing, supermarkets, e-commerce, etc.), so trade unions have sought to respond. One example takes us back to the 1890s, when the American Knights of Labor organised in Britain. By 1999, the American union, the Association of Flight Attendants, was recruiting members at London's Heathrow Airport, and as such had affiliated to the British TUC.

Having explored the cultural and aesthetic aspects of the badge, the technical processes and innovations that produce them will now be given some consideration in Chapter 5.

Notes

1   Billy Bragg, singer/songwriter, 1980s.
2   For a general overview of the history, development and uses of the button badge, see Setchfield, *The Official Badge Collectors' Guide.*
3   P. Peacock, *Buttons For The Collector*, Bath, David & Charles, 1972, p. 80.
4   Ibid., p. 82.
5   Gorman, *Banner Bright*, p. 48.
6   It should be noted however, no badges were issued for the fifteenth anniversary in 1999. Rick Sumner of the Justice For Mineworkers Campaign, through whom most of the NUM badges are now sold for fund-raising purposes, explains that it was not possible to find a British badge manufacturer who would have the badges made in Britain rather than China where labour costs are cheaper and non-union (personal communication, 1999).
7   For example, see M. Merritt, 'Your Verdict on Craze that's big Business', Brighton *Evening Argus*, 17 September 1979, pp. 2–3.
8   If anything, the situation is worse today. Recent high media profile cases of fatal racial and suspected racial attacks include Stephen Lawrence, Michael Menson, Ricky Reel, and Howard and Jason McGowan.
9   D. Widgery, (1986) *Beating Time: Riot 'n' Race 'n Rock 'n' Roll,* London, Chatto & Windus.
10   There is a copious literature on the history and course of the 1984–85 miners' strike and its aftermath. The following are a selective but representative selection. 1).National studies: L. Sutcliffe and B. Hill, *Let Them Eat Coal: the political use of social security*

during the miners strike, London, Canary Press, 1985; P. Wilsher, D. Macintyre and M. Jones, *Strike – 358 days That Shook The Nation: a battle of ideologies Thatcher, Scargill and the Miners*, London, Coronet, 1985; D.Reed and A. Adamson, *Miners Strike 1984–1985: people versus the state*, London Larkin Publications 1985, S. Milne, *The Enemy Within: the secret war against the miners*, London, Pan, 1994. Local studies: A.Thornett (ed.), *The Miners Strike In Oxford*, Oxford, Oxford Miners Strike Support Group, 1985, J. Williams, N. Dickinson and L. Jaddou, *Hanging On By Our Fingernails: the struggle at Lea Hall Colliery 1984–1987*, Nottingham, Spokesman Books, 1987. Photo-texts: R. Huddle, A. Phillips, M. Simons and J. Sturrock, *Blood Sweat And Tears: photographs from the great miners strike 1984–1985*, London, Artworker Books, 1985; I. Jedrzejczyk, R. Page, B. Prince and I. Young, *Striking Women:communities and coal*, London, Pluto Press, 1986; C. Salt and J. Layzell, *Here We Go! women's memories of the 1984–85 miners strike*, London, Co-operative Retail Services Ltd, 1985.

11   For examples, see the collection of National Museum of Labour History, Manchester and Seaton, *Justice For Mineworkers Badge Collectors' Guide*.

12   For examples, see, for example, N. Clark, 'Worn with Pride Union Badges', *Labour Research*, 1987, February, pp. 19–20.

13   TUC collection, London.

14   Which is the same thing, not to be confused with the militancy of that term as applied to the 1890s.

15   Smith, *Emblems Of Unity*, p. 239.

16   Leeson, *United We Stand*, pp. 39, 68. Between 1879 and 1889 three concerted efforts were made by branches to have an emblem made, but not until 1897 were they successful.

17   This of course mimics the corporate rebranding of formally identifable industries such as British Steel as Corus; British Gas as Centrica and for business purposes at least, the Post Office as Consignia. See, e.g. the Midlands commuter free paper *Metro*, 1 January 2001, p. 15.

18   Clark, 'Worn with Pride ...', p. 20.

19   See L. Malvern, *The End of the Street*, London, Methuen, 1986 for a full account of the dispute.

20   For example, the long-running lockout and dismissal-based disputes at Keetings and Senior Colemans engineering companies, and Morris Curtains in the 1980s. There were many others.

21   J. Pilger, 'They Never Walk Alone', *Guardian Weekend*, 23 November 1996, pp. 14–23; S. Miller, 'Reminder Of Old-Fashioned Struggle', *Guardian*, 10 September 1996; S. Milne, 'Uphill Struggle For Forgotten Strikers'; *Guardian* 1997, reproduced in *Trade Union Badge Collectors' Newsletter*, No. 61, September 1997. See also the television documentary *Dockers: Writing The Wrongs* and the dramatisation of the dispute *Dockers,* both screened on Channel Four, 11 July 1999.

22   Milne, 'Uphill Struggle ...'; A. Beckett, 'Poles Apart At Magnet', *Guardian G2*, 16 March 1998, pp. 1–3.

23   Milne 'Uphill Struggle ...'.

24   Ibid.

25   S. Milne, 'Battered Unions Cut Adrift', *Guardian,* 14 September 1996, p. 1; S. Milne 'How Unions Found They Were On The Menu', *Guardian Comment*, 14 September

1996, p. 3. See also 'Blair and the TUC', *Guardian Comment*, 14 September 1996; 'Union Dues', A. Culf, 'BBC Drama Puts Labour In A Spin', *Guardian*, 14 September 1996; *Guardian Weekend*, (letters page) 7 December 1996.

26   R. Thomas and T. Hunter, 'Unions Strike Out In New Direction', *Guardian Jobs and Money*, 7 September 1996, pp. 1–3.

27   M. Halsall, 'Monks Aims At 5m "Union Wannabes"', *Guardian*, 10 September 1996, p. 8.

28   Beckett 'Poles Apart At Magnet', p. 3. Other expressions of contemporary worker dissatisfaction are expressed humorously and subversively; a Rotherham gardener, unfairly sacked during the winter for instance, sewed bedding plants in such a way as to spell out the word 'Bollocks' come the spring. *Trade Union Badge Collectors' Newsletter*, No. 70, January, 2000. Elsewhere, 30 staff made redundant at the Ibstock Himley brick plant, near Dudley, on being instructed by management 'to make sure the last batch of bricks were up to scratch before leaving', produced 30,000 bricks with the same expletive impressed in their surface. They were distributed to the company's customers before the prank was realised, *Guardian*, 29 March 2000.

29   See Gorman, *Images of Labour*, p. 33 for illustration and history.

30   *Labour*, August, 1949, p. 269.

31   See A. Redpath in *Trade Union Badge Collectors' Newsletter*, No. 68, Summer, 1999.

32   L.Tickner, *The Spectacle Of Women: images of the suffrage movement 1907–1914*, London, Chatto & Windus, 1987; T. Campbell, *100 years of Women's Banners* (second edition), Dyfed, Wales, Women For Life On Earth, 1990; D. Atkinson, *The Purple, White and Green: suffragettes in London 1906–1914*, London, Museum of London, 1992; T. Campbell and M. Wilson, *Each For All and All For Each: a celebration of co-operative banners*, Manchester National Co-operative Education Association, 1994.

33   I. McDonald, *Vindication! A Postcard History of the Women's Movement*, London, Bellew Publishing, 1989.

34   Devine, 'Who Dares', p. 60.

35   'Spooning Up History With A Selhurst Veteran'.

36   Which is reproduced as the frontispiece of the book on their history. See N.H. Cuthbert, *The Lacemakers Society*, Nottingham, Amalgamated Society of Lace Makers and Auxilliary Workers, 1960.

37   A. Marsh, V. Ryan and J. Smethurst, *Historical Directory of Trade Unions Volume 4*, Aldershot, Scolar Press, 1994, p. 480. For further reference to women's representation in labour history and women's iconography, see E. Hobsbawm, 'Man and Woman in Socialist Iconography', *History Workshop Journal*, 1978, No. 6, Autumn, pp. 121–138; S. Alexander, A. Davin and E. Hostettler, 'Labouring Women: a reply to Eric Hobsbawm', *History Workshop Journal*, 1979, No. 8 pp. 174–182; A. Davin, 'Feminism and Labour History' in R. Samuel (ed.), *People's History and Socialist Theory*, London, Routledge, 1981, pp. 176–181; L. Tickner, *The Spectacle of Women* ...

38   P. Martin, 'The National Union of Domestic Workers', *Trade Union Badge Collectors' Newsletter*, No. 35, 1992, October, p. 11.

39   Ibid.

40   For a further example of such negative action in the labour movement in this period, see M. Dresser, 'The Colour Bar In Bristol, 1963', in R. Samuel (ed.), *Patriotism: The Making and Unmaking of British National Identity, Volume 1: History and Politics*, London, Routledge, 1989, pp. 288–316.

41   J. Rose, *One Hundred Years of King's Cross Aslef*, London, King's Cross branch ASLEF, London, 1986, p. 48.

42   *Morning Star*, 23 June 1987.

43   The Mond–Turner talks were held between Sir Alfred Mond of ICI representing the employers and Ben Turner of the TUC in 1927 in the aftermath of the 1926 General Strike. The purpose was to find a way of avoiding such a situation again by finding more effective machinery for unions and employers to settle differences. The talks came to little especially against the background of vindictive Conservative anti-trade union legislation in 1927 which remained on the statute book until after the Second World War.

44   For further reference to these and other Irish-related trade union badges, see the leaflet issued for the exhibition *In Solidarity*, held at The Ulster Museum, Belfast from 7 February to 22 April 1984.

45   D. Pretty, *The Rural Revolt That Failed*, p. 105.

46   For the union's full history, see D. Pretty, 'Undeb Gweithwyr Mon: Anglesey Workers Union (Part One)', *Transactions of the Anglesey Antiquarian Society and Field Club*, 1988, pp. 115–148; D. Pretty, 'Undeb Gweithwyr Mon: Anglesey Workers Union (Part Two)', *Transactions of the Anglesey Antiquarian Society and Field Club*, 1989, pp. 43–79; D. Pretty, *The Rural Revolt That Failed*.

47   This, though, cannot have been a unanimous view in the labour movement, even at that time, as an 'East Coast District' key chain fob exists of the National Union Of Gas Workers and General Labourers, based in Hull, dating from between 1889–1916 (See K. Sinclair, op. cit.).

48   A. Redpath, personal communication, 13 January 1998.

49   Smith, *Emblems Of Unity*, pp. 160, 67, 130.

50   Ibid., pp. 134–135.

51   Ibid., p. 75.

52   Ibid., p. 79.

53   Ibid., p. 81.

54   Ibid., p. 240.

55   Ibid., pp. 45–46.

56   'Trade Union Badges', *Man and Metal*, 1965, November, pp. 326 327.

57   Trade Union Printing Services publicity sheet, 1999.

58   For example, W. Hutton, *The State We're In,* London: Jonathan Cape, 1995; C. Lasch, *The Revolt of The Elites And The Betrayal Of Democracy*, New York: Norton Publishers, 1995.

59   See G. Ritzer, *The MacDonaldization Of Society* (new millennium edition), London, Sage, 2000. Ritzer shows how the rise of the MacDonald's fast food chain has become universally adopted as a model for the global standardisation of industrial and commercial process, practice and employment, etc.

Chapter 5

The Manufacturers

[The] Token of Thanks [badge]: 'was produced by Billy Seaton / Steve Peak in 1985. The badge was produced so that people could buy supporters [of the miners during the 1984/5 strike] the badges as a way of saying thank you. The centre of the badge depicts a miner holding his wife, girlfriend, daughter or supporter which speaks for itself. There may be plans to produce the badge in solid silver in 1987 but this depends on orders'.[1]

Mention has been made in Chapter 1 of the role of George Tutill's company in badge production. The whole question of manufacturers, however, is still sorely under-researched.[2] In the 1980s, many enamel badge manufacturers resided in the jewellery quarter of Birmingham, in which city there were estimated to be some fifty companies.[3] Many are old established firms such as J.R. Gaunt established in the 1750s. There have been numerous badge-producing firms, many of which remain largely unknown, such as Denton and Down; Caville; Simpson and Collins; Jewellery Metal Company, Dublin; London Badge; L. Simpson & Co. Ltd., London; Coffer Ltd., London and Northampton; Firmin, London; and Collins, London.[4] Many of these are now only names on the reverse of badges, but more investigation could yield another Tutill's and supply valuable information on the badge's origin. It is known that the firm of Henry Slingsby of Nuneaton produced many badges for friendly societies for instance, but little else. Some manufacturers, like H.B. Sale of Constitution Hill, Birmingham, are known largely from old adverts in the labour press.[5] Some like H.W. Miller, ceased trading in the early 1960s; others, like John Pinches of London (who ceased producing badges in the early 1970s) were absorbed by other companies (in the latter case, by the American Franklin Mint, in order to manufacturer artistic medals). Famous Birmingham badge companies often found on the reverse of badges include: A.E.W.; The Birmingham Medal & Badge Co.; Butler; Gladman & Norman; J.R. Gaunt Ltd; W.O. Lewis (Badges) Ltd.; Manhattan Windsor Ltd; Marples and Beasley; Parry; T.N. Priest & Co.; Vaughtons; W. Reeves & Co.; R.E.V. Gomm and Morton T. Colver.[6] One of these companies, R.E.V. Gomm, printed a detailed account of the manufacturing process of enamel badges. First, the process of design and creation of the die:

The manufacture usually commences initially with a coloured drawing to the actual size for the customers' inspection, which after approval reaches the hands of the die sinker, who cuts the required outline, in reverse, on plastic sheet, enlarged five times, so that as far as it's practical all details can be incorporated. This outline is then transferred by a reducing pantograph machine to the face of the actual soft metal die, a piece of cylindrical steel, and appropriate areas cut away. The lines and letters that will appear in metal on the badge being flush with the surface and the areas to contain the enamel being recessed and matted, the finished die on completion being treated and hardened. The die is now ready to receive the metal for stamping, which is carried out, either on a manually assisted drop stamp or a hydraulic press, the latter being more suitable for larger quantities. The material used is gilding metal, comprising 90% copper and 10% zinc, any higher proportion of the latter resulting in melting during firing and if pure copper is used, transparent enamels such as red will assume appearance due to the darkening of the copper when heated. In the case of a new die, a clipping tool will now be required to cut the badge to shape. This is made by hand sawing a stamping to shape, fixing to the end of a metal punch, which is machined to the outline. A tool bed is then made into which the stamping will rest and into which the punch will pass, this operation being accomplished in a hand press, the shaped badges dropping through the bed. Fittings to retain the pins on the reverse are then soldered in place on the stampings which are cleaned in acid, ready for enamelling.

Second, the enamelling and finishing process:

Enamel is a form of glass, obtained in powdered form, which is mixed with water to form a paste and placed with a pen into the appropriate sections of the badge for the particular colour required and fired onto the metal with a hand held gun, from below, until the enamel visually fuses. It is not usually possible to coat multi-coloured badges with more than two colours simultaneously, as spillage may occur between the sections, so the badges are cleaned between each firing in acid, to ensure that the surface is free from scale thus allowing the colours in the subsequent firing to fuse cleanly. The coloured badge now presents a lumpy appearance, with no letters or lines visible, this being rectified by careful grinding on an endless band to remove the surplus enamel from the metal areas and results in a flat surface to the badge. The final enamel process is to fire once again, so that the surface of the enamel runs thus eliminating the scratch marks of the grinding process.

Pins are now inserted into the fittings, the metal areas are polished on a circular electric mop to smooth the grinding scratches on the metal areas. The articles are then electroplated in either chromium or gilt finish, this process only depositing the finish on the metal areas leaving the coloured enamel untouched. The badges are now ready for inspection and despatch.

The quality and precision with which some older badges were made is exemplary of the engravers' and enamellers' art. As Greg Smith wrote in his introduction to his book on Australian trade union badges:

When the small scale is considered, who could not be impressed by the intricate details on the locomotive and viaduct on the 1892 issue of the NSW Locomotive Engine Drivers and Cleaners Association; or the image of the actor on the stage, complete with scenery and footlights, as issued by the Australian Federated Theatrical Employees Association;

or the ornate design incorporating the old-fashioned lace-up boot of the Australian Boot Trade Employees Federation?[7]

Some 550 fine examples of the pre-1940 enamel badge makers' art are to be found, in colour, in one recent publication, many of which are 'delicate cut-out figural badges with rich and colourful enamelling, often with contrasting and transparent and opaque enamels, which included relief moulding, below the enamelled surface, lending realism to the badge's design'.[8]

The firm of Toye, was established in 1685, and was once the major rival to Tutill's for banners. The firm was established by Guillaume Toye, a Huguenot weaver who escaped to London disguised as a cattle dealer, at the time of Louis XIV's purge of French Protestants. He settled in Bethnal Green (then Hope Town) and made his name by weaving glistening embellishments for military uniforms. With the introduction of the rifle, however, this stopped as such adornments became easy targets when worn. A descendant, William Toye's eldest son, built a new factory at Bethnal Green and 'started producing regalia [in the late nineteenth century] beautifully embroidered and hand-painted banners and ornamental sashes for friendly societies and the emergent trade unions'.[9] In the 1890s, the firm also turned to metal work and began making trophies and medals. In 1956, the firm of George Kenning and Spencer was taken over by Toye to form what is today Toye, Kenning and Spencer.[10]

The firm of Fattorini had a near monopoly on trade union badges at one time, its name being found on the back of more badges than any other; it had offices in many parts of the country. The Fattorini family in fact had two distinct firms competing with each other, Fattorini and Sons Ltd. and Thomas Fattorini Ltd: 'Both firms bought most of their vast stocks of badges from Birmingham factories, and both were large enough to insist on having the name "Fattorini" stamped on what they sold'.[11] Frank Setchfield's research has revealed that the addresses given on the reverse of Fattorini badges can help date them. He provides the following list:

Fattorini and Sons, Bradford (up to 1916)
Fattorini and Sons, Barr Street, Birmingham (1916–1983)
I. Fattorini, Skipton (1886)
T. Fattorini, Skipton (1886–1934)
T. Fattorini, Preston (1903–1928, shop)
T. Fattorini, Hockley Street, Birmingham (c.1916–1927)
T. Fattorini, Regenet Street, Birmingham (1927 to date)
Frank Fattorini, Birmingham (A breakaway from T. Fatorini which ceased trading in the 1970s, exact dates unknown)
A. Fattorini, Harrogate (1931) (A shop, still trading, but not currently involved in making badges).[12]

An information leaflet published by the firm of Thomas Fattorini in the 1980s, gives further details (see Appendix 4). The complexity of dates and family members presumably seeking to strike out on their own makes it difficult to pinpoint exact dating. Records in the Public Record Office (PRO) do however show that Thomas Fattorini had registered a firm in Knowsley Street, Bolton, Lancashire by June 1914, and by November 1917 had premises in Caroline Square, Skipton; Hockley Street, Birmingham and Holborn, London. A Mr John Robert Griffin seems to have become proprietor of at least some of these premises, according to a deed of application, dated 25 March 1920. We also find in the PRO, a certificate to the firm of Walter Francis Gaunt of Warstone Parade Works, Birmingham, granting a second five-year extension of copyright, although on what is uncertain, on 5 September 1922.[13]

These and other firms have been making badges for many years. In a survey by *Labour Research,* it was found that the firms of Gaunt and Marple and Beasley, at least, did recognise unions, whilst Fattorini's had no trade union recognition, but did not think it relevant even though they had been making the TUC's and other unions' badges for many years.[14] Fattorini in fact, made many of the Durham lodge NUM strike badges. Rumour has it that once the lodges discovered that Fattorini was a non-union firm and indeed contributed financially to the Conservative Party, they withdrew their orders, and allegedly in some cases returned the badges unpaid for. In an article in the *TGWU Record,* the outsourcing of badge production to Third World countries and the slave labour used to make the badges was attacked: 'Some unions preach one thing, calling for the use of organised labour, and practise another by using suppliers who use and exploit cheap foreign or non union labour. This can put good union members on the dole.'[15] In at least one instance it is reported that Fattorini's were guilty of this practice. Rick Sumner, the chair of the National Justice For Mine Workers Campaign

> ... tells of the time when the GCHQ campaigners asked a company called Fxxxxxxi if the badges would be made in the UK. They were assured that they were and the order went ahead. Some time later they asked for the dies back! They were told it would be very difficult and expensive to have it sent back from East Asia![16]

Given the emphasis that has been placed on clamping down on child exploitation in Third World countries on an international level, this seems to be an oversight too close to home to ignore.

The comparatively new firms that issued many union badges in the 1980s were Adams Badges of Finsbury Park, London and Badges Plus in Birmingham. Adams seem to have issued the majority of the ASLEF badges made by branches since 1980, of which there have been several hundred. Badges Plus was set up in 1976 by two brothers, Stephen and John Peak, both of whom at one time worked for Fattorini's, and whose work force is fully unionised, although in more than one union.[17] Badges Plus have issued around three-quarters of the badges for miners and supporters, issued both during and after the 1984/5 miners' strike.[18] Other manufacturers issuing them were Fattorini's, mainly in Durham; Marples and

Beasley, mainly in Nottinghamshire. Adams Badges and Reeves also made some.[19] The Peaks' father was a member of the AEU for forty years and active in the Labour Party.[20]

They have pioneered a sort of three-dimensional effect for their badges, by using a softer gilding metal and also by using surface paints to colour the metal borders that define the design of the badge. During the miners' strike they issued badges to the miners in advance, receiving payment once they had sold them themselves. Their first union issue was for the National Union of Tailors & Garment Workers in 1976. Most of the artwork is provided by the clients and the badges can be made any size, from that of a match head upwards. Stephen Peak estimated in 1987 that forty per cent of all the company's work was derived from trade unions and that as much as eighty per cent of new business came from trade unions.[21] In 1998, Badges Plus were manufacturing '1000 to 3000 badges a day according to the complexity of the design'.[22]

During the miners' strike, the graphics department at *The Morning Star* was used to produce large tin badges sent directly to the picket lines and to visiting delegations to London. This made available imagery and propaganda serving as a morale booster in a very short space of time.[23] Another group arising from the situation in the 1980s was the 'Strike Graphics' cooperative which emerged during the 1986/87 Wapping dispute. They produced badges and other items for the pickets for fundraising. After the end of the dispute they decided to continue as a co-operative making badges and publicity items for the broad left of the labour movement.[24] Badges had become relatively costly to produce, especially in small numbers, but with the development of the cooperative, and more widespread distribution, they became a vital part of the trade union movement in its campaign to rejuvenate and defend itself against the Thatcherite onslaught. With new competition to the established manufactures emanating from below, and from the labour movement itself, the concept of the enamel badge and cheaply produced iconography has been revived.

An ordinary gilt and enamel badge throughout the 1990s was generally sold by the union for between fifty pence and five pounds depending on the level of subsidy granted (if any), the manufacturer used and the quantity ordered. For instance, an advert for the embroidered blazer badge of the Amalgamated Society of Woodcutting Machinists, dating from between the 1930s and 1950s, was at pains to point out that: 'This is a service to members and without making any profit whatever we are retailing these badges at 6s 6d each.'[25] In the 1980s, with the National Union of Public Employees (NUPE) at least, the issuing of badges could be a contentious issue. Motions were proposed for the free issue of badges to all new members as an aid to recruitment. Opposition was based largely on the cost of doing so. An opponent to the free issue of badges at the 1980 conference also claimed that 'What is more, I am sure that if these badges are given to everyone they will be chucked in a drawer and you will see little kids wearing them in the street.'[26] Also at the 1980 conference, the finance secretary noted that 'Doubt has been expressed as to whether, if a badge was issued to every new member, he should actually wear it. With our present system of selling badges, we sell at approximately a third of the cost, our net expenditure at the moment comes to about £7,200 per annum.' The motion was defeated that year.[27] At NUPE's 1982 conference, the assistant finance secretary stated 'The cost of one badge to the union is 26p plus postage, plus stationary, plus VAT. It costs about 30p per badge and we sell them at 10p, so there is a net loss to the union of 20p per badge.' Amid allegations that if NUPE's executive committee stayed in cheaper hotels at conference time and curtailed their fraternal foreign visits to other unions, the cost of issuing the badges gratis to new members would easily be affordable, the motion was carried.[28] At the 1988 conference, a motion moved by Stockton Hospital Branch called for the introduction of a round 'deluxe' as opposed to the then current small, pointed triangular-shaped badge for the reasons stated in Chapter 3. The assistant finance secretary at this time noted 'In 1981 we were spending about £27,000 a year on badges; 1983 £50,000; and if this was implemented, it would be about £100,000.'[29] However, the motion for the provision of a free round badge was carried. The cost to unions as clients can be anything from thirty pence to four pounds per piece, depending on the firm used and an additional cost for the engraving of a die from which to strike the badges may also be charged for separately.[30] As the small independents challenge the established firms, the costs may fall even further. What direction the enamel badge may take is uncertain, but at the moment there seems very little that could challenge it in simplicity, durability and versatility. The upsurge of collectors of trade union badges from within the movement over the last decade has shown the desire for iconography and the reclaiming of one's own history as represented by it. This forms the content of the next chapter.

Notes

1   Seaton, *Justice For Mineworkers*, p. 6.
2   For information on the manufacturing process, materials and the development of badge-making technology etc., see Setchfield, *The Official Badge Collectors' Guide*, pp. 1–21.
3   Interview with Stephen Peak of Badges Plus, 1987.
4   Setchfield, *The Official Badge Collectors' Guide*, p. 15.
5   A pictorial advert for H.B. Sale appeared in a 1914 issue of the *Daily Herald*, and ran for several weeks, reproduced in the *Trade Union Badge Collectors' Newsletter*, No. 73, Autumn, 2000.
6   Setchfield, *The Official Badge Collectors' Guide*, p. 14.
7   Smith, *Emblems Of Unity*, p. 16.
8   Sequin, *The Graphic Art of the Enamel Badge*, p. 8.
9   Toye Kenning and Spencer information leaflet, 1986.
10 Ibid.

11   P. Carter, 'Finding And Collecting Enamelled Badges', *Treasure Hunting*, 1995a, January, p. 30.
12   Setchfield, *The Official Badge Collectors' Guide*, p. 14.
13   PRO BT/53/30; Cert No. 638232; BT 53/56; Cert No. 662341; Cert No. 662342; my thanks to Joe Fleming for providing this information.
14   Clark, 'Worn With Pride', p. 20.
15   M. Pentelow, 'Badger The Non-Union Badge Makers Out of Business', *TGWU Record*, 1997, December, p. 30.
16   P. Carter, *Trade Union Badge Collectors' Newsletter*, No. 63, May, p. 3.
17   Peak, interview, 1987.
18   Sadly, a few years ago however, Badges Plus decided to sue the NUM for non-payment of monies owed (R. Sumner, personal communication, 25 January 1999).
19   This is based on the named manufacturers on the reverse of some four hundred badges issued for the NUM between 1984 and 1988. It was rumoured at the time, that the miners' strike had actually saved one Birmingham manufacturer (where most badge manufacturers are based) from bankruptcy (Clark, 'Worn With Pride', p. 20).
20   Peak, interview.
21   Ibid.
22   Pentelow, 'Badger The Non-Union Badge Makers', p. 30.
23   Sid Brown, *Morning Star*, personal communication, 1985.
24   Strike Graphics leaflet, 1987.
25   Reproduced in *Trade Union Badge Collectors' Newsletter*, No. 44, 1994, June.
26   NUPE 1980 Report, p. 332.
27   Ibid., p. 331.
28   NUPE 1982 Report, p. 382.
29   NUPE 1988 Report, p. 367.
30   Peak, interview, 1987; Clark 'Worn With Pride', p. 20.

Chapter 6

Collect and Display: Post Function

For one thing, it [the industrial revolution] transformed and expanded the range of items treated as collectibles. The phenomenon of aestheticization of the obsolete was made possible by the Industrial Revolution, notably by the rise of a newly prosperous bourgeoisie, which led to a widespread new interest in objects for the home, and to the democratisation of collecting, once the province of kings, princes and the Church.[1]

The emblems of the union became multifarious and more outwardly displayed as trade union confidence and membership grew from the 1940s. This is demonstrated through the numerous large metal car badges designed to be fixed to the radiator grill and the often elaborately embroidered, woven blazer pocket badges which also flourished in post-war years with unions as diverse as the Boilermakers Society and NALGO. The National Union of Agricultural Workers even had two kinds of car badge: 'one with a standard, the other with a grill type fixing'. At 35 shillings each, an advert in a 1963 issue of the union's paper *Landworker* advised 'those who would like both types to decorate their cars and advertise the union, should write to head office.' From the 1950s, ties, cufflinks and headscarves bearing the union logos began to make an appearance. From here, developed the contemporary T-shirts, sweatshirts and baseball caps sporting union slogans and motifs, no doubt inspired by transatlantic innovations, as Britain became more Americanised after the Second World War.

In 1994, to commemorate the tenth anniversary of the great miners' strike of 1984/85, a large art-quality poster was produced which pictured over two hundred lapel badges from every pit that had been closed under successive Conservative governments. These came from the collection of just one ex-miner. That, by this point, the lapel badge could have come to take on such significance, not just as an utilitarian object in the workplace, but as highly symbolic and often emotive collectable is a story in itself. The growth in the collecting of trade union badges is a part of the burgeoning of contemporary collecting at all levels during the 1980s and 1990s.[2] The very term 'labour history' is itself highly unstable, and what is encompassed by it is hotly contested.[3] Some academics and museum practitioners shy away from the term altogether, protesting its inadequacy, whilst others never recognised or engaged with it in the first place. There is a preference instead, to talk about the history of work,[4] which it is felt is less exclusive.

Collectors

There would seem to have been badge collectors since antiquity. Writing on the cult of Saint George, one author notes that:

> The survival of pilgrim badges probably bought at Windsor may suggest that St. George was venerated by a wide social mix during the late medieval period, for these relatively cheap devotional objects would have been affordable to all but the poorest people. However, it is difficult to know whether the survivals of such tokens reflects a genuine groundswell of popular interest in an individual saint, for pilgrims are known to have amassed the badges of shrines as a kind of hobby, just as some people today collect badges from towns and countries they have visited without necessarily feeling any real regard for each particular place.[5]

We know also that there have been collectors of labour ephemera in the past. We know of Walter Southgate, who began collecting trade union ephemera in 1905, and Henry Fry who began doing likewise during the Second World War, because they were founders of the National Museum of Labour History (NMLH).[6] We also get glimpses into the otherwise undocumented collecting activities of people like Will Sherwood, a veteran member of the National Union of General and Municipal Workers, who had by 1937, been collecting minerals and gems for forty years, and who had a 'practically complete collection of British trade union badges'.[7] One or two of today's trade union badge collectors began in the 1950s and 1960s.[8] Historically, how many other individuals have been engaged in collecting the material culture of the trade union movement is open to conjecture. The chinks of light shed accidentally on the incidental records of lives of ordinary people as above, suggest that it is not an entirely recent activity, although as a 'phenomenon' which it has become since the miners' strike of 1984/85, in Britain at least, it probably is so.[9]

By the 1970s, a core group of some dozen serious collectors were in regular contact and were actively seeking out trade union badges. Around 1981, there was an early attempt at a collectors' organisation, which met a number of times at the NMLH when still based in Limehouse Town Hall, London, but the group failed to take off. By 1985, however, there was a sufficient popular collecting interest to start a bimonthly newsletter, the *Trade Union Badge Collectors' Newsletter* (TUBCNL). National meetings were later arranged, and the organisation became known as the Trade Union Badge Collectors' Society (TUBCS). The upsurge in the collecting of trade union badges had come about principally because of the nature of Thatcherite economic policy which saw the running down of traditional industries and the rise of commerce. This was most notably highlighted by the miners' strike of 1984/85, an event which led many people to collect trade union badges, as travelling miners and supporters made and exchanged badges as symbols of solidarity and remembrance. One collector, Andy Smith, who had been a trade union member since 1966, began collecting trade union badges after the 'People's March For Jobs' passed through his home town of Loughborough in 1981. A local newspaper article reported 'His interest developed into something of a passion at the time of the miners' strike when badges were produced to raise money for strike relief.'[10] Another collector, Bill Patterson, began collecting after he became a full-time trade union officer with the Iron and Steel Trades Confederation in 1988. He would meet officers from other unions who would give him badges as fraternal tokens. He states as his reasons for collecting:

> It's a hobby, it's interesting, it's history, it's research, it's fun. It keeps me sane and helps me unwind. On high moral ground it's saving working class history which in most instances gets thrown in the dustbin and lost to future generations. It's not about completing the *set*, as that's impossible. It's about a sense of pride in *my* movement. [emphasis in original]

The seemingly serendipitous nature of collecting is often subconsciously conditioned by other experiences which collecting exemplifies in material terms. Sometimes it seems not to be so, such as the young man converted to socialism by 'reading copies of the socialist paper *Forward* left by his neighbours for use in the communal staircase toilet!'[11]

Both liberals and the left continually made comparisons between Thatcherism, and the 1930s and hunger marches, etc. The significance of the miners' struggle in contemporary terms caused many to reflect on this and project their feelings onto the iconography of labour's past. In so doing, they sought to preserve it by collecting its ephemera, principally the badges.[12] It is perhaps easy to forget now how complete Thatcherism's grip on the country appeared in the mid-1980s. First, the Falklands War of 1982, in conjunction with Thatcher and Tebbit's crackdown on unemployment benefits at the time, had caused many younger people to wonder if military conscription was not far off. Second, Thatcher's regime adopted a total anti-union stance. This, as mentioned in Chapter 4, witnessed numerous cases of employer-manipulated strikes in order to get the workforce out of the building, declare them sacked, and then replace them with cheaper, non-union labour with the blessing of Thatcherite labour law. Many trade union activists started collecting badges and symbols of the movement as a result. Collecting served first as a way of physically preserving the memory and motivations of trade unions, in a period in which it was feared that they could at any time be made illegal (which happened at GCHQ in 1984).[13] In addition, collecting was a way of reaffirming faith and belief in the principles and causes of trade unions to the self, of which collecting is a psychological extension.[14] We seek to manifest physically the imperatives and concerns, values and principles that we feel and hold, so we can project onto them externally those same ideas, and have them reflected back at us, as a means of reassurance of their legitimacy. Most often this happens when we perceive a decline or loss of those values, or the threat of radical change to our accepted social and personal norms. Hence we discover one reason why popular collecting in general burgeoned in the 1980s and 1990s, and why trade union badge collecting became so popular from the mid-1980s onwards. Steve Lynch, a collector from Hull of both trade union and bus company badges, is a good example of this tendency:

> I started collecting bus company badges mostly because my father had been a trolley bus driver in Hull in the 1960s, and with all the changes since, I realised that soon there would be nothing left to remember those days by ... I simply collect badges for the interest. They are a piece of history and something which I feel should be preserved.[15]

Parting with a collection which has been painstakingly built up over many years again exemplifies the way in which collections are regarded as an extension of ourselves and a physical manifestation of our values. Nick Wetton, one of the original group of modern collectors of trade union badges, found in 1990, that with the arrival of a new baby, he needed a new house. To raise the deposit he resolved to sell his collection by auction at Glendinning's in London. He confessed:

> To be honest, I was really sick about it. I did not dare go to the badge sale. I would have changed my mind and asked the auctioneer to withdraw them. I began collecting in 1975 and I had reached about 2,500 badges. Many of them were from smaller craft unions which have now gone out of existence, either through amalgamation or winding up. The collection represented a big chunk of my life. The badges from unions which have gone out of existence have now largely disappeared from the collectors' market and many people know nothing at all about them. When I first began collecting, there were not many people interested in union badges. It was throwaway material costing virtually nothing from the junk boxes of dealers' stalls. For years, a friend and I had a stall at Charring Cross market in London and a lot of my material came from there. It was a blow when the site was sold for redevelopment and the dealers had to relocate at London Bridge and Camden Passage.[16]

In collecting generally, it is not so much about finding something, as the hunt for it, what Susan Pearce has usefully termed 'the kiss of possession'.[17] Like a kiss, the process of making a find must be repeated in order to enjoy it anew, because in itself, the moment of discovery cannot be made to last. Ruth and Edmund Frow demonstrate this in their account of a long search for a copy of Gammage's *History Of The Chartist Movement*, a book which they had often asked for, but believed they would never find:

> After a time, the question became academic and we knew we would never achieve the happiness of owning a Gammage. But one day in Steedman's [book shop] in Grey Street, Newcastle, one of us was up the ladder while the other worked over the lower shelves. Suddenly there was a strangled cry and the ladder shook. White and shaken, we both checked the top shelf, and there for a reasonable sum, was a copy of Gammage. We paid our money and went for a coffee to restore our frayed nerves. But a dimension had gone from our lives. It's not the kill, but the chase that is most fun.[18]

The *TUBCNL* was initiated in 1985 by a Liverpool collector, Paul Cosgrove and from 1990 to 1997 was run by the late John Hammond.[19] The newsletter served not only as a means of contact between collectors, but also a forum for the exchange of information, which as Paul Cosgrove had stated in the first issue of the newsletter, had become important because of the number of badges then being produced and of those beginning to collect them. Although it has sometimes been hard to get people to write articles for the newsletter, much important and interesting information was brought to light by amongst others, Peter Carter, Andrew Redpath, Keith Sinclair and Joe Fleming. Annual meetings of subscribers were arranged, and John Hammond's hard work on compiling the catalogue *Trade Union Badges*, currently in its fourth updated edition, was his legacy to the recording of labour's material culture. There are also other smaller groups working along similar, though more specific lines to the TUBCS such as the National Mining Memorabilia Association with some ninety members in 1998. We might call these 'contact groups' and should perhaps be seen as an extension of such organisations as the Society for the Study of Labour History, North-West Group for the Study of Labour History, Irish Labour History Society, History Workshop, etc. Since the 1960s, these organisations have provided a forum for the discussion and dissemination of ideas and research into labour history between academics and those working in museums, libraries and the heritage sector. A number of those active in the TUBCS are also members of some of these groups.

In other countries, collecting trade union ephemera seems to be the province of one or two individual collectors with significant collections, rather than a group, such as David Yorke in Canada and the late Greg Smith in Australia. One comparable organisation however, is the American Political Items Collectors (APIC). This organisation is largely concerned with the collection of the material culture of past presidential campaigns, but within it has a Labor History Chapter specialising in collecting American trade union material. Some ten newsletters were published under the title *Solidarity For Ever*, until 1992 when it ceased publication; it was then revived in 1998.[20] Canadian collector David Yorke began collecting trade union badges as an extension of his collection of political cause badges from his student days. He finally decided to focus exclusively on trade union material when he found that such material was not being collected by anyone else, including the unions themselves:

> ... it gradually occurred to me that there was an interesting part of the history of our unions that wasn't being collected. I was surprised to discover that on the one hand, few unions had kept a good historical collection of the non-paper items they had issued, and on the other hand that many of those items could still be located by digging here and there.[21]

Dealers and Sources of Acquisition

There is a substantial (and growing) literature on the environments and contexts of popular collecting.[22] Often, the source of acquisitions for a collector come from exchanging with other collectors, but their origins are numerous. Typically, one collector, Bill Patterson, cited trade union offices, trade union members, auctions, dealers' lists, antique and collectors' fairs, car boot sales and friends. He 'allows' himself £40 a month to spend on his hobby. 'Reasonable' spending limits are observed by many collectors as a means of self-legitimation of their activity. In so doing, they often create a tension between their limitations and the exceeding of them by the required prices from dealers or numbers of finds unexpectedly made at any one time. As such, dealers are both demonised and sanctified depending on what the collector can afford. None the less, Bill Patterson finds prices in the secondary market to be relatively stable over a period of time:

> I have a number of old dealers' catalogues, i.e. 1970s, and I have found YMA [Yorkshire Miners Association] and DMA [Durham Miners Association] in these at £2–3 in 1972. This would be around 10–15% of a week's wages, so £30–£40 nowadays is about relative, it just seems more (don't tell the dealers!). I like to think that if I find a badge at 50p, one at £10 and one at £16.50, then on average, each costs £9, much more acceptable than three at £16.50

On a somewhat different tack, the metal-collecting fraternity have recently turned their attention to buried objects of the twentieth century. Since the introduction of the Treasure Act, which requires them to report finds of more than a hundred years old, they have been attracted to the material culture of the twentieth century, rather than the more arcane finds they have been prone to search for. This includes trade union badges (as well as badges in general), which have become increasingly written up in *Treasure Hunting*, the detectorists' main magazine.[23] Likely sites for finds are posited, how to access them, and when. In this sense, the finding, collecting and selling of trade union badges is spread across a wider interest cadre, perhaps with a different agenda. As I asserted in *Popular Collecting*, it is all the more important that collectors of all kinds, including museums, come together, not as cultural competitors, but as allies in sharing knowledge and information.[24]

Pearce neatly sums up the underlying motivation in popular collecting generally, which is especially relevant to historical material such as trade union badges:

> The notion that objects carry the past with them (as separable from their action in the past) is itself the operation of a particular symbolic way of viewing the world. Symbolic things share the assumption that an integral relationship exists between modes of being, in this case, the physical collection and what is believed to be the invisible reality of the past. Here the objects are not just seen as simple epistemological signs – carriers of information about what happened – but rather as mystical bridges between imagination and the past regarded as eternally present and presentable through its physical traces.[25]

I argued in *Popular Collecting* that if this holds good for collectors, it has been equally applicable to museum collections.[26] As such, we have seen a number of exhibitions and displays, such as those described by King (cited in the Introduction), of banners, emblems and badges, which have presented the spectacle of their visual beauty and curiosity, as in itself self-evident of the culture that produced them. That this is now seen by museums as inadequate to convey the context of the experience of working-class life, only serves to point up the woeful lack of engagement with the subject and its material culture in the past.

Museums

Institutionally, we hear occasionally of instances such as those in 1821, when Henry 'Orator' Hunt, the radical leader of 'Peterloo' fame, proposed to establish 'Hunt's Radical Museum', to display the gifts he had received from radical groups around the country during his imprisonment.[27] The People's Palace Museum in Glasgow, established in 1898, had an active policy of collecting labour movement artefacts (other than as 'curios'): 'In 1900 antiquarians were depositing banners of the trade unions of the 1830s with the museum.'[28] Some wealthy Victorian philanthropists indulged their interest in the working classes by collecting aspects of working-class material culture. Such an example was Henry Willett of Brighton. Willett was known to address crowds of six hundred workmen on 'The Level' (a stretch of open ground in central Brighton) and give readings from 'semi-political novels such as *Alton Locke*'.[29] He collected variously in the field of ceramics and first exhibited at the Brighton Museum in 1873. The extensive Willett Gallery is still part of the permanent exhibits, displayed in the way in which Willett wished it to be. As the gallery's textual panel states 'Willett commented that the themes: "while confessedly arbitrary, have been chosen in most cases, not because the specimens happen to have been made by a certain man at a certain time or place, but because of the greater human interest which they represent".' The categories covered in Willett's collection of naively decorated pottery include radical politics of the eighteenth and nineteenth centuries, such as commemorative tableware celebrating Sir Francis Burdett, John Wilkes and Tom Paine, the 1832 Reform Act, professions, trades, friendly societies, early trade unions and fraternal bodies, the Napoleonic wars, agriculture, literature and the arts.

However, labour history collections were largely confined to such specialised and sectionally interested institutions as the Tolpuddle Martyrs' Museum in Dorset, opened on the occasion of the centenary of their transportation, in 1934, and comprising one medium-sized room.[30] Instances of trade union displays in museums seem to have been initiatives of art historians, focusing on that aspect of the material culture. Klingender's exhibition *The Engineer In British Life*, staged in 1947, is one such example. In this, he drew attention to the art of the worker-artist, James Sharples, designer of the Amalgamated Society of Engineers early emblems.

It is notable that the NMLH (est. 1975), was the end-product of a group of collectors, the Trade Union, Labour, Co-operative, Democratic History Society (TULC
as it was known), formed in the 1950s. This group, based in Reigate, Surrey, staged
a number of exhibitions, without the guidance of museum professionals or labour
historian specialists, resulting in a mixed reception.[31] They were, however, perhaps
the first organisation to promote the collecting of labour ephemera in the widest
sense, and to attribute a cultural and historical value to it. That such material has an
educational value is now self-evident.[32] Folk-life museums of the inter-war period
were the first attempts at showing the lives of ordinary people, but were still largely
concerned with rural change, preservation and above all 'crafts' techniques, rather
than conditions or organisations of workers.[33] Industrial museums, from the 1960s
onwards, were largely concerned with technology not people.[34] Until the mid-
1980s, however, labour history was largely ignored in museums. Many museum
professionals felt that they would be straying into 'dangerous politically sensitive
areas',[35] or simply that it was too marginal an interest to attract anyone.[36] In the
specific case of the early NMLH, when based in the old Limehouse Town Hall in
east London, the Liberals described the museum as 'disgusting and outrageous ...
Some of us would argue that the museum provides no service to the public – it
provides a service to the Labour Party and trade unions. It is of a very dubious
nature as far as charitable status is concerned.'[37] In Copenhagen, the proposition for
a labour history museum was met with similar oppropbrium and indifference,
before setting itself up in 1982:

> The museum was created primarily in response to a social demand to make workers'
> history visible in Danish museums. Existing museums were approached but few ven-
> tured further into discussing the subject other than to observe that a museum of this kind
> would presumably grow into a combination of flags-and-banners museum and an institu-
> tion for retired trade union presidents. They held aloof – and the outcome was that the
> Workers' Museum was established as an autonomous institution.[38]

As Trustram points out, controversy often accompanies the presentation of labour
history, and it sometimes stimulates debate.[39] By the 1970s, 'although few museums began to seek out labour history material, many were now willing to accept
material "discovered" by amateur enthusiasts.'[40] It was, no doubt, felt to be safer to
stage exhibitions of the regalia of friendly societies, as in Coventry,[41] and in 1988 at
Buckingham County Museum in the exhibition, *Standards High*. Even small displays in single glass cabinets in libraries, such as that held at Brighton Reference
Library in 1986 made a contribution to awareness of and interest in such material
culture. The *Standards High* exhibition represented 'standards' of many social
organisations such as friendly societies, Mothers' Unions, Scouts and Girl Guides,
as well as political and trade union material. It was 'intended to show how many
different organisations have felt the need for symbolic unity given by flags and
banners, and also to demonstrate the varied skills which have been used to produce

them'.[42] These sort of displays presented spectacle on a grand scale, especially when the regalia included ceremonial axes and similar material, without raising the eyebrows of the politically sensitive. In the mid-1980s, institutions such as the National Museum of Labour History and the Working Class Movement Library became more prominent. The NMLH had been in abeyance for some years since its ejection from its east London premises.[43] It allegedly suffered from the same lack of curatorial discipline as the original TULC. However, it was still impressive enough for seasoned teachers to feel it to be of significant value to their pupils.[44] It also suffered from chronic under-funding, with staff for a period working for virtually nothing,[45] and survived due largely to the enthusiasm of its first curator, Terry McCarthy. It finally found a permanent home in the refurbished old Mechanics Institute, venue for the first meeting of the TUC in 1868, and of a number of *TUBCNL* meetings, in Manchester. These premises are now used solely for administration and conferences, the collections having been transferred to the refurbished Pump House on the outskirts of the city centre and where all exhibitions are held. The NMLH became a subscriber to the *TUBCNL* and has benefited accordingly from the information shared in it. This demonstrates how a private body of ordinary enthusiastic people can make history as well as expose and preserve it. In 1997, the NMLH won financial backing from the Heritage Lottery Fund (HLF) to extend its pilot scheme of identifying and cataloguing all known banners of working-class movements, in conjunction with the Ancient Order of Foresters Friendly Society and Co-operative Movement.[46] This parallels John Hammond's and the TUBCS's survey of all known British trade union badges, and also highlights the relevance of both when cited together. Britain would seem to be the only country with any track record in the exhibiting of labour's material culture. An Australian exhibition, *Badges of Labour, Banners Of Pride*, held at the Museum of Applied Arts and Sciences in 1984/85, and the *Symbols And Images of American Labor* exhibition held at the National Museum of American History in 1988,[47] seem to be exceptions rather than the rule. Industrial heritigisation however, has been more prominent. At the Australian Workers' Heritage Centre in outback Queensland, based on the site of the Great Shearers' strike of 1891 and part of the 'outback tourism trail' 'visitors can experience the hardships and the victories of the workers who helped built [sic] this nation.'[48] Near the town of Forbach, in the department of Lorrain in eastern France, is one of the country's largest and now redundant coal centres. In common with many British former coal mines, it is in the process of being transformed into a museum. Initially, as part of the industrial regeneration programme *Expo Forbach 2000*, a major bilingual (French and German) exhibition *The Adventure of Work: of tools and men*, running throughout 2000, sought to explore the rise and decline of industry in various ways. One of the exhibits, *42 Strike Objects*, was a photographic exhibit by Jean-Luc Moulène which looked at objects made by workers in occupation of their factories and sold for fund raising and publicity purposes:

After several months' research, the photographer Jean-Luc Moulène put together several strike objects and photographed them to build an unusual strike exhibit, but which is also deeply meaningful. Made by strikers who got back the means of production of the firms and factories they occupied, each of these objects expresses the rebellion and the anger of the workers movement. These original manufactured products which have been subverted, form, thanks to Jean-Luc Moulène's lens, the living memory of some of the greatest hours of social protest of the past century. By using visual codes borrowed from the world of communication, the photographer manages to catch the perfect way to define those objects in all their starkness: close ups and natural light. As a result, we can see a watch engraved with the memory of the Lip conflict, a packet of red Gauloises [cigarettes, usually sold in a blue packet] made by the CGT [Confederation of General Workers] during the 1982 strikes of the SEITA [French tobacco company] and an issue of *Parisian Libéré* printed during the occupation of the factory during the great strike of 1975, a timer, a scarf and a version of the Monopoly board game 'Unemployedopoly'.[49]

However, different approaches have been adopted in other countries to interpret and communicate concepts and experiences of 'work'. The Danish Arbejdermuseet or Workers' Museum in Copenhagen, opened in 1984 in what was formally the central meeting place for Copenhagen's labour movement, built in 1879. Although funded partially by the Danish labour movement, there already existed an extensive Danish archive of labour's material culture, the Labour Movement Library and Archive. The museum therefore decided to concentrate on the material culture of ordinary people's everyday lives, and in 1998 had some 12,000 objects in its collections. As its director, Peter Ludvigsen notes, 'To a large group of working-class families, leisure time and family life have played a far more important role than working life or organizational life.'[50] Its four main exhibits exemplify living conditions for working-class Danes from the 1870s to the 1950s. However, exhibitions such as the 1993 'Led By The Nose – An Exhibition of Smells', museologically explores work through a non-material and finer sensory perception. When the restaurant was restored to its original 1892 condition such considerations were already present:

> We sell old-fashioned Danish dishes, beer and aquavit to enable visitors to taste workers' cultural history as well as see it. In 1989, when the restaurant had been open for a year, we offered the traditional raw salted herring with brown bread at the same price it had been sold for in 1892 ... .[51]

To an even greater extent, Sweden's Museum of Work at Norrköping, housed in a former textile mill, the Strykjärnet building, has only one permanent exhibition, which examines the working life of a female warp-winder, who worked there between 1927 and 1962. It instead concentrates on temporary and travelling art installations, photographic exhibitions and oral history projects, as the information leaflet asserts: 'The Museum of Work is part of our society's memory. There's nothing passive about it – it's a living memory, rich, cross-disciplinary, deeply immersed in its culture. A memory open to everyone through exhibits and libraries, courses and seminars.' And as one 23-year-old female visitor was moved to write in the visitors' book:

> I am but one of many unemployed souls
> The need for friends. Life is fragile.
> My daughter, my heart.
> My mood swings up and down
> Unemployment strangles my ability
> To make a difference.[52]

In similar vein, the French *Adventure of Work* exhibition, also included an exhibit based around an unemployed Frenchman, Jean Osinski:

> In order to give life to his project Jean-Michel Bruyère [one of the exhibition's directors] came to the Bassin Houiller to reconnoitre and in his walks was guided by an unemployed person from Forbach, Jean Osinski. As time went by, Jean-Michel Bruyèr decided to make this random companion the central focus of his reflections and thoughts. Jean the inactive, the unemployed who spends his time in Forbach on his own or with his dog, to the hours spent in the cafes of Forbach. As an essential counterpoint to the exhibit *The Adventure of Work*, the Jean Osinski project creates an event around the unemployed person. This project consists of several stages; a museum of Jean Osinksi is open, the netsurfers of the world can follow his every move through a web cam placed in his bedroom. A performance organised on 26th October 2000 will conclude this journey of several months. A catalogue of the correspondence between Jean Osinski and Jean-Michel Bruyère will be published.[53]

Thus we discover alternative ways of evoking engagement with historical archives and statements about work in its broadest sense that do not rely so heavily on material culture *per se*, and which are not derived from organisation at all, but rather from individual experience of the workplace or its lack of it, without qualification of category. The case for material culture however, is usefully put by Harry Rubenstein, curator at the National Museum of American History, writing on the 'Symbols And Images Of American Labor' exhibition of 1988 (see Figure 6.1):

> Because workers of the past left few written documents, their portraits, emblems, graphics and other images fill a gap in our understanding of how workers saw themselves, what concerns they had, and how their own attitudes towards their worklife and their place in society have changed over time.[54]

Rubenstein argues that a trend for workers to have themselves photographed holding tools of their trade (men and women) in mid-nineteenth-century America, reflected pride in occupation. This he believes was replaced, as industrialisation expanded, by industrial organisation, in which the material culture which such organisations produced, such as membership emblems, banners, sashes and badges,

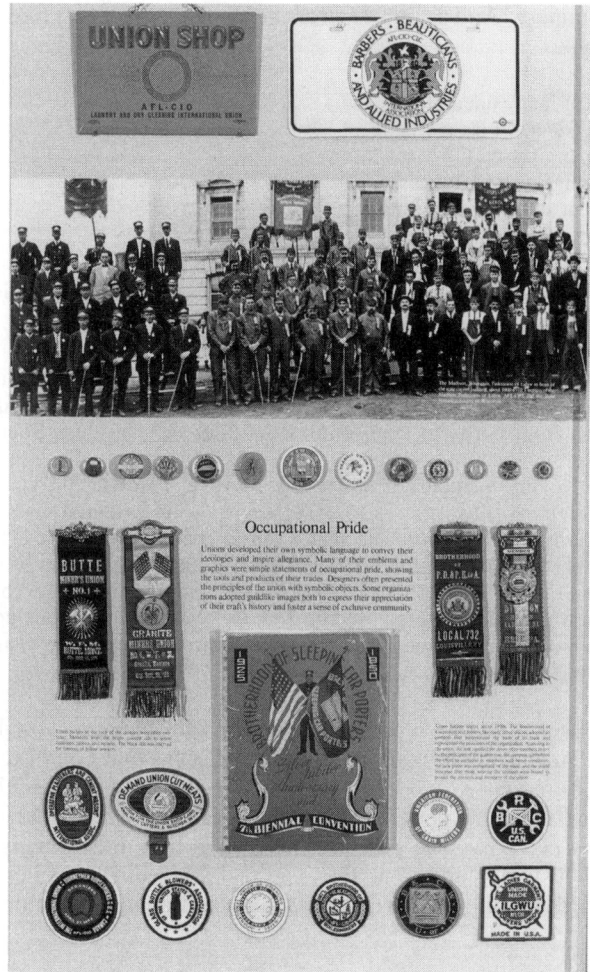

Figure 6.1   *Symbols and Images of American Labor* **exhibition. National Museum of American History, Smithsonian Institute, Washington, DC 1988. Badges and ribbons from the exhibition are contextualised through the contemporary photograph of the workers wearing some of them. Perhaps this particular panel is rather too near the 'stamp album' form of display disapproved of by some museum professionals, but highly evocative and visually stimulating to the visitor.**
Reproduced with permission of the National Museum of 'American History'.

reflected this same self-esteem.[55] He further explores the nature of the corporatisation of industrial promotion through various visual media:

> These popular portrayals of expanding industry and assembly lines promoted corporations' achievements in creating and organizing production. What is missing from these dramatizations was the role and skills of the individual workers ... This ... projected a positive image for managers who purchased, organized and controlled the machinery, and a diminished status for the workers who made it function.[56]

As such, workers, through organisation, created a body of visual and material culture which asserted their self-worth and value in such processes. In this context, then, the lapel badge represented the material reflection of, and vessel in which was kept, this personal value and sense of self-worth; it was an assertive symbol of individual human existence in the midst of mechanical and capital processes which threatened to swamp them. Hence, whether we adopt a material or non-material approach to labour history, we are essentially examining working-class perceptions of the self, articulated through popular materials and language, which themselves reflect the cultural beliefs and ethos of their environments in time.

Clearly, museums have long since ceased to be the gloomy, dusty, glass-cabinet dominated environments that some once were. This may seem too obvious to need stating to some, but to many whose only memories of museums are obligatory school trips indifferently attended, it is not so. To many others, museums are alien territory. As recently as 1990, Myna Trustram, the NMLH's head curator, recounted a quip in the *New Statesman and Society*, about the TGWU, that 'the union needs an urgent spring-clean: or else rapid removal to an honoured but dusty place in the Museum of Labour History'. She continued:

> The implication here is that once something is in a museum it is the end of the story, there is no interaction with present issues. But we do not see the National Museum of Labour History as labour history's graveyard and we do not plan to provide any 'dusty places' for any unions, no matter how honoured. We would rather collect from an alive and kicking T and G[57]

Many museums, it was noted, originated from mechanics institutes of the 1820s and 'received collections of working class collectors of shells, curiosities and fossils'; furthermore:

> Museums were intended to educate – they dealt with the new natural sciences and helped to promote industrial development and good design. They tended not to deal with the history of particular people, rather they were intended to broaden the experience of their visitors, not to increase their self-awareness. Museums became set in this mould and, as fashions changed, many museums did not. It is from the largely stagnant 1920s and '30s that the public image of museums as dead, dusty places derives.[58]

The point is that museums are, even under trying financial circumstances, more often than not, vibrant and engaging places which have over the last twenty years made great strides in terms of accessibility (in all senses of the word) and in being meaningful to the widest public possible. When objects find their way into museums, they are taken out of the context in which they were intended for use, be that a badge, a banner, or a protest leaflet. None the less, sensitively interpreted, they continue to inform us about those contexts and cultures which produced them, causing us to question, explore and sometimes even marvel. At their best, social and labour history museums strive to 'convey a sense of resistance, that people have made their own history within the power relationships imposed on them', and it is accepted that 'we are engaged in a subjective practice, but one which can be disciplined by constant referral to our audience.'[59] This is a statement of validity of public history (that is, history derived from the experience of everyday living, and our interaction with the processes of engagement with our immediate environment). In museums this can be done with as subtle a shift in emphasis as talking about 'glassmakers not glassmaking, miners not mining, dockers not docks etc.',[60] or in the case of the *George Edwards Celebration*, at the Norfolk Museum of Rural Life (a temporary Exhibition), commemorating the 150th anniversary of the birth of the agricultural workers union's founder in 1983: 'No longer are we just a farmer's museum.'[61] Other areas of an extended labour movement into wider socialised areas such as the cooperative movement, offer more scope for the revealing and interpreting of women's history, both as organisations such as the Women's Co-operative Guild and as consumers.[62]

In recent years, for a variety of reasons, some more valid than others, museums have rejected the centrality of objects to their missions. The advent of information technology, massive cuts in funding and the resulting cuts in staff have expedited this trend. Lack of storage space, and a positive commitment to a more focused collecting policy have also affected it. Museums, at least social history museums, now regard themselves more as centres for interactive communication than the telling of narrative stories. Today, it is largely collectors who make the headway in preserving the material culture, often to the indifference of museums. On occasion, such collections become significant. They grow into national archives. Such is the case of the Working Class Movement Library.

The Working Class Movement Library (WCML) is centred on the collections of Ruth and Eddie Frow, dedicated collectors of working-class literature and political pamphlets.[63] They soon found however, that:

> ... we could not stop at books if we wanted to reflect the interests and history of the labour movement. We had to expand our ideas to encompass periodicals, songs, prints, pamphlets, cartoons, badges, inscribed pottery, photographs, recorded interviews and all aspects of working class culture from about 1770.[64]

Originally, their house in Kings Road, Old Trafford, became from 1956, a living library and museum, and was registered as a charitable trust as early as 1959.[65] The landing walls were covered in framed membership emblems of trade unions from the nineteenth century, whilst the walls in all the rooms were covered in bookshelves.[66] Manchester City Council finally ensured a permanent site for the collection in Salford and financial provision for its upkeep and curatorship. The WCML was another favourite meeting place for TUBCS meetings.

There is still precious little museological recognition of the importance of the material culture of the labour movement. This lack even necessitated a call for this recognition in museums.[67] In 1997, however, museums from Scandanavia, Britain and Germany, defining themselves as labour museums, came together to form 'WORKLAB' – The International Association of Labour Museums. This was partly inspired by the creation of several new labour museums over the last fifteen to twenty years.[68] As such, more recognition of their importance is likely to follow, as well as better information on the different interpretations and encounters with labour in all forms in a museological context.

There is still widespread misunderstanding about museum practice which holds that material donated to a museum is somehow spirited away, never to see the light of day again. This arises from lack of knowledge about what museums do, about permanent and temporary exhibitions and about permanent display and reserve collections. As Ludmilla Jordanova notes 'Museums have significant silences; their processes of selection, management and interpretation, are rarely accessible to the general public and remain unimagined by them.'[69] This has been the fault largely of museums themselves, and only in recent years have reflexive and reflective displays, often initiated by installation artists, questioned the nature of what museums do.[70] One collector of more than thirty years standing is uncertain what ultimately to do with his collection:

> I am still weighing whether it best goes to a union central, with the hopes that they take good care of it, or to a museum or university collection, with the hopes that it does not disappear from sight and that unionists will still have good access to it.[71]

There are however, significant holdings of labour history material in local museums pertaining to the locality of the museum. These holdings are often viewed as local rather than labour history and are accessioned and used as such. It may be surprising therefore to learn, that Britain's most prestigious national museum, the British Museum, an otherwise bastion of high culture, has a significant holding of trade union badges and medals, five hundred in 1987,[72] held in its Department of Coins and Medals. Even more surprising is that trade unions, such as the NUM, should consider the British Museum as a suitable depository for its material, rather than the more obvious NMLH.[73]

The British Museum in fact, made a small, but notable step forward in raising the museological legitimacy of labour's material culture, when it staged the exhibition *British Trade Union Badges,* to coincide with the sixtieth anniversary of the General Strike, between 19 May and 17 August 1986. The prestige of the museum

legitimised acquisition and display of such material for other museums, and simultaneously signalled to extra-mural interest groups (collectors, dealers, etc.), acknowledgement of the importance of such material. It was also important in that it
sought to trace the lineage of trade union emblems from freemasons, friendly and
benevolent societies:

> The first half of the display is concerned with the variety of badge forms and functions.
> Many of the symbols derive from the example of earlier associations: livery companies,
> Masonic and friendly societies. The variety of symbols is matched by the variety of
> purposes to which the badges bearing them are put. The fortunes of unions – formations,
> dissolutions, amalgamations – can be traced in the badges. The second half looks at a
> number of union campaigns in recent years and examines the role of the badge. The
> recent miners' strike, the issue concerning trade unions at GCHQ and the dispute at
> Wapping bring the selection right up to date.[74]

This sought to show that such organisations, though diverse in practice, shared a
common iconographical, ritualistic and often structural heritage. The wealth of old
and rare badges and medals used for this purpose had often been donated to the
museum in the nineteenth or early twentieth centuries. This implied that acquisition
of such material, often by wealthy patrons of the museum at the time, may well
have held a certain social anthropological fascination for them. This in itself would
make an intriguing study of a sub-strand of Victorian social imperialistic ideology,
although the museum has only actively collected trade union badges since 1966.[75]
Around the same time, the Irish Labour History Society (ILHS) were staging
exhibitions of Irish trade union badges, banners and ephemera. First, in 1984, they
staged the *In Solidarity* exhibition at the Ulster Museum, Botanical Gardens, Belfast. Then in 1986 they presented *The Parliament of Labour*, to commemorate the
centenary of Dublin Trades Council at the Dublin Civic Museum. The leading
authority in the ILHS as far as the trade union badges are concerned is Francis
Devine, a research officer for the former Irish TGWU, now the Services, Industrial
and Professional Trade Union (SIPTU). As a collector and historian, he is to the
material culture of Irish labour, what Hammond and Gorman were to the British.
Like the TULC, the ILHS would perhaps be regarded as 'preservationists' in the
Hobsbawmian sense. As Myna Trustram, curator of the NMLH pondered, when
discussing the nature of labour history and its artefacts: 'It is tempting to think that
it was all a lot more straightforward for the members of the TULC. Their motivation, I suspect, stemmed from a desire to preserve the evidence of labour's past and
to use that evidence to instruct and inspire.'[76] This is not to suggest that such
sentiments are meant pejoratively, but for so long, organisations like the TULC as
well as individual collectors, were seen as eccentric. In the 1980s when museums
woke up to the potential and validity of such material as was being collected
outside of museums, it suddenly became culturally important. It is such organisations that provide a coherent and collective focus for research; they bring the

importance of the objects to both academic and general notice, even if cultural appropriation was too often the end result. In this, study and research groups, such as the TULC and ILHS, bridge a gap between private collector and museum professional, and are a useful vehicle by which both can be brought together. The focus of all of these exhibitions was widened in 1988 by Andy Durr, a lecturer at what is now the University of Brighton, whom we first met in Chapter 1, when he staged his exhibition: *Popular Art: The Emblems And Associations of Mutual Aid.* This exhibition looked at the emblems and material culture of friendly societies, freemasons and other pre-trade union organisations.[77]

There was also a fundamental questioning of the nature, definition and interpretation of 'labour history', even of the very term itself, both in museum and academic circles at this time.[78] Historians of women, ethnicity and the family rightly felt that there was room for their inclusion in the field, which they claimed was still focused on white, male trade unionism[79] as was examined in Chapter 4. Second, there was a strong move from museums, notably the People's Palace in Glasgow, for the incorporation of other non-union or labour movement working-class history to be included, such as dog racing and football. Also, the anti-conventional labour history of popular conservatism[80] was argued for both academically and as display in museums. History exhibitions in museums had too often in the past used objects, the material culture of the labour movement, as little more than illustrations to vast panels of graphics and text, or 'book on the wall exhibitions'.[81] The private collections of trade unionists are one way in which wider communal bonds can be achieved. New history is unearthed and made public, by tracing the events and occasions that the badges represent.[82] Doing so is natural to many collectors who are curious about the context in which their badges were made. Conventionally in collectors this has been seen as 'fetishistic' by museum curators, whilst their own label for the same interest is 'specialist'.[83] The People's Palace in Glasgow are keen to relate the personal as well as the organisational representation of their trade union badge collection:

> Whenever possible, we try to put trade union badges in a similar [personal] context. We have, for example, the badges of Robert Townsley (1892–1974) a shop steward in Weir's of Cathcart during the Great War and the industrial unrest of 1919 and 1926. His 'On War Service' badge, his ILP badge and Keir Hardie button were also important to him, and we display these badges with his Amalgamated Society of Engineers and other trade union badges.[84]

Organisations such as the Amalgamated Engineering and Electrical Union (AEEU), that have their own permanent displays, incorporate the union within the industry in which they organise, thus contextualising the displays. This has also been done in some exhibitions, for example, the use of trade union banners and emblems as examples of agricultural art.[85] Significant private collections of trade union badges have now found willing museum homes.[86] Trade unions themselves house their own collections, one of the earliest of which was formed by John Martin, the late general secretary of the National Union of Lock and Metal Workers.[87] Others include the collection, on permanent display at Unison's head office, the TUC's collection, those of unions that formed the TGWU at their London headquarters and a similar collection of former unions, absorbed into the ISTC at Swinton House, London. These collections have grown from private missions to save the labour movement's ephemera, every bit as much as any museums. Therefore, if museums are valuing these collections as worthy of inclusion, they should also be equally concerned with maintaining contact with other collectors and outside bodies in which they organise, for the furtherance of knowledge in general.

Museum and Collector Relationships

In 1985, the TUC hosted the first museum seminar on labour history in museums, papers from which were subsequently published in 1988. Amongst the museum delegates was one private collector, John Smethurst and one 'preservationist', John Gorman. The summary in relation to private collectors of the material culture of labour history, stated that:

> Several speakers criticised them because they could not ensure the long-term survival of their collections. John Smethurst claimed that when he began collecting in the 1950s, none of the museums or archives he approached were interested in labour history material. John Griffin's concept of 'pastoral' care depended on a close relationship between curators and the bodies or individuals which owned labour history objects; those who owned such things may well treasure them but without professional advice they could do damage through ignorance.[88]

John Gorman stated that he believed it was 'legitimate for enthusiasts to collect multiples – badges, emblems, posters etc., but that "one-offs" when discovered, should be eventually returned to the movement'.[89]

The relationship between museums and collectors of the material culture of popular culture had been virtually non-existent, and even when the first progressive moves were made to bring them together, there were institutional reservations.[90] The TUBCS from 1990 made a deliberate attempt to hold meetings in museum surroundings, holding conferences at both the NMLH and the WCML in Manchester and Salford respectively. The effect was to cause both institutions to subscribe to the TUBCNL and enhance a friendly and mutually rewarding relationship. This was a reflection of a wider museum willingness to value and recognise the popular collections of ordinary people, and afford them a collective display in museums through the immensely popular democratic practice (and phenomenon) of 'The People's Shows'.[91] Frequently, badges including trade union badges, formed part of these. As long ago as 1979, the exhibition *Pinned Down*, held at the Midland Art

Group, Nottingham, relied on badge collectors to form the exhibition, including trade union badges. The burgeoning of popular collecting generally from the mid-1980s onwards, and in this specific sense of this book, of trade union badges, brought collectors closer to museums. Both gained insight to the value of each other's expertise as a result. Around the time that the TUBCNL was formed, museums began to appear which took on board both the People's Palace ethos of inclusive labour history and which were centred on the locality. The Merseyside Museum of Labour History (est. 1986), now part of the Museum of Liverpool Life; The People's Story in Edinburgh (est. 1989) and The Story Of Hull And Its People (est. 1990)[92] are all good examples. They were constituted partly through lessons learned in the challenge of the heritage industry from the turn of the 1980s. Museums had now realised that they had to be entertaining attractions as well as centres of knowledge and research. In 1994, Moore wrote:

> Curators have an opportunity to co-operate with academic labour historians on a level that has not existed before. At the same time this would encourage museum historians to gain the confidence to believe that their work, and the exhibition form, can be as valuable in historiographic terms as the work of academics.[93]

In an academic sense, there has been little written on trade union badges. They have tended to be used as illustrations to other subjects. Museums, as institutional collectors, were largely indifferent to the ephemera of the labour movement (with certain exceptions as noted above) until the 1980s. Although there have been written accounts of curatorial practice towards it in journals and briefing papers of the museum profession,[94] philosophical articles have been comparatively rare.[95] The importance of the private collector in this equation seems to have been left out. I argued in *Popular Collecting* that a mutual knowledge-sharing nexus between museums and collectors, especially through their collective organisations, is necessary for an informed and democratic approach to the collection and interpretation of material culture in the twenty-first century.[96] The burgeoning in popular collecting since 1980 and the formation of collectors' organisations and publications has led to an extra-mural cadre of collectors and a considerable collective knowledge in the material culture of the everyday that museums lack. In many ways now collectors and museums are on a level of parity, and will increasingly come to perform a wider interpretative role. The TUBCS and the NMLH and WCML are a good example of this process.

Dealing

Many long-established trade union badge collectors will nostalgically recall the heady days of the 1970s and early 1980s, when old and rare badges could be obtained free, simply by writing to national, regional and branch offices of trade unions. Often, such gems had been 'resting' in an office drawer, file or store for decades, and still looked brand new.[97] As the interest in collecting grew, so such stocks dwindled. New badges became more desirable as a result, and a healthy trade in them emerged. These new badges have tended to fall into three categories: firstly, those issued for use by the union membership. These are variously issued by national, regional or even branch offices of unions. These are usually sold at cost price to interested buyers within the labour movement, although some are restricted to members only. Second, badges are issued for sale, in order to raise funds for workers in dispute, or as souvenir commemoratives after the dispute is over. These are made as widely available as possible to the public in general, although again some differentiating colour or design feature may be incorporated into a small number of them, and distributed only to participants in the events they commemorate (as touched on in Chapter 4). Finally, there are those badges that are issued to commemorate anniversaries of events and individuals within the labour movement. Sometimes these are sold for straight profit, or with a percentage of profits going to a worthy labour cause. The growth in interest in trade union badges and its associated material culture naturally led to a rise in price on the secondary market, where most older badges were by now obtained. The NMLH at one time even considered reproducing 'classic' badges for sale at reasonable prices, because of the demand for old badges.[98] There emerged a small group of traders, many in London, who began to specialise in dealing in badges generally, with a number of client–patron relationships being established. Concomitantly, some activists employed the entrepreneurial spirit of the age,[99] to act as commissioning agents for the design and implementation of manufacturer of badges from trade unions (Just Badges and Strike Graphics being two examples).[100]

During the early 1990s a number of 'reproduction' badges from the 1984/85 miners strike began to appear, struck in colours which were different from the originals. These were offered for sale from various sources at reasonable prices. The response from collectors was mixed. Some felt it would benefit newer collectors who had not been able to get the originals, whilst others were outraged by the idea of replicas of any kind, feeling that it cheapened the reverence with which they should be perceived. Some even felt them to be 'fakes'. These badges none the less sold well amongst collectors and served to show the growth of interest in collecting them by the mid-1990s.[101] This example also poses a question; what is 'real'? The copies were struck from original dies after all. The particularism already noted in relation to the use of the badge, is here seen to carry over to its collection. Rather like the nature of history itself, of which the badge is often seen as an envoy, there is no absolute reality of any given version. Museums and collectors are crucial both as aids to understanding and as investigators, for the revealing of material artefacts and oral and written accounts of involvement and witness to events of the past (distant and recent) in everyday experience. The trade union badge, especially over the last two decades, is a good example of a vehicle for drawing collectors and museums together. This can only be to their mutual advantage and to the advantage of future generations for whom the esoteric interests of a few enthusiasts in the twentieth century will be a far more mainstream source of British and international public history.

Notes

1 B. Danet and T. Katriel, 'Glorious Obsessions, Passionate Lovers and Hidden Treasures: collecting, metaphor and the romantic ethic', in S.H. Riggins (ed.), *The Socialness Of Things: Essays on the socio-semiotics of objects,* Berlin: Mouton de Gruyter, 1994, pp. 23–61.

2 See R. *Belk Collecting In A Consumer Society,* London, Routledge, 1995; J. Elsner and R. Cardinal (eds), *The Cultures of Collecting,* London, Reaktion Books, 1994; S. Pearce, *On Collecting,* London, Routledge, 1995; S. Pearce, *Collecting In Contemporary Practice,* London, Sage, 1998; P. Martin, 'Tomorrow's History Today: Postmodern Collecting', *History Today,* 1996, Volume 46, No. 2, February, pp. 5–8; P. Martin, *Popular Collecting and the Everyday Self: the reinvention of museums?,* London, Leicester University Press.

3 See, for example, K. Moore, 'Labour History In Museums: Development and Direction', in S. Pearce (ed.), *Museums and the Appropriation of Culture,* London, Athlone Press, 1994, pp. 142–173.

4 G. Kavenagh, in conversation, 1998.

5 S. Riches, 'Seynt George … On Whom Alle Englond Hath Byleve', *History Today,* Vol. 50, No. 10, October, 2000, p. 50.

6 Gorman, *Images of Labour,* pp. 11–13.

7 'The Unorganised Are Now Organised: Will Sherwood looks back over forty years of trade union service', *Labour,* 1937, September, p. 19.

8 For example, John Smethurst, Peter Carter, Eddie and Ruth Frow all based in Manchester.

9 The collecting of trade union badges is not confined to Britain: one Australian trade union badge collector, Greg Smith, collected for thirty years for instance. It does though, seem to be a particularly British passion. One American authority wrote to say that 'For years and years these [union buttons] were ignored by American collectors, but in the last five years there has been a growing interest in labor related items, although dues buttons are not much in demand' (T. Hake, personal communication, 1998).

The union label, however, which was much more widely used in America than Britain, does have a reasonably strong collecting interest there.

10 Newspaper feature reproduced in *Trade Union Badge Collectors' Newsletter,* No. 51, 1995, November.

11 E. King, 'Labour History At The People's Palace', in V. Bott (ed.), *Labour History In Museums,* London, Society For The Study of Labour History/Social History Curators Group, 1988, p. 14.

12 See also Cusack 'Is Size Important?'.

13 There is perhaps a comparison with Henry Fry, one of the founders of the NMLH. He began collecting the material culture of the labour movement in 1942, another peril-

ous time for trade unions, when the outcome of the Second World War was far from certain. It can only be conjecture, as he left few records (see Gorman, *Images of Labour*, pp. 11–12), but his collecting activities may have been spurred on by the possibility of a German victory, which would then eradicate all record of the British labour movement.

14   See R. Belk, 'Possessions And The Extended Self', *Journal of Consumer Research*, 1988, Vol. 15, September pp. 139–168; S. Lancaster and M. Foddy, 'Self Extensions: A Conceptualisation', *Journal For The Theory of Social Behaviour*, No. 18, 1988, January, pp. 77–94; P. Martin, *Popular Collecting and the Everyday Self*, pp. 26–47.

15   T. Law, 'Meet The Badge Man', *Hull Daily Mail*, 2 August 1997, p. 38.

16   H. Hawkes, 'Union History Under The Hammer', *Birmingham Evening Mail*, 22 September 1990.

17   Pearce, *On Collecting*, p. 173.

18   E. Frow and R. Frow, 'Travels With A Caravan', *History Workshop Journal*, 1976, No. 2, p. 181.

19   Currently run by Peter Carter.

20   R. Oestreicher, personal communication, 1998.

21   D. Yorke, personal communication, 1998.

22   See for example, R. Maisel, 'The Flea Market as an Action Scene', *Urban Life and Culture*, 1974, Vol. 2, No. 4, January, pp. 488–505; G.R. Hermann and S.M. Soiffer, 'For Fun and Profit: an analysis of the American garage sale', *Urban Life*, 1984, Vol. 2, No. 4, January, pp. 397–421; C. McCree, 'Flea Markets', *Psychology Today*, 1984, Vol. 18, No. 3, pp. 46–53; B. Gordon, 'The Souvenir: messenger of the extraordinary', *Journal of Popular Culture*, 1986, Vol. 20, No. 3, pp. 135–146; S. Soiffer and G. Hermann, 'Visions of Power: ideology and practice in the American garage sale', *Sociological Review*, 1987, No. 35, pp. 48–83; M. Glancy, The Play World Setting of the Auction', *Journal of Leisure Research*, 1988, Vol. 20, No. 2, pp. 135–153; C.S. Smith, *Auctions: The Social Construction of Value*, Hemel Hempstead, Harvester Wheatsheaf, 1989; J. Sherry, 'A Sociocultural Analysis of a Midwestern American Flea Market', *Journal of Consumer Research*, 1990, No. 17, pp. 13–30; N. Gregson and L. Crewe, 'Beyond The High Street and the Mall: car-boot sales and the new geographies of consumption in the 1990s', *Area*, 1994, No. 26, pp. 261–267; N. Gegson and L. Crewe, 'The Bargain, The Knowledge and the Spectacle: making sense of consumption in the space of the car-boot sale', *Environment And Planning D: Social Space*, 1997, Vol. 15, pp. 87–112; N. Gregson, L. Crewe and B. Longstaff, 'Excluded Spaces of Regulation: car-boot sales as an enterprise culture out of control?', *Environment And Planning A*, 1997, Vol. 29: pp. 1717–1737; N. Gregson and L. Crewe, 'Performance and Possession: rethinking the act of purchase in the light of the car boot sale', *Journal of Material Culture*, 1997, Vol. 2, No. 2, pp. 241–263; P. Martin, *Popular Collecting and the Everyday Self*, pp. 130–143; S. Pearce and P. Martin, *The Collectors' Voice, Volume 4: Contemporary Collecting*, Aldershot, Ashgate Press, 2002.

23   Carter, 'Finding and Collecting ... '; T. Walker, 'Collecting Golliwog Badges', *Treasure Hunting*, 1995, September, pp. 4–5; E. Fletcher, 'Detecting And Collecting The Twentieth Century', *Treasure Hunting*, 1997, November, p. 39; E. Fletcher, 'Detecting And Collecting The Twentieth Century Part Two', *Treasure Hunting*, 1997, December, p. 38.

24 Martin, *Popular Collecting*, pp. 99–129.
25 Pearce, *Collecting In Contemporary Practice*, pp. 160–161.
26 Martin, *Popular Collecting*, pp. 99–129.
27 J. Belchem, *Henry 'Orator' Hunt: Henry Hunt and English Working-Class Radicalism*, Oxford, Clarendon Press, 1985, p. 152.
28 King, *Labour History ...* op. cit., p. 12. In a slightly wider context, the Victoria and Albert Museum staged an exhibition of pottery and ceramics of 'popular art' – *A collection of pottery and porcelain illustrating British History*, suitably in Bethnal Green, in 1899, based on the collections of Henry Willett. This included pots that were made for sale to members of the Friendly Society of Cordwainers of England, Friendly Association of Cotton Spinners and the Society of United Journeymen Couriers (Durr MS, p. 2). Much of the Willett collection is on permanent display at Brighton Museum and Art Gallery, and also includes similar objects commemorating, for example, John Wilkes and the 1832 Reform Act.
29 J. Rutherford, 'Henry Willett As a Collector', *Apollo*, 1982, March, p. 176.
30 See D. Horne, *'The Great Museum: The Representation of History*, London, Pluto Press, 1984, pp. 137–9.
31 D. Rubinstein, 'The Second Labour History Exhibition', *Bulletin of the Society for the Study of Labour History*, 1966, No. 12, Spring, p. 21.
32 For example, see J. Bellamy 'The Use of Trade Union Emblems and Banners In Teaching', *Social History Curators' Newsletter*, 1990, No. 18, pp. 15–16.
33 G. Kavanagh, *History Curatorship* , Leicester, Leicester University Press, 1990, pp. 22–31.
34 Kavanagh, *History Curatorship*, pp. 42–43.
35 N. Mansfield, 'The George Edwards Celebration', in Bott ed. op. cit. p. 8.
36 E. King, *The People's Palace and Glasgow Green* Glasgow, Richard Drew publishers, 1988, p. 116.
37 T. McCarthy, 'The National Museum of Labour History', in Bott (ed.), *Labour History in Museums*, p. 18.
38 P. Ludvigson, 'A Workers' Museum in Copenhagen', *Museum International*, Oxford, Blackwell, No. 188, 1995, Vol. 47 No. 4, p. 40.
39 M. Trustram, 'Dealing With Controversy at the National Museum of Labour History', *Worklab Newsletter*, 1998, pp. 9–11.
40 Moore, 'Labour History In Museums ... ', pp. 147–148.
41 D. Janes, 'The Philosophy Behind Collecting Labour History Material' in Bott (ed.), *Labour History in Museums*, p. 1.
42 'Green Arrow', 'Between Ourselves', *Forester's Miscellany*, 1988, April, p. 92.
43 For its origins, early history and subsequent fortunes, see Gorman, *Images of Labour*; M. Trustram, 'The National Museum of Labour History (Manchester, England) and the National Banner Initiative', *Worklab Newsletter* 1998b, No. 1, April, pp. 12–14; N. Mansfield, 'The political situation of workers museums in the UK: the case of the National Museum of Labour History', *Worklab Newsletter*, 1999, No. 2, February, pp. 27–28, 30.
44 C. Gibbs, 'The National Museum of Labour History', *History Workshop Journal*, 1980, No. 10, pp. 191–193.
45 Gibbs, 'The National Museum of Labour History', p. 193.
46 Trustram, 'The National Museum of Labour History (Manchester, England)' ... p. 14.

47   S. Molloy, 'Labor History Exhibit', *Solidarity Forever*, newsletter of the American Political Items Collectors' Labor History Chapter, 1988, Summer: 1; Rubenstein, 'Symbols and Images of American Labor: Badges of Pride'; Rubenstein, 'Symbols And Images of American Labor: Dinner Pails and Hard Hats', *Labor's Heritage*, 1989, July, pp. 34–49.

48   Australian Workers Heritage Centre website <http://www.alp.org.au/workers/about.htm> accessed 2 July 2000.

49   Visitors Guide, *L'Aventure du Travail: Des Outils et des Hommes* (translation, M.S. Delâge-Martin), Musée due Bassin Houiller Lorrain, 2000, p. 48.

50   A. Vasstrim and P. Ludvigsen, 'Documentation in a Social History Museum: the Workers' Museum in Copenhagen', *Cahiers d' étude Study Series*, ICOM Committee for Documentation (CIDOC), No. 3, December, 1996, p. 20.

51   P. Ludvigsen, 'Links Between Museums and the Public: Introducing the Workers Museum', ICOM MPR, No. 1, 1992, p. 8.

52   Museum of Work, Norrkoping, Sweden *Visitors Guide* (English).

53   Visitors Guide, *L'Aventure du Travail: Des Outils et des Hommes*, p. 50.

54   Rubenstein, 'Symbols And Images: Badges Of Pride', p. 36.

55   Ibid., pp. 36–41.

56   Rubenstein, 'Symbols and Images: Dinner Pails and Hard Hats' op. cit., p. 43.

57   M. Trustram, 'The National Museum of Labour History', *Social History Curators' Group Journal*, 1990, No. 18, p. 7.

58   Janes, 'The Philosophy Behind Collecting Labour History', p. 1.

59   Trustram, 'The National Museum of Labour History', p. 7.

60   L. Knowles, 'The Portrayal of Labour History In Museum Displays', *Bias In Museums*, 1990, Museums Professionals Group Transaction 22, p. 10.

61   Mansfield, 'The George Edwards Celebration', p. 9.

62   See for example, G. Wade and K. Lunn, 'The Portsea Island Co-Op Museum', *Social History Curators Group Journal*, 1990, No. 18, p. 14.

63   E. Frow and R. Frow, 'Travels With A Caravan', pp. 177–182; E. Frow and R. Frow, 'The Working Class Movement Library', *Social History Curators' Group Journal*, 1990, No. 18, pp. 13–14.

64   Frow and Frow, 'The Working Class Movement Library', p. 13.

65   Frow and Frow, 'Travels With A Caravan', p. 182.

66   Personal visit in 1985.

67   Moore, 'Labour History In Museums ...', 1994.

68   P. Ludvigson, editorial, *Worklab Newsletter*, 1998, No. 1, p. 3.

69   L. Jordanova, *History In Practice*, London, Edward Arnold, 2000, p. 145. For a specific example of such a silence, see J. Stanley, 'Putting Gender Into Seafearing: Representing Women in Public Maritime History', in H. Kean, P. Martin and S. J. Morgan (eds), *Seeing History: Public History in Britain Now*, London, Francis Boutle, 2000, pp. 81–103.

70   See e.g. M. Beard and J. Henderson, 'Please Don't Touch The Ceiling: the culture of appropriation', in S. Pearce (ed.), *The Appropriation of Culture*, pp. 5–42.

71   D. Yorke, personal communication, 1998.

72   Clark, 'Worn With Pride ...', p. 20.

73   The Scottish Colliery Enginemen, Boilermen and Tradesmen's Association (SCEBTA), a section of the NUM, donated one of its rare long-service badges to the British

Museum in the 1980s. It emphasised that this was the only award of the badge outside of the union (SCEBTA, personal communication, 1989).

74 P. Attwood, curator of coins and medals, British Museum, leaflet guide to the exhibition in 1986.

75 Clark, 'Worn With Pride', p. 20. The Department's more recent acquisitions have been published in a series of occasional papers: P. Attwood, *Acquisitions of Badges (1978–1982)*, Occasional paper No. 55, Department of Coins and Medals, British Museum, London, 1982; P. Attwood, *Acquisitions of Badges (1983–1987)*, Occasional paper No. 76, Department of Coins and Medals, British Museum, London, 1990.

76 Trustram, 'The National Museum of Labour History', p. 6.

77 See Chapter 1.

78 This was usefully summarised in Moore, 'Labour History In Museums ...'.

79 Davin, 'Feminism and Labour History'; G. Porter, 'Putting Your House In order: representations of women and domestic life' in R. Lumley (ed.), *The Museum Time Machine*, London, Routledge, 1988, pp. 102–127; King, 'Labour History ...'; Trustram, 'The National Museum of Labour History'; Moore, 'Labour History In Museums ...', p. 161.

80 P. Martin, 'The Vermin Club 1948–1951', *History Today*, 1997, Vol. 47, No. 6, June, pp. 17–22; 'The Tories and the People: Mass Conservatism 1867–1997', exhibition, National Museum of Labour History, Manchester, 25 September 1998–17 January 1999.

81 Moore, 'Labour History in Museums'.

82 For example, Martin, 'The Vermin Club'.

83 Martin, *Popular Collecting*, p. 128.

84 King, 'Labour History', p. 13.

85 D. Spargo, *This Land Is Our Land: aspects of agriculture in English art*, London, Royal Academy of Art, 1989, pp. 108–109.

86 Both the National Museum of Labour History and the National Railway Museum in Britain bought up private collections during the 1990s.

87 It passed to his son on his death some years ago. Its exact location is now obscure, but is believed to be in London. (information from NUL&MW, 3 February 2000).

88 V. Bott, summary in Bott (ed.) *Labour History In Museums*, p. 22.

89 Gorman, 'What To Collect', in Bott (ed.), *Labour History in Museums*, p. 5.

90 Martin, *Popular Collecting*, p. 110.

91 Martin, 'Tomorrow's History ...'; Martin, *Popular Collecting*, pp. 105–113; Jo Digger 'The People's Show At Walsall', unpublished MA dissertation, Department of Museum Studies, University of Leicester, 1995; R. Fardell, 'From Australiana To World War Memorabilia: The People's Show Festival At Harborough Museum', unpublished MA dissertation, Department of Museum Studies, Leicester University; J. Lovatt; 'The People's Show Festival 1994', in S. Pearce (ed.), *Experiencing Material Culture In The Western World*, London, Leicester University Press, 1997, pp. 196–254.

92 See E. Frostick, 'Worth A Hull Lot More', *Museums Journal*, Vol. 91, No. 2, February, pp. 33–35.

93 Moore, 'Labour History In Museums ...', p. 168.

94 For example, Bott, *Labour History In Museums*; Knowles, 'The Portrayal of Labour

History ...'; H. Coutts and H. Clark, 'Telling The Story', *Museums Journal*, Volume 89, No. 8, August, 1989, pp. 30–32; S.N. Mastoris (ed.), *Social History Curators' Group Journal* No. 18, 1990–91; H. Clark and S. Marwick, 'The People's Story – Moving On', *Social History Curators' Group Journal*, No. 19, 1991–92, pp. 54–65.

95 For example, M. Trustram, 'Which History, Whose History?', *Northwest Labour History*, No. 15, 1990–1991, pp. 16–25; Trustram 'The National Museum of Labour History' op. cit.; Moore, 'Labour History In Museums ...'.

96 Martin, *Popular Collecting*, pp. 99–129, 144–149.

97 For instance, one collector, on being notified of a union branch moving offices, arrived to find a number of its badges floating away in the gutter!.

98 Clark, 'Worn With Pride', p. 20.

99 A resurgence in the use of banners and iconography generally was a characteristic of the 1980s labour movement in Britain, inverting the entrepreneurial spirit for its resistance to Thatcherism. One example was Red Wedge Banners. This was a part of the pop artists Billy Bragg ('wearing badges is not enough') and Paul Weller's 'Red Wedge' arts initiative, which offered a platform to the Labour Party to communicate with youth. Red Wedge Banners was established in 1983. Thaila Campbell, a feminist antinuclear activist, who commissioned banners for CND, local Labour Parties, etc. was another example. Jonathan Fell 'works in a more modern idiom' ('Sign Language', *Labour Party News*, 1987, November/December, p. 20) with avant garde designs for Labour Parties, etc. At the 1987 Labour Party conference there was a Red Wedge/Arts For Labour stall setting out their wares. The inheritors of the original George Tutill company, Chippenham Designs, began to do good trade with local trade union branches, and Gorman's 1973 book, *Banner Bright* was republished, suitably updated to incorporate the new demand, in 1986; in other articles he restated his original case for their preservation (J. Gorman, *Banner Bright*, London, Scorpion Books (3rd edition)1986), which by now was almost accepted as a given amongst union activists, art historians and collectors alike; J.Gorman, 'Trade Union Banners', *Artseen*, No. 14, December 1986/ January 1987, pp. 10–11. The popularity of trade union badges was recognised by Manchester City Council. The programme of the 1988 annual Manchester Trade Union week ran a competition to name the unions featured on badges which comprised the front cover (the author won first prize, part of which included the photograph of the badges!). The GMB meanwhile, for its centenary conference in 1989 in Brighton, published its conference information with reproductions of suitable historic certificates and designs from its past.

100 During 1986 and 1987, a large number of enamel badges were produced in support of the Wapping dispute between Rupert Murdoch's titles and the print union's National Graphical Association (NGA) and Society of Graphical & Allied Trades (SOGAT). The majority of them were issued by John Breen of the NGA, and bought in great numbers by collectors. Breen ultimately presented the dies from which the badges were struck, together with representative examples of the finished badges, to the NGA on the eve of the amalgamation between the NGA and SOGAT to form the Graphical, Print and Media Union (GPMU). They now reside in a display case in the foyer of the GPMU's head office. Wonderful enamel badges, commemorating May Day, were also made in the late 1980s, designed by Strike Graphics, which again highlights the use of such material as a defensive weapon and morale booster.

101   At least one rare NUM badge from the 1984/85 strike, the South Kirby 'Second To None' badge, which was at the time changing hands for up to £60, was bought by one woman as a parting gift for her soon-to-be-divorced husband, whilst another woman bought a copy of the same badge as a wedding present for her fiancé!.

Chapter 7

This Is What I Am

People use them [badges] to maintain identity in a rapidly changing environment like the
NHS to remember the past from whence they came. Also so many hospitals/schools of
nursing are now gone forever and 'Trusts' are NOT issuing badges (cost saving measures)
and hence people are feeling very insecure etc. Badges offer a link with the past.[1]

For more than a century, the badge in one form or another has played a crucial part
in trade unions. During this time it has evolved from its cryptomasonic origins and
grown from being a secretly carried symbol of belief, worn *inside* jackets or
elsewhere with discretion, to an overtly displayed mark of a felt security. The
iconography progressed from arcane and exclusive craft symbolism to inclusive
and easily understood symbols of unity through strength, be they clasped hands or
lath bundles. Mottoes and maxims changed from craft-based, defensive conservatism such as 'united to protect, not combined to injure' to the universal Marxist
maxim 'workers of the world unite', which before the First World War even the
former 'Railway Servants' and relaunched agricultural labourers union asserted on
their badges. As such, the badge more than any other form of material culture,
mirrors the growth of trade unionism in Britain. From clandestine origins, to
legally constituted organisations, unions proudly asserted their recognition by employers and governments and their independence and confidence through the iconic
pride emblazoned on the lapel of the ordinary member. The union badge was an
outward indication of an inward stability and resolve. Indeed, it soon took on the
mantle of civic achievement or public service when used as an award for long
membership of or active service in the union. It became a celebratory symbol of
pride, a souvenir or memory capsule when used to commemorate the 'jubilee
outing', as did the National Union of Lock and Metal Workers before the Second
World War or the Amalgamated Engineering Union after it, for instance. All of
which can be read as allegorical of the way in which trade unions were once
culturally cemented in local communities along with the cooperative movement,
working-men's clubs and friendly societies, as the organisational sinews of a proudly
self-conscious collective identity.

In more recent decades, a myriad array of badges have appeared denoting officials within unions, anniversaries and other events, political and cause factions
within unions, local disputes and committees, gender and occupational groups and
sections, etc. The causes of the past have been re-invoked in the iconography of the
new, linking the past with the future and therefore promoting the need to act in the

present. This burgeoning of the union badge has not arisen in a vacuum. As work has changed and occupations diversified, as women have come to comprise a major part of the permanent work force and the importance of gender and racial equality and opportunity has become recognised, so demand has grown for recognition of individual roles within collective activity through the use of the badge to denote it. The largest British trade union, UNISON, by 2000, could boast of a very large selection of badges, which not only identified the different occupational groups embraced within it, but also a large number of generically designed logo badges with the various regions or districts of the union appended to them. Thus can be seen the assertion of local identity within the context of the national, rather like parochial Second World War home front organisations, members want to be seen to be 'doing their bit' at a local level whilst feeling a part of a large national organisation. The local or regional representations of trade unionism worn on the lapel help enable bonding with and encourage participation in, or feelings of belonging to, what otherwise might seem in such a large national organisation, a remoteness from local conditions.

The use of the badge, in contemporary British society at least, serves to highlight the cyclical nature of history. As the contraction of industry and the expansion of services and the professions has intensified through globalisation, so the process is mirrored in the badges of unions organising in them, both graphically or iconically in membership badges and in the use of the protest and dispute or commemorative badge. Therefore this decline and rise is better represented iconographically than the material culture that remains of the protests against the rise of industry in the eighteenth century. The ephemeral and clandestine nature of the followers of the apocryphal 'Ned Ludd' and 'Captain Swing' in the early nineteenth century have left us little in terms of material culture of their activities; there is an equal paucity of material culture from the displaced hand-loom weaver 'Blanketeers' and other victims of industrialisation. The early trade unions which arose to organise those engaged in the new industrial processes left material culture such as rule books, tramping cards and commemorative pottery and are amongst the best representation of the transformation of society at this time.

For future historians of our own period of socio-economic transition, the trade union badge should prove a significant part of the story, synoptically documenting as it does the resistance to unfettered free market forces and the fight for stability in a world, which in our own lifetimes at least, does often seem to have 'turned upside-down'. The badge in contemporary society chronicles the issues that affect people's daily lives and advocates the principles that individuals and progressive organisations feel should be upheld and fought for in order to consolidate and maintain both their retrospective and future self-perceived role and place in society. They illustrate in imagery, maxims and slogans the changing pattern of society and its infrastructure, socially, politically, industrially, commercially and economically. They underline specific causes prevalent at any particular time and magnify them. The Iron and Steel Trades Confederation offer an example of this change. They chose for the venue of their 1992 annual conference, the Sparrenduin Conference Centre in Belgium. Describing the design of the conference badge for this conference, they state in a note for delegates:

> We, the ISTC, who continue in those metal making skills, have chosen Belgium as the venue for our Annual Conference as a token of commitment to a united Europe. Thus the Celtic figure, the link between the past and the future, holds his iron sword in one hand and his shield carrying the European symbol in the other.

Further research needs to be undertaken in the area of badge manufacturers, especially the old, well-established ones, which may well yield more evidence in relation to the extent that the badge was used in the early years. Patents and registrations held at the Public Record Office seem to be one useful source for this, and one or two collectors have already made attempts in this direction. As many of these firms themselves have in recent years folded or amalgamated, more company records are lost. Stephen Peak (see Chapter 5) related to me in the 1980s how many old dies of badges long since defunct, and paperwork pertaining to them, were regularly disposed of in the larger badge manufactories in Birmingham's jewellery quarter, in order to make room for newer ones. The same urgency therefore needs to be attached to the investigation and, dare I say, 'rescue' of such material, as is given to the early designs and moulds of pottery which are held in such high esteem. John Gorman is rightly respected for his research and salvage work on trade union banners, but by the time he was active, as he told me himself, and which he noted in *Banner Bright*, he was hearing stories of old banners being fed as fuel to the office boiler. Even in the late 1980s, one of the last officials of the Pressed Glass Makers Society in north-east England, told me how he had himself chosen what he thought important from the union's records when it was wound up and deposited them with the local library, whilst making a bonfire of the rest in his back garden!

Any attempt to rescue commercial material like old badge dies or paper records pertaining to customers, etc., should be conducted in conjunction with professionals such as archivists, industrial historians and archaeologists, and museum staff. The relationship between popular collectors and museum staff, as I argued in *Popular Collecting and the Everyday Self*, could be a lot more trusting, but as I have sketched out in Chapter 6, the alliance in Britain at least between collectors and labour history museums and research bodies has improved markedly throughout the 1990s. Many trade union badge collectors, however, feel sceptical about leaving material to museums, because it is unlikely to go on immediate and permanent display. It is up to museum practitioners, at least in the environments discussed in Chapter 6, to take advantage of their mutual interest with collectors, to try to explain the nature of museum practice. In this way, collectors' organisations and museums become symbiotic and over the longer term will, I feel, merge as a wider and more fluid conceptual manifestation of 'museum'.

Ultimately, what I have tried to show is how the badge iconically has acted as a kind of coded language. I have sought to use it as a vehicle for drawing attention to the material culture of the everyday and how it bears on how we live and what we understand through it. The curiosity of a worker as to the nature of a badge, seen on the lapel of another, could easily lead to the opening of a debate or a discussion of the merits of the union it referred to and the sense of joining it. The badge is one thing that members of a union will ask for and still has this attraction or even fascination.[2] The course of events described in this book have all taken place in a very public arena; the very point of the badge being to advertise or even proselytise for the union. This then is a very public history, but which has in the widest public sense, gone unnoticed or uncommented upon. Like ancient public wall plaques or monuments which testify to locally long-defunct events, communal presences or individuals, the union badge has gone unnoticed because of its public ubiquity. Deeper readings of such material therefore reveal to us the complexity that is so often involved in what is assumed to be simplistic or trivial.

The visual legacy of the union badge is an attractive and evocative social and cultural display of battles fought, honours awarded, issues and themes adopted in the movement, and the changing patterns of rising and declining industries and occupations. Historically it acts as a touchstone with time and creates an empathy with the people who wore it and the causes they fought for. They are a public historical statement, helping to promote history as made by the people and thus counteracting 'great men' theories of history which still periodically come into fashion. They are an invaluable source of trade union values and worth. They can sum up a mood, or reveal an intensity felt over certain issues. The badge is imperative to the effective engagement with and communication of the history of the labour movement and working class as a whole. It continues to act as a material chronicle of contemporary society and the fundamental changes that the very notion of 'work' is currently undergoing. It will no doubt continue to act in this way in the future as workplaces and workforces change and the boundaries between work and leisure dissolve or become more fluid. As Ruth and Eddie Frow of the Working Class Movement Library have said:

> One of the things we have tried to do is to show the very diverse ways in which working class culture develops ... The main reason for this [the collection] is that it can inspire people to know that others before them have struggled and fought for a cause and it can help to solve current problems if correctly applied.[3]

With the union badge as part of this culture, there seems no better way to end than on that note.

Notes

1   E. Wilkinson, personal communication, 12 May 2000.
2   An instance of the badge's attraction to the membership *per se* involves some novel inter-union rivalry from the mid-1980s. NUPE (now part of UNISON) and the GMB were competing in one town for members. NUPE, as part of their recruitment propaganda, claimed that they were the better union, as they gave their badges away free, whereas the GMB charged for theirs. The GMB official apparently toyed with the idea of asking for the charge to be dropped, as the move was having a positive effect for NUPE! (K. Pickering, in conversation, Ruskin College, Oxford, 1987). More recently, an activist in UNISON related that:

> One of the health branches in Cumbria obtained a large number of health care sectional badges from me, and gave them out to members as part of the sign up campaign (we recently had to get all members to sign up to remain union members, under law). Another health care branch produced a branch badge and only sent it to members when a completed sign up form was received in the branch office, it also encouraged a large number of non-members to join the branch. (A. Redpath, personal communication, 1998)

> Conversely, Terry Thomas, an ex-AEU member, recalls that in the 1950s and 1960s the wearing of the union badge was considered by the younger members as something that old men did. It was the older members who wore the badge, which may have been seen in the sense of a British Legion badge, as something 'fuddy-duddy' or un-hip by the younger members (T. Thomas, in conversation, Ruskin College, Oxford, 1987).

3   *Morning Star*, 3 January 1987, pp. 6–7.

Appendix 1

Selected Replies To The *Labour Research* Survey

In October and November 1986, Nick Clark of *Labour Research*, conducted a postal questionnaire of TUC-affiliated trade unions, canvassing their opinions on and use of the lapel badge in their respective unions. The findings were incorporated in his article in the February 1987 issue of *Labour Research*. Below are some of the more significant replies that Clark received, in terms of their pertinence to issues raised in this book.

Amalgamated Engineering Union (AEU):
It is an item we have been able to sell to the members and even if there were not a clear demand for badges we believe that the value of our identity/logo represents very valuable free publicity.

Association of Professional Executive Clerical and Computer Staff (APEX):
We believe union badges were introduced to identify the wearer as a union member and so instil pride for being involved in the trades union movement. The use of badges is a tradition which members and lay officials feel is particularly important.

Banking, Insurance and Finance Union (BIFU):
We find they are of value to identify active union members. Also useful to give out to visitors from other unions.

Engineers and Managers Association (EMA):
Like all badges, it is useful in that a member who wears it is readily recognised by another and is a stimulus to the inquisitive.

Greater London Staff Association (GLSA):
The badge acts as a good advertisement for the union. They are a small part of the history of the labour movement and are to be encouraged.

National Graphical Association (NGA):
Members show considerable interest in the badges and we are regularly receiving requests for further supplies.

National Union of Footwear, Leather and Allied Trades (NUFLAT):
Our view is that they give a sense of identity with fellow trade union members and their aims and objectives. They also show a fraternity in both human and industrial relations and a bond of friendship within the international family of trade unionism.

National Union of Lock and Metal Workers (NUL&MW):
We encourage as many members as possible to purchase a badge especially representatives and to wear the badge at work and at union meetings. We believe they represent a part of trade union history.

National Union of Mineworkers (NUM):
They are an expression of the importance of understanding the historical traditions and experiences of the trade union and labour movement ... They are a useful and important means of expressing a visible identity with the organisation and assist towards the development of a collective trade union consciousness.

Technical, Administrative and Supervisory Staff (TASS):
We believe it is essential to have a badge which projects the appropriate image to the men and women whom the organisation seeks to recruit. Badges are also an economic way to promote solidarity or good relations with other organisations at home and abroad.

Union of Communication Workers:
It is our belief that our badge is a valuable asset in making our members feel a part of the union ... In our uniformed grades we have an agreement with the post office that our badge is the only unofficial adornment allowed on a uniform and many of our postmen (and women) wear their trade union badges every day of their working lives. To many of these members – as well as members of the public – it is part of the uniform.

Appendix 2

The Badge and Medallion in Song and Rhyme

The following are the full lyrics to the song 'The Colour Bar Strike', mentioned in Chapter 4. It was written by Charlie Mayo and recorded by Ewan Mcoll and Peggy Seager on *Industrial Ballads*, and reproduced in Rose's, *One Hundred Years of King's Cross ASLEF* (1986, pp. 48–50):

The Colour Bar Strike

My union badge shows two joined hands
with a lighted flame in common fight
but trouble's brewing in the sheds
for both these working hands are white

But working hands are white and black
and the work they do is just the same
but fear and ignorance come in
to break the grip and dim the flame.

The shunters broke the grip one day
The King's Cross goods yard went on strike
not in a fight for better pay
but a coloured man they did not like.

They did not like the coloured man
they would not work with him they said
In truth it touched their overtime
but to a colour bar it led.

The colour bar strikers soon went back
Jim Figgins led the NUR
and when they asked for his support
he said 'we'll have no colour bar'.

Jim Figgins said get back to work
this is a strike we'll not support
This is the kind of ignorance
the unions have always fought

But though the union won that fight
the pressures there are rising higher
smoke rises in the engine sheds
and where there's smoke, there's always fire.

Men, don't let smoke get in your eyes
kindle that flame and keep it bright
to proud tradition still be true
and make those joined hands black and white.

The following rhyme was composed by Mr W. Franks in honour of Mr C.H. Hague of Manchester No. 6 Branch of the Transport Salaried Staffs Association (TSSA), who had been a member since 1922, and was awarded TSSA's gold medallion, the Association's highest award, which was presented by Tom Bradley MP, TSSA president in 1968. It was published in the *TSSA Journal*, November 1968, p. 12:

The Gold Medallion

Not achieved through the power of a
strong right arm
or the explosive dash down some
athletic track,
nor yet for some prodigious leap
as high or as broad as a farm hay
stack.

Neither achieved for a 'courier'
service
currying favour for work done,
not yet for digging pits for others
or propelling himself into the sun.

But for service to the underprivileged
class
with the ability and the ferocity that would
dispel a plague
loyalty to the association he has
willingly served
the gold medallion is awarded to
Charles Harry Hague.

Appendix 3

The KOKURO/ITF Survey Questionnaire and Unions in Countries Which Replied To It

8 November 1993

Dear Friends
<u>Wearing of Trade Union Badges On Duty</u>
Our Japanese affiliate, the National Railway Workers' Union – KOKURO, has informed us that its members employed by JR companies have been disciplined by company managements for wearing union badges during working hours. While KOKURO has obtained favourable decisions from District Labour Relations Committees, the companies have refused to accept these decisions and KOKURO will now pursue the case through the courts.

In order to assist KOKURO, I should be grateful if you would answer the following questions:-

1. Are your members allowed to wear your union's badges during working hours?

2. If "Yes", is this by specific agreement between your union and railway management?

3. Is the maximum size of the badge prescribed? If "Yes", what is the size?

4. If a written agreement exists regarding the wearing of badges or if company regulations prohibit it, please supply a copy of the text.

5. If the wearing of badges is prohibited, what disciplinary action has been taken by railway management against employees who continue to wear them?

6. Please send examples of union badges which your union members wear during working hours.

175

On behalf of KOKURO, I thank you in advance for your assistance.

Yours fraternally,

Graham Brothers
Assistant General Secretary (ITF)

Australia:	Public Transport Union
Austria:	HTV
	Gewerkschaft der Eisenbahner
Britain:	Associated Society Of Locomotive Enginemen & Firemen (ASLEF)
	Transport & General Workers Union
Canada:	National Automobile, Aerospace & Agricultural Implement Workers Union
Denmark:	Dansk Jernbaneforbund
	Dansk Metalarbejderforbund
France:	Fédération des Cheminots
Fiji:	Figi Sugar And General Workers Union
Germany:	Vervoers Bund FNV
	Gewerkschaft Öffentliche Dienste, Transport und Verkehr Hauptvorstand
Ghana:	Railway Enginemen's Union
Greece:	Federation Panhellenique Des Cheminots
Hong Kong:	Mass Transit Railway Operating Department Staff Union
India:	All India Railwaymen's Federation
Israel:	Histadrut – General Federation of Labour In Israel
Luxembourg:	FNCTTEEL – Landesverband
Norway:	Norsk Jernbaneforbund
	Norsk Lokomotivmannsforbund
Spain:	UGT
Switzerland:	Schweizerischer Eisenbahner-Verband (SEV)
Sweden:	Statsanstalldas Forbund
Turkey:	Railway Workers Trade Union Of Turkey
USA:	International Association of Machinists and Aerospace Workers

Appendix 4

The History of Thomas Fattorini Ltd.

The following is the transcript of a publicity leaflet printed by Thomas Fattorini Ltd. in the 1980s:

<u>General & History of the firm of</u>
<u>THOMAS FATTORINI LTD</u>

The original Fattorini came to England from Northern Italy in the early part of the nineteenth century (after the Napoleonic wars). He was established as a jewellery and watchmaker in North Yorkshire and over the years opened a number of retail jeweller shops in that area.

Later the methods adopted for selling items such as barometers and clocks to the local farming communities led to the development of mail order in this country and this side of the business outpaced the retail side in the first forty years of this century.

Around 1900, the shops in the north were increasingly being asked to supply badges for new clubs, such as the burgeoning Football Association clubs and manufacture of this type of item commenced in Bolton, Lancashire. However, this was an unsuitable locale for metal production and a small factory was opened in Birmingham's jewellery quarter just before WWI. This was moved in 1929 to larger premises in Regent Street – still in the jewellery quarter – and now our head office.

In the 1930's the retail shops were sold and the company concentrated on mail order from Skipton and badge, insignia and trophy manufacture in Birmingham.

Although the mail order side moved from Skipton to Manchester during WWII, Skipton Castle maintains our links with that area and is our registered office today.

Over twenty years ago, a manufacturing unit was opened in Manchester, and now all the company's plastic injection and screen printing is carried out there, although we disposed of the Manchester mail order warehouse some fifteen years ago.

In recent years, a further factory, very close to our Regent Street, Birmingham premises, was purchased to house expanding production facilities and in November 1983, we completed the purchase of Fattorini and Sons Ltd (a firm which, whilst sharing our surname, had no connection with us, apart from having been founded by a relative of our founders about one hundred and fifty years ago).

We are now specialists in the design and production of National Honours and Awards.

Civic and association insignia
Military uniforms, accoutrements and swords
Club and association membership badges
Plastic personal and identification badges
Nursing and Hospital badges
Superior quality badges for superior cars (Rolls-Royce, Lotus, Aston Martin, Morgan etc.)
General Gold and Silversmiths.

Appendix 5

Explanations of Two Badge Designs

The Irish Customs and Excise Union, letter to author 12 October 1987

I have pleasure in enclosing our union badge which, as you can see, features the griffin who, in mythology, kept guard over hidden wealth. The body is that of a lion and its claws, head and wings that of a powerful eagle. This emblem was first used by the union in 1971. In legend the griffin (or gryphon), guarded the wealth of Scythia from the Arimaspians, the one-eyed people. Milton mentions them in *Paradise Lost*:-

'As when a Gryphon, through the wilderness,
Pursues the Arimaspian, who, by stealth,
has from his wakeful custody purloined,
the guarded gold'.

Scythia was a country in what is now South West USSR, and it lay roughly between the Carpathians and the Don. The country had valuable gold mines which were envied by the Arimaspians, a barbarous people who lived in the mountains to the North East. The griffin is the emblem of watchfulness, courage, perseverance and rapidity of execution and, as such, is considered very appropriate to represent the ICEU.

Yours sincerely,

Martin McDonald,
General Secretary

Union of Communication Workers (UCW), handbill, London 1987

The design of the UCW badge consists of the Caduceus or winged staff of Hermes, with a panel of red enamel with the letters "UCW" in white at the head. The original caduceus was simply in olive black ornamented at the end with garlands. On an ancient vase Hermes can be seen with this simpler type of symbol. This was presented to him by Apollo in exchange for the lyre which he is reputed to have invented. Mercury, which was the Roman name for the same god (Hermes was the

Greek name) is sometimes referred to in classical literature as the Caducifer, or one who carried the Caduceus. The Caduceus was a herald's staff, and Mercury carried it as the herald of the gods. In Greek the person sent as an ambassador to treat for peace was called a Caduceator. Mercury's rod was supposed to be endowed with the power of deciding all quarrels and of bestowing great eloquence upon its possessor – two very useful qualities for a peace ambassador. It might be well if some duplicates of this rod could be issued to a few of our present-day [c.1987] diplomats. The two serpents which inter-twine themselves round the rod have been restrained from fighting and reconciled by its peacemaking powers. "L'Empriere" suggests, however, that they may symbolise prudence. The rod is supposed also to be vested with resurrectionary powers. The pine cone which is often shown is the repository of health-giving power. The wings are the symbol of diligence or, alternatively, speed. If any members of the UCW place their faith in mascots therefore, they could hardly do better than invest in a UCW badge. Mercury, the bearer of the Caduceus, was the son of Jupiter and Mars, who was a daughter of Atlas. He is sometimes represented with his foot upon a tortoise; the lyre which he exchanged for the Caduceus was made of tortoise shell. On other occasions he is shown as seated on a crayfish.

Bibliography of Principle Works Cited

Achten, U., Reichelt, M. and Schultz, R. (1986) *Mein Vaterland ist International: internationale illustrierte Geschichte des 1. mai 1886 bis heute*, Berlin, Asso Verlag.

L'Aventure du Travail: Des Outils et des Hommes, Visitors Guide, Musée due Bassin Houiller Lorrain, 2000.

Alexander, S., Davin, A. and Hostettler, E. (1979) 'Labouring Women: a reply to Eric Hobsbawm', *History Workshop*, 8, pp. 174–82.

Allen, V.L (1958) 'The National Union of Police and Prison officers', *Economic History Review*, Vol. X1, (1), pp. 133–43.

American Federation of Labour, (1911) *International Label Department Directory*, Washington, DC, AFL.

Atkinson, D. (1992) *The Purple, White & Green: suffragettes in London 1906–1914*, London, Museum of London.

Attwood, P. (1982) *Acquisition of Badges (1978–1982)*, Occasional Paper No. 55, Department of Coins and Medals, London, British Museum.

—— (1990) *Acquisition of Badges (1983–1987)*, Occasional Paper No. 76, Department of Coins and Medals, London, British Museum.

Bagwell, P. S. (1963) *The Railwaymen: the history of the National Union of Railwaymen*, London, George Allen & Unwin.

Bailey, W. Milne (ed.) (1929), *Trade Union Documents*, London, G. Bell & Sons.

Beard, M. and Henderson, J. (1994) 'Please Don't Touch The Ceiling: the culture of appropriation' in Pearce, S.M. *The Appropriation of Culture*, Vol. 4 of New Research in Museum Studies series, London: Athlone Press, pp. 5–42.

Beer, M. (1984) *A History Of British Socialism*, London, Spokesman.

Belchem, J. (1985) *Henry 'Orator' Hunt: Henry Hunt and English Working-Class Radicalism*, Oxford, Clarendon Press .

Belk, R. (1988) 'Possessions And The Extended Self', *Journal Of Consumer Research*, Vol. 15, September, pp. 139–68.

Belk, R. (1995) *Collecting In Contemporary Society*, London, Routledge.

Bird, S. (1985) 'The British Workers Sports Association 1930–1960', *Bulletin of The Society for the Study Of Labour History*, No. 50, Spring, pp. 7–9.

Blaenau Ffestiniog Women's Support Group (1986) *We Stand Together: Blaenau Ffestiniog 1985–1986 – seven months on the slate*, Wales, Blaenau Ffestiniog Women's Support Group.

Boney, K. (1962) 'The Liverpool Society of Bucks', *Apollo: the magazine of the arts,* January, p. 8–10.

Bott, V. (ed.) (1988) *Labour History in Museums,* London, Society For The Study of Labour History/Social History Curators Group.

Brake, T. (1985) *Men of Good Character,* London, Lawrence & Wishart.

Bromley, J. and Child, H. (1960) *The Armorial Bearings of the Guilds of London,* London, Frederick Warne & Co..

Brunel, C. and Jackson, P.M. (1966) 'Notes on tokens as a source of information on the history of the labour and radical movement, part one', *Journal of the Society For The Study of Labour History,* No. 13, Autumn, pp. 26–36.

Buhle, P. and Sullivan E.B. (1998) *Images of American Radicalism,* Massachusetts, Christopher Publishing House.

Bundock, C.J. (1959) *The Story of The National Union of Printing, Bookbinding and Paper Workers,* Oxford University Press.

Cahn, W. (1972) *A Pictorial History of American Labor,* New York, Crown Publishers.

Campbell, T. (1990) *100 Years Of Women's Banners* (second edition), Dyfed, Wales, Women For Life On Earth.

—— and Wilson, M. (1994) *Each for All and All for Each: a celebration of Co-operative banners,* Manchester, National Co-operative Education Association.

Carpenter, M. (1980) *All for One,* Surrey, COHSE.

—— (1988) *Working for Health: a history of COHSE,* London, Lawrence & Wishart.

Chaplin, P. M. (1982) *The Thames from Source to Tideway,* London, Whittel.

Citrine, W. (1933) *How We Will Commemorate The Dorsetshire Labourers Centenary,* TUC, London.

Clark, N. (1987) 'Worn With Pride–Union Badges', *Labour Research,* February, pp. 19–20.

Clarke, A. (1999) *Tupperware: The Promise of Plastic in 1950s America,* Washington/London, Smithsonian Institute Press.

Clayson, A. (1997) *Hamburg: Cradle of British Rock,* London, Sanctuary Press.

Coates, K. and Topham, T. (1991) *The History of the Transport and General Workers Union Volume One: the making of the Transport and General Workers Union, the emergence of the labour movement 1870–1922,* Oxford, Blackwell.

Corfield, A.J. (1964) 'Docker's Trade Unionism In Liverpool', *TGWU Record,* December.

Cooper, W.G. (1984) *The Ancient Order of Foresters Friendly Society: 150 years 1834–1984,* Southampton, Hampshire, AOF.

Cox, N. and Cox, A.(1994) *The Tokens, Checks, Metallic Tickets, Passes And Tallies of Wales 1800–1993: Two Hundred Years of Welsh Paranumismatic History,* Cardiff. .

Cummings, D.C. (1905) *The History of the United Society of Boilermakers and Iron and Steel Shipbuilders,* Newcastle upon Tyne, USBI&SS.

Cuthbert, N.H. (1960) *The Lace Makers Society*, Nottingham, Amalgamated Society of Lace Makers and Auxiliary Workers.

Danet, B. and Katriel, T. (1994) 'Glorious Obsessions, Passionate Lovers and Hidden Treasures: collecting, metaphor and the romantic ethic', in Riggins, S.H. (ed.) *The Socialness Of Things: Essays on the socio-semiotics of objects,* Berlin: Mouton de Gruyter, pp. 23–61.

Dash, J. (1969) *Good Morning Brothers*, London, Lawrence & Wishart.

Davin, A. (1981) 'Feminism And Labour History', in Samuel, R. (ed.), *People's History and Socialist Theory*, London, Routledge, pp. 176–81.

Deetz, J. (1977) *In Small Things Forgotten: the archaeology of early American life*, New York, Anchor Books.

Devine, F. (1984) 'Who Dares Wear The Red Hand Badge?', *Liberty*, Journal of the ITGWU, June.

Diehl, H. (1986) *An Index of Icons in English Emblem Books 1500–1700*, Oklahoma, University of Oklahoma Press.

Digger, J. (1995) 'The People's Show at Walsall', unpublished MA thesis, Department of Museum Studies, University of Leicester..

Doyle, P. and O'Down, J. (eds) (1986) *The Parliament of Labour: 100 years of the Dublin Council of Trade Unions*, Catalogue prepared for an exhibition in The Dublin Civic Museum, 7 October–31 December 1986, Dublin, Irish Labour History Society.

Dresser, M. (1989) 'The Colour Bar In Bristol, 1963', in Samuel, R. (ed.), *Patriotism: the making and unmaking of British national identity,* Vol. 1: History and Politics, London, Routledge, pp. 288–316.

Durr, A. (1983) 'The Origin of the Craft', *Ars Quatuor Coronatorum*, Vol. 96, pp. 170–83.

—— (1987) 'Rituals of Association and the Organisation of the Common People', *Ars Quatuor Coronatorum*, Vol. 100, pp. 88–108.

—— (1988a) 'Popular Art: The Emblems And Associations of Mutual Aid', Unpublished manuscript, Brighton..

—— (1988b) *Popular Art: The Emblems and Associations Of Mutual Aid*, exhibition catalogue, University of Brighton.

Emery, N. (1998) *Banners of the Durham Coalfield*, Gloucestershire, Sutton Press.

Erixon, S. (1949) *Stockholm's Hamnarbetare*, Stockholm, Nordisk Rotogravyr.

Fardell, R. (1995) 'From Australiana to World War Memorabilia: The People's Show Festival at Harborough Museum', Unpublished MA thesis, Department of Museum Studies, Leicester University.

Fevyer, W.H., Wilson, J.W. and Cribb, J. (2000) *The Order of Industrial Heroism*, Guildford, Surrey, Orders and Medals Research Society.

Foner, P. S. and Schultz, R. (1986) *Das Andere Amerika*, Berlin, Elefanten Press.

Freeman, R. (1948) *English Emblem Books*, London, Chatto & Windus, 1967 edition.

French, J.O (1965) *Plumbers in Unity*, London, PTU.

Froggatt, D. (1986) *Railway Buttons, Badges & Uniforms*, London, Ian Allen.

Frow, E and Frow, R. (1976a) 'Travels With A Caravan', *History Workshop*, No. 2, pp. 177–82.

—— (1976b) 'Trade Union Emblems', *North-West Group for the Study of Labour History*, No. 3, pp. 29–31.

—— (1980) 'Badges of The Engineers', *AUEW Journal*, August.

Fuller, K. (1985) *Radical Aristocrats*, London, Lawrence & Wishart.

Gardiner, J. (1996) *Checks, Tokens, Tickets and Passes of County Durham and Northumberland*, Darlington (self-published).

Geertz, C. (1973) *The Interpretation of Cultures*, New York, Basic Books.

Glancy, M. (1988) 'The Play World Setting of the Auction', *Journal of Leisure Research*, Vol. 20, No. 2, pp. 135–53.

Godwin, A. (1979) *The Friends of Liberty*, London, Hutchinson.

Gombrich, E.H. (1972) *Symbolic Images*, Oxford, Phaidon Press (1985 edition).

Gordon, B. (1986) 'The Souvenir: messenger of the extraordinary', *Journal of Popular Culture*, Vol. 20, No. 3, pp. 135–46.

Gorman, J. (1973) *Banner Bright*, London, Allan Lane .

—— (1985) *Images of Labour*, London, Scorpion.

—— (1986) *Banner Bright*, London, Scorpion (revised and updated, 3rd edition).

Gosden, P. H.J.H. (1961) *The Friendly Societies in England 1815–1875*, Manchester, Manchester University Press.

Graves, V. (ed.) (1987) *Trade Union Badges*, Milton Keynes. A compilation of photocopied articles on badges from various sources..

Greaves, C. Desmond (1982) *The Irish Transport & General Workers Union: The Formative Years*, Dublin, Gill & MacMillan.

Gregson, N. and Crewe L. (1994) 'Beyond the high street and the mall: car boot fairs and the new geographies of consumption in the 1990's', *Area 26*, pp. 261–7.

—— (1997a) 'The bargain, the knowledge and the spectacle: making sense of consumption in the space of the car boot sale', *Environment and Planning D: Social Space*, Vol. 15, pp. 87–112.

—— (1997b) 'Performance and Possession: rethinking the act of purchase in the light of the car boot sale', *Journal of Material Culture*, Vol. 2, No. 2, pp. 241–63.

—— and Longstaff, B. (1997) 'Excluded spaces of regulation: car boot sales as an enterprise culture out of control?', *Environment And Planning A*, Vol. 29, pp. 1717–37.

Griffin, A.R. (1981) *The Notts Coalfield 1881–1981*, Nottingham, Moorland Publishing.

Hake, T. (1972) *The Button Book*, New York, Daffran House.

—— (1987) *Political Buttons, Book III 1789–1916*, Pennsylvania, Hakes Americana and Collectible Press.

Hammond, J. (1991) *Trade Union Badges*, Worthing, Private publication (first edition).

Haunch, T.O. (1969) 'English Craft Certificates', *Ars Quatuor Coronatorum*, Vol. 82, pp. 169–263.

Hawkins, R.N.P (1989) *A Dictionary of Makers of British Metallic Tickets, Checks,Medalets, Tallies and Counters 1778–1910*, London, Baldwins.

Hebdidge, D. (1985) *Subculture: The Meaning of Style*, London, Methuen.

Hermann, G.R. and Soiffer, S.M. (1984) 'For Fun And Profit: an analysis of the American garage sale', *Urban Life*, Vol. 12, No. 4, January, pp. 397–421.

Higginbottom, S. (1939) *Our Society's History*, Manchester, London, Amalgamated Society of Woodworkers.

Hobsbawm, E.J. (1949) 'General Labour Unions In Britain 1884–1914', *Economic History Review*, second series, No. 1, pp. 123–42.

—— (1959) *Primitive Rebels*, Manchester, Manchester University Press.

—— (1978) 'Man and Woman in Socialist Iconography', *History Workshop Journal*, No. 6, Autumn, pp. 121–38.

—— (1984) *Worlds of Labour*, London, Weidenfeld & Nicholson.

—— (1997) *On History*, London, Weidenfeld & Nicholson.

Horn, D. (1984) *The Great Museum: the re-presentation of history*, London, Pluto.

Huddle, R., Phillips, A., Simons, M. and Sturrock, J. (1985) *Blood, Sweat and Tears: photographs from the great miners strike 1984–1985,* London, Artworker Books.

Hutton, W. (1995) *The State We're In,* London: Jonathan Cape.

Hyman, R. (1971) *The Workers Union*, London, Clarendon Press.

Irish Transport and General Workers Union (1959) *Fifty Years Of Liberty Hall*, Dublin, ITGWU.

Iron & Steel Trades Confederation (1965) 'Trade Union Badges', *Men and Metal*, November, p. 326.

—— (1972) 'Gold, Silver and Silk Badges for Steelworkers', *Man and Metal*, Vol. 49, No. 7, July, p. 172.

Jefferson, H. (1892) *The Platform (Volume One)*, London, MacMillan.

Jedrzejczyk, I., Page, R., Prince, B. Young, I. (1986) *Striking Women: communities and coal*, London, Pluto Press .

Kavanagh, G. (1990) *History Curatorship*, Leicester, Leicester University Press.

Kean, H., Martin, P., Morgan, S. (eds) (2000) *Seeing History: Public History Now in Britain*, London, Francis Boutle.

Kellet, J.R. (1958) 'The breakdown of guild and corporation control over the handicraft and retail trade in London', *Economic History Review*, 2nd series, Vol. 10, pp. 381–94.

Kemp-Ashraf, P.M. (1984) *The Life And Times of Thomas Spence*, Newcastle-Upon-Tyne, Frank Graham .

Kiddier, W. (1930) *The Old Trade Unions*, London, George Allen & Unwin.

Kightly, C. (1986) *The Customs and Ceremonies of Britain: an encyclopaedia of living traditions* London, Thames and Hudson.

King, E. (1988) *The People's Palace and Glasgow Green*, Glasgow, Richard Drew.

Klingender, F.D. (1947/1968) *Art and the Industrial Revolution*, (Elton, A. ed.) London, Evelyn Adams & Mackay.

Knoop, D. and Jones, G.P. (1933) *The Medieval Mason: an economic history of English stone building in the later middle ages and early modern times*, Manchester, Manchester University Press.

Lasch, C. (1995) *The Revolt of the Elites and the Betrayal Of Democracy*, New York: Norton Publishers.

Leech, Sir Bosdin (1907) *The History of The Manchester Ship Canal*, London, Sherriton & Hughs.

Leeson, R.A. (1971) *United We Stand*, Bath, Adams & Dart.

—— (1979) *Travelling Brothers: the six centuries road from craft fellowship to trade unionism*, London, George Allen and Unwin.

—— and Dobson, C.R. (1980) *Masters And Journeymen: a prehistory of industrial relations 1717–1800,* London, Croom Helm.

Lloyd, M. (1995) *Military Badges and Insignia*, London, Grange Books .

Loftus, B. (1978) *Marching Workers*, Dublin, Arts Council of Ireland.

Lovatt, J.R (1997) 'The People's Show Festival 1994', in S. Pearce (ed.), *Experiencing Material Culture in the Western World*, Leicester, Leicester University Press, pp. 196–254.

Lovell, J. (1969) *Stevedores and Dockers: a study of trade unionism in the port of London 1870–1914,* London, MacMillan.

McCree, C. (1984) 'Flea Markets', *Psychology Today*, Vol. 18, No. 3, pp. 46–53.

McDonald, I. (1989) *Vindication! A postcard history of the women's movement*, London, Bellew.

McDougall, I. (1985) *Labour in Scotland*, Edinburgh, Mainstream Publishing.

Mace, R. (1999) *British Trade Union Posters*, Gloucestershire, Sutton Publishing.

Maisel, R. (1974) 'The Flea Market as an Action Scene', *Urban Life And Culture* Vol. 2, No. 4, January, pp. 488–505.

Malvern, L. (1986) *The End of the Street*, London, Methuen.

Marsh, A. and Ryan, V. (1980) *Historical Directory of Trade Unions, Volume 1*, Hampshire, Gower.

—— (1984) *Historical Directory of Trade Unions, Volume 2*, Hampshire, Gower.

—— (1987) *Historical Directory of Trade Unions, Volume 3*, Hampshire, Gower.

—— and Smethurst, J.B. (1994) *Historical Directory of Trade Unions, Volume 4*, Hampshire, Scolar Press.

Martin, P. (1992) 'Spain's Other Olympics', *History Today,* Vol. 42, No. 8, August, pp. 6–8.

—— (1994) 'Badgering the Union', *History Today*, Vol. 44, No. 1, January, pp. 9–12.

—— (1995) 'Collectors, Museums and Community', *Museological Review*, Vol. 1, No. 2, pp. 77–86.

—— (1996) 'Tomorrow's History Today: post-modern collecting', *History Today*, Vol. 46, No. 2, February, pp. 5–8.

—— (1997) 'The Vermin Club: 1948–1951', *History Today*, Vol. 47, No. 6, June, pp. 17–22 .

—— (1999) *Popular Collecting and the Everyday Self: the reinvention of museums?*, London, Leicester University Press .

Mayo, E., (ed.) (1984) *American Material Culture: the shape of things around us*, Ohio, Bowling Green State University Popular Press..

Meglaughlin, J. (1990) *British Nursing Badges, Volume One: an illustrated handbook*, London: Vade Mecum..

Mental Hospital and Institutional Workers Union (1931) *Twenty First Anniversary History*, Manchester, MH&IWU.

Milne, S. (1994) *The Enemy Within: the secret war against the miners*, London, Pan.

Minnitt, S. and Young, D. (1990) *Tickets, Checks and Passes from the County of Somerset*, Taunton, Somerset County Library And Museum Services.

Moffrey, R. H (1910) *A Century of Oddfellowship: being a brief record of the rise and progress of the Manchester Unity of Independent Order of Oddfellows*, Manchester, G.M. and Board of Directors IOOF..

Moore, K. (1994) 'Labour History In Museums: development and direction', in Pearce, S.M. (ed.) *Museums and the Appropriation of Culture*, London, Athlone Press, pp. 142–73.

Mortimer, J.M. (1973), *The History of The Boilermakers Society, Vol. 1: 1834–1906*, London, George Allen & Unwin.

Moyes, W. (1974) *The Banner Book,* Newcastle upon Tyne, Frank Graham.

Muller, C. (1978) *James Sharples und Das Zertifikat der Amalgamated Society of Engineers: Studien zur Bildkultur Britischer Gewerkshaften*, Hamburg.

National Railway Workers Union of Japan (KOKURU) (1994) *Report on an International Survey of Wearing Trade Union Badges,* London, International Transport Workers Federation (English and Japanese text).

National Union of General and Municipal Workers (1939) *Fifty Years (1889–1939)*, London, NUG&MW.

National Union of Vehicle Builders (1972) *The Badge Emblems and Banner of the National Union of Vehicle Builders 1834–1972,* London, N.U. Vehicle Builders. .

Nicholson, J. (1934) *A Hundred Years of Vehicle Building 1834–1934: centenary of the National Union of Vehicle Workers*, London, NUVB.

Oestreicher, R. (1981) 'From Artisan to Consumer: Images of Workers 1840–1920', *Journal of American Culture* 4, pp. 47–64.

O'Neill, T.P. , (1976) 'Irish Trade Union Banners', in O'Danachair, C. (ed.) *Folk and Farm: essays in honour of A.T. Lucas*, Ireland, Royal Society of Antiquaries of Ireland, pp. 177–99.

Osborne, W.V. (1912) *Sane Trades Unionism*, London, Collins.

Peacham, H. (1966) *Minerva Brittanica or a Garden of Heraldic Devises* (1612 facs.), Leeds, Scolar Press.

Peacock, P. (1972) *Buttons for the Collector*, Newton Abbot, David & Charles.

Pearce, S.M. (1995) *On Collecting in the European Tradition*, London, Routledge.

—— (ed.) (1997) *Experiencing Material Culture in the Western World*, Leicester University Press.

—— (1998) *Collecting in Contemporary Practice*, London, Sage.

—— and Martin, P. (2002) *The Collectors' Voice: Vol. 4 Contemporary Collecting*, Aldershot, Ashgate Publishing.

Pelling, H. (1956) 'The Knights of Labor in Britain 1880–1901', *Economic History Review*, second series, Vol. IX, Nos 1, 2 and 3, 1956–57, pp. 313–31.

—— (1963) *A History of British Trade Unionism*, London, MacMillan.

Plunkett, J. (1978) *Strumpet City*, London, Arrow .

Porter, G. (1988) 'Putting Your House in Order: representations of women and domestic life', in Lumley, R. (ed.) *The Museum Time Machine*, London: Routledge, pp. 102–27.

Pretty, D.A. (1988) 'Undeb Gweithwyr Mon: Anglesey Workers Union (Part One)', *Transactions of the Anglesey Antiquarian Society and Field Club*, pp. 115–48.

—— (1989a), 'Undeb Gweithwyr Mon: Anglesey Workers Union (Part Two)' *Transactions of the Anglesey Antiquarian Society and Field Club*, pp. 43–79.

—— (1989b) *The Rural Revolt That Failed: farm workers trade unions in Wales 1889–1950,* Cardiff of Wales Press.

Pugh, A. (1951) *Men of Steel: by one of them*, London, Iron and Steel Trades Confederation.

Radford, F.H. (1951) *Fetch the Engine*, London, Fire Brigades Union.

Raynes, J.R. (1921) *Engines and Men*, (Associated Society of Locomotive Engineers and Firemen), London, Goodall & Suddick.

Reed, D. and Adamson, A. (1985) *Miners' Strike 1984–1985: people versus state*, London, Larkin Publications.

Reeves, A. (1984) *Badges of Labour Banners of Pride*, Sydney, George Allen & Unwin, .

—— (1988) *Another Day Another Dollar: working lives in Australian history*, Victoria. McCulloch Publishing.

—— (1992) *A Tapestry of Australia: The Sydney Wharfies Mural*, Sydney, Waterside Workers Federation.

Reynolds, G.W. and Judge, A. (1968) *The Night the Police Went on Strike*, London, Weidenfeld and Nicholson.

Rose, J. (1986) *One Hundred Years of King's Cross ASLEF*, London, ASLEF.

Rubenstein, H.R. (1989a) 'Symbols and Images of American Labor: Badges Of Pride', *Labor's Heritage*, April, pp. 36–51.

—— (1989b) 'Symbols and Images of American Labor: Dinner Pails And Hard Hats', *Labor's Heritage*, July, pp. 34–49.

Rudkin, O. (1927) *Thomas Spence and His Connections*, London, George, Allen & Unwin.

Russell, D. (1988) 'The Emblem and Authority', *Words and Image*, Vol. 4, No. 1, pp. 81–7.

Russell, M. (1966) *Men Along The Shore: The International Longshoremens Association and its history,* New York, Brussel & Brussel .

Rutherford, J. (1982) 'Henry Willett as a Collector', *Apollo,* March, pp. 176–81.

Sage, J. (1951) *Memoirs of Josiah Sage,* London, Lawrence & Wishart.

Salt, C. and Layzell, J. (1985) *Here We Go!: women's memories of the 1984/85 miners strike,* London, Co-operative Retail Services Ltd..

Schnapper, M.B. (1972) *American Labor: A Pictorial Social History,* Washington D.C., Public Affairs Press.

—— (1975) *American Labor: A Bicentenial History,* Washington, DC, Public Affairs Press.

Schroeder, F.E.H (ed.) (1981) *Popular Culture in Museums and Libraries,* Ohio, Bowling Green University Press..

Seaton, B. (1987) *Justice for Mineworkers Badge Collectors' Guide,* Nottingham, Private publication.

Senior, B. (1964) 'Association Badges', *Numismatic Circular,* London, Spink and Sons, Vol. 72, May, pp. 105–106.

Sequin, K. (1999) *The Graphic Art of the Enamel Badge,* London, Thames & Hudson.

Setchfield, F. (1986) *The Official Badge Collectors' Guide,* London, Longman.

Sexton, J. (1936) *Life of a Docker's M.P,* London, Faber & Faber.

Sherry, J. (1990) 'A sociocultural analysis of a Midwestern American flea market', *Journal of Consumer Research,* 17, pp. 13–30.

Slate Miners Support Group (1986) *United We Stand,* Blaenau Ffestiniog.

Smethurst, J. (1976) 'The Manchester Banner Makers', *Northwest Group for the Study of Labour History,* No. 3, pp. 17–28.

—— and Devine, F. (1981) 'Trade Union Badges – Mere Emblems or Means of Membership Control?', *Soathar,* Journal of the Irish Labour History Society, No. 7.

Smith, C.S. (1989) *Auctions: the social construction of value,* Hemel Hempstead, Harvester Wheatsheaf.

Smith, G. (1985) 'Badges Trace the History of NSW Railways', *Australian Coin Review,* June, pp. 25–6.

—— (1991) 'Badges of the NSW General Strike 1917', *Journal of The Numismatic Association of Australia,* Vol. 5, pp. 53–6.

—— (1992a) *Emblems of Unity: badges of Australia's trade unions,* New South Wales, Little Hill Press Pty Ltd..

—— (1992b) 'Union Badges of the 1913 Ferry Strike', *Australian Coin Review,* October, pp. 34–5.

Smith, G.M (1969) *Joe Hill,* Salt Lake City, University Of Utah Press.

Smith, J.R. (1970) *The Hatters,* Denton, Amalgamated Journeymen Felt Hatters, Felt Hat Trimmers & Wool Formers Societies.

Soiffer, S. and Hermann, G. (1987) 'Visions of power: ideology and practice in the American garage sale', *Sociological Review,* 35, pp. 48–83.

Spargo, D. (1989) *This Land Is Our Land: aspects of agriculture in English art*, London, Royal Agricultural Society.

Spedden, E.R. (1910) *The Trade Union Label*, Baltimore, John Hopkins University Press.

Spoor, A. (1967) *White Collar Union* (NALGO), London, Heinemann.

Stubbs, J. and Haunch, T.O. (1983) *Freemason's Hall: The Hall and Heritage of the Craft,* London, The United Grand Lodge of England.

Sutcliffe, L. and Hill, B. (1985) *Let Them Eat Coal: the political use of social security during the miners' strike*, London, Canary Press.

Sutherland, W. and Sutherland, W.G. (1898) 'Emblems of the Friendly Societies of Great Britain', in Sutherland, W. and Sutherland W.G. (eds), *The Sign-Writer and the Glass Embosser*, Manchester, The Decorative Art Journal.

Suthers, R.B. (1929) *The Story of NATSOPA 1889–1929*, London, NATSOPA.

Swift, J. (1947) *History Of The Dublin Bakers and Others*, Dublin.

Taplin, E. (1986) *The Docker's Union: A Study of the National Union of Dock Labourers 1889–1922*, Leicester University Press.

Taylor, P. (1998) *Collecting Anodised Cap Badges*, London, Pen and Sword Books.

Thornett, A. ed. (1985) *The Miners' Strike in Oxford*, Oxford, Oxford Miners' Support Group.

Tickner, L. (1987) *The Spectacle Of Women: images of the suffrage movement 1907–1914*, London, Chatto & Windus.

Topham, T. (1996) 'The Unofficial National Docks Strike of 1923: the Transport and General Workers Union's first crisis', *Historical Studies In Industrial Relations*, No. 2, Keele, Keele University Centre For Industrial Relations, pp. 27–64.

Trade Union Badge Collectors Newsletter, 1985–2000. A full set is available for consultation in the library of Ruskin College, Oxford.

Transport and General Workers' Union (1977) *The Story of The TGWU*, London, TGWU.

Tucket, A. (1967) *The Scottish Carter*, London, George, Allen & Unwin.

Tung, M. (1987) 'From Heraldry to Emblem: a study of Peacham's use of heraldic arms in Minerva Brittanica', *Word and Image*, Vol. 3, No. 1, pp. 86–93.

Turner, B. (1920) *A Short History of the General Union of Textile Workers*, Heckmondwike, Labour Pioneer & Factory Times Printing Department.

Webb, S. and B. (1950) *History of Trade Unions*, London, Longman.

Weir, R. (1996) *Beyond Labor's Veil: the culture of the Knights Of Labor*, Pennsylvania State University Press.

Whiting, J.R.S. (1972) *Commemorative Medals,* Newton Abbot, David & Charles.

Whitfield, W. (1980) 'Against the Wind Their Banners Streamed', *Embroidery*, Vol. 31, No. 2, pp. 43–4.

Widgery, D. (1986) *Beating Time: Riot 'n' Race 'n Rock 'n' Roll,* London, Chatto & Windus .

Williams, C. (1981) *One Hundred Years of Progress 1881–1981* (Derbyshire miners), Derby, NUM.

Williams, G.A. introduction to Gorman, J. (1973) *Banner Bright*, London, Allen Lane, pp. 1–19.

Williams, J.E. (1961) *The Derbyshire Miners*, London, George, Allen & Unwin.

Wilkinson, F. (1997) *Badges of the British Army: an illustrated reference guide for collectors*, London, Arms And Armour Press.

Wilshire, P. , Macintyre, D. and Jones, M. (1985) *Strike – 358 Days That Shook the Nation: a battle of ideologies; Thatcher, Scargill and the Miners*, London, Coronet.

Williams, J., Dickinson, N. and Jaddou, L. (1987) *Hanging on by your Fingernails: the struggle at Lea Hall Colliery 1984–87*, Nottingham, Spokesman.

Williamson-Latham, R. (1994) *British Military Badges and Buttons*, Buckinghamshire, Shire Publications.

Winter, J. (1996) 'Public History and Historical Scholarship', *History Workshop Journal*, No. 42, Autumn, pp. 169–172.

Wittkower, R. (1977) *Allegory and the Migration Of Symbols*, London, Thames & Hudson, 1987 edn.

Index